S.R. Bissette's Blur
(Complete Edition)
Volume 1: Video Views
1999-2000

Also by Stephen R. Bissette

Aliens: Tribes
We Are Going to Eat You! The Third World Cannibal Movies
Comic Book Rebels (with Stanley Wiater)
The Monster Book: Buffy the Vampire Slayer
(with Christopher Golden, Thomas E. Sniegoski)

edited by Stephen R. Bissette
Taboo 1-9, Taboo Especial

Also from Black Coat Press:

edited by Stephen R. Bissette

Green Mountain Cinema I:
Green Mountain Boys

S. R. Bissette's Blur
Volume 1: Video Views
(1999-2000)

by

Stephen R. Bissette

A Black Coat Press Book

S.R. Bissette's Blur (Complete Edition) Volume 1 and all its contents Copyright © 1999, 2000, 2007 Stephen R. Bissette. Cover illustration Copyright © 2007 by Stephen R. Bissette.

Cover design: Jon-Mikel Gates
Packaged by SpiderBaby Grafix & Publications.

To contact the author, please write to:
Stephen R. Bissette, PO Box 157, Windsor, VT 05089, or visit: www.srbissette.com

A complete set of the original *Brattleboro Reformer Arts & Entertainment* sections, featuring *Video Views* and my miscellaneous articles, and an almost-complete set of *VMag* are preserved in the Stephen R. Bissette Collection in the HUIE Library at Henderson State University in Arkadelphia, Arkansas. *The Reformer* is also accessible via microfiche at the Brooks Memorial Library in Brattleboro, VT.

Visit our website at www.blackcoatpress.com

ISBN 1-934543-23-8. First Printing. September 2007. Published by Black Coat Press, an imprint of Hollywood Comics.com, LLC, P.O. Box 17270, Encino, CA 91416. All rights reserved. Except for review purposes, no part of this book may be reproduced or transmitted in any form or by any means, electronic or mechanical, including photocopying, recording or by any information storage and retrieval system, without permission in writing from the publisher. The stories and characters depicted in this book are entirely fictional. Printed in the United States of America.

For Marjory

Acknowledgements:

These reviews and essays were originally published in *The Brattleboro Reformer*, *VMag*, *The Chicopee Herald* and *The Reminder*.

My thanks to my respective editors and publishers, particularly Chris Nixon (my first *Brattleboro Reformer Arts & Entertainment* editor), Willow Dannible (my second), and Jon Potter (the current *Reformer A&E* editor); Steve Murphy (*VMag* and a comrade-in-arms from my comics days/daze); and G. Michael Dobbs (*The Chicopee Herald*, *The Reminder*, and the dearest and closest friend of 'em all).

Thanks to Alan Goldstein for asking me to tackle the column back in '99; sorry they weren't all positive reviews, Alan, but I never did listen to Thumper's mother. Thanks to everyone at First Run Video, including our customers. Thanks most of all to April Stage (now April Anderson), then-manager at First Run and beloved fellow employee. April "kept me honest" in this process, insisting that I do not ignore the latest Julia Roberts or Sandra Bullock opus, try as I might. Thanks, too, to the many fellow independent video store owners, members of the New England Buying Group, and the various studio reps who provided insights, opinions, and screeners whenever necessary, and often when they weren't necessary.

Thanks to Scott Shaw!, for permitting me to incorporate his online comicon.com posts about *Yellow Submarine* into my review of that film (see page 49-50).

Special thanks to Jon-Mikel Gates for his excellent cover design from my spastic artwork; thanks, Jon!

Thanks to then-Marjory Bleier—now Marjory Bissette—who put up with me throughout this manic two year+ saga and opened my eyes to the pleasures of films (and life) I might otherwise have skirted.

Thanks to my then-teenage offspring Maia Rose and Daniel, who also made sure I stay tuned to many movies I might have otherwise passed over or missed altogether. You may have given me many gray hairs, but you kept me young.

Finally, thanks to Jean-Marc and Randy Lofficier, who made these collections possible.

SRB

Introduction

FOCUS

I'm a devotee and reader of collected movie reviews, and have been since my junior high school years in the late 1960s. Like most children of the late '50s and early '60s, my first beloved film publication was *Famous Monsters of Filmland*. Though I can't and won't elevate Forrest J. Ackerman's pun-filled writing into the pantheon of great cinema critics, I can honestly say I owe it all to Forry.

The stirring of my earliest critical thought on cinema, though, owes a greater debt to *Famous Monsters of Filmland*'s competitor on the newsstand, *Castle of Frankenstein*, which from its earliest issues demonstrated a far more adult orientation to the monsters and movies we so loved. Thus, I have to say without hesitation that Calvin T. Beck (the erstwhile, opportunistic editor/publisher of *Castle*), Bhob Stewart, and Joe Dante, Jr. were the first critics I came to trust and depend upon. Looking back, their writings still resonate, including the briefest of their capsule reviews, which easily outstrip their mainstream equivalents (from *TV Guide*—for which, it turns out, Bhob Stewart wrote capsules!—to Steven Scheuer's *Movies on TV* to Leonard Maltin's *TV Movies*). In fact, when it came to the horror, sf, and fantasy films I loved so, *CoF*'s reviews were the antidote to Scheuer's *Movies on TV* (which was suspect from my first exposure when Scheuer dismissed Ray Harryhausen's glorious *20 Million Miles to Earth* as a "blob" movie) and *The New York Times* TV listing capsules (which copped out on almost all genre films by ending their usually sarcastic non-reviews with, "your move"). In fact, invaluable and handy a reference as it was, Scheuer's book almost put me off capsule reviews for life: they too often expressed nothing, and were occasionally simply wrong in a way that implied the films being summarized hadn't even been seen. Thankfully, *CoF* taught me the value of even the briefest shorthand, alerting me to countless films and filmmakers I otherwise never would have known of. In doing so, Beck, Stewart, and Dante expanded my horizons by steering my attention to the films of Orson Welles (lionized at every turn in *CoF*), underground cinema, film *noir*, and dark gems like *Leave Her to Heaven*, *Night of the Hunter* and *The Fool Killer*.

Like many junior-league movie lovers, I kept a scrapbook of clippings from the newspapers. I didn't tear up or clip from my monster magazines—those were totems too precious for cutting!—but I did save movie items from the local newspapers and *TV Guides* (expanding my vocabulary with words like "antediluvian," which was used in one memorable *TV Guide* capsule for *Godzilla, King of the Monsters*). The first of my movie scrapbooks gathered the most lurid movie ads from the local papers, first targeting the ads for films I had seen. But it wasn't long before the more enticing forbidden fruit dominated each page: the increasingly lurid ads for the movies I couldn't, or wasn't permitted, to see, pre-16th birthday and the earning of my driver's license. These were increasingly accompanied by capsule synopsis from the *TV Guide* from the channels we didn't get—hence, a growing list of "must see" films that remained tantalizingly out-of-reach—and the *Catholic Tribune*'s updated listing of current films, categorized per their moral movie ratings. Like the *TV Guide* capsules of films I couldn't see, the *Catholic Tribune* listings became crucial for the allure of their forbidden fruit, particularly those films that represented (gasp!) *sin*. As years went by, the latter became a private "must see" checklist of sorts, with the "Condemned" films being the most compelling, as I'd long since realized the best horror films inevitably ended up on that blacklist. My final scrapbook gave way to a mix of the coolest drive-in double-feature ads, Judith Crist's one-page *TV Guide* movie review column, and (best of all) reviews clipped from the copies of *Variety* I was allowed to pick up from the local Waterbury, VT radio station (WDEV) offices when they were done with them. There was a no-nonsense, market-savvy pragmatism to the *Variety* reviews that was new to me, scribed with a straightforward industry insider's perspective that spoke volumes. Simply put, I learned a great deal from the most perfunctory of *Variety* reviews, packed as they were with succinct, connect-the-dots insights about the studios, producers, distributors, and creative individuals making the films. As I outgrew scrapbooks, the *Variety* and *The New York Times* reviews continued to be of great interest to me, gathered thereafter in file folders alongside filed reviews and ads clipped from the Boston papers (the *Herald* and the *Globe*).

By this time, published collections of reviews were much sought-after additions to my modest home library. James Agee's seminal *Agee on Film* was the first of these I recall purchasing. I loved the book: it impressed upon me the enormous value of a critic's work when read, sequentially, as a coherent whole. Whether I knew the films being written about or not (steering me inevitably to late-night TV viewings of those films I had never seen before), whether or not I found myself in agreement with Agee's opinions and/or world view, there was a mesmerizing power in a singular informed voice summarizing, on a weekly basis, a chronology of films from a distant past (primarily the 1940s). There was an immense fascination for me in reading Agee's attentive recognition of Val Lewton's RKO horrors (beginning with *The Cat People*, 1942), and his delight in finding a new Lewton production. By this time, I'd already scoured the *Periodical Index* and enough dusty back issues of *Time*, *Newsweek*, and *The Saturday Review* in the Waterbury Library to know how rarely horror films were reviewed by the mainstream magazines and critics of the 1940s, '50s and early '60s, and how disdainfully those few reviewed were treated. Agee had no such prejudice against the genre, and Agee's loving essays on comedy and comedy stars (particularly those of the silent era) prompted me to catch any and all TV broadcasts and area revivals of the films of Chaplin, Keaton, Laurel & Hardy and the Marx Brothers. And so it went: as with *CoF*, I availed myself of the opportunity to see any film Agee's reviews had opened my eyes to. Thus, my cinematic education expanded beyond my initial fixation on horror, sf, fantasy, and monster movies.

Soon, Agee's tome was joined on my shelves by the first Pauline Kael collection, *I Lost It at the Movies*, and paperback gatherums of John Simon, Judith Crist, and Renata Adler's columns and reviews. These books considerably enriched my junior high and high school years, prompting me to dig even more passionately into the stacks of 1940s and '50s magazines in the Waterbury Library attic and basement, all the while savoring and tearing choice pieces from the *Sunday New York Times* Arts section (Vincent Canby became a particular favorite of mine among the current critics, recognizing as he did the considerable virtues of, for example, Piers Haggard's *Blood on Satan's Claw* and Harry Kumel's *Daughters of Darkness*, films his fellow mainstream critics either reviled off-hand or ignored altogether). The books, though, were key. These collected reviews and essays were far more valuable than the capsule reviews in Scheuer's *Movies on TV*.

Most surprising to me was the fact that those critics I disagreed with—who often infuriated me (Simon filled the bill, loathing as he did almost every film I loved at that time)—became vital, as their distinctive voices and the consistency of their critical thinking led me to treasure their writings, whether I shared their opinions or not (again, Simon was foremost among these). There was a perverse glee in reading and rereading the scathing reviews of those films dearest to me: Arthur Penn's *Bonnie & Clyde*, Sergio Leone's spaghetti westerns, Stanley Kubrick's *2001: A Space Odyssey* and Nicolas Roeg and Donald Cammell's *Performance*, for example, drew nothing but negative reviews. These were evidence of my own awakening critical perspective—how could these literate, insightful writers not see what I was seeing, feel what I was feeling?—not to mention amusing in and of themselves. *Time*'s condescending review of *A Fistful of Dollars* remains hilarious reading, as does Simon's absolute revulsion for *The Good, the Bad, and the Ugly*, which prompted his gross distortion of even the most innocuous lines of dialogue to make the film seem more repugnant (did he mishear, or deliberately misinterpret? It didn't matter). Thankfully, these prejudices didn't inform every text: there were, after all, the rare positive reviews of Lewton's horror films in *Agee on Film*, and Pauline *Kael's Kiss Kiss Bang Bang* included an excellent essay on horror films, including a great analysis of Georges Franju's *Eyes Without a Face*, aka *The Horror Chamber of Dr. Faustus*, couched amid Kael's observations of the audience attending the film. Elsewhere in the book, Kael demonstrated a firm grasp of what made Jack Clayton's *The Innocents* tick, citing my favorite shot (artfully articulating why it was such a haunting image), and her evocative short reviews of eclectic fare concluding the book embraced curios like Karel Zeman's *The Fabulous World of Jules Verne*.

By the time I was a teenager, the best of these books, to my mind, was Jonas Mekas' *Movie Journal*, a collection of Mekas's *Village Voice* columns tracing the key years of the American underground film movement. Mekas's beguiling writings opened an eye on a world of films I'd never heard of in the backwoods of Vermont: more forbidden fruit to be tracked down and savored in the coming years. Mekas's columns also awakened my grasp of venues and markets: writing in a consciously poetic manner that was both open and utterly subjective, Mekas eschewed the artifice of all other critics. He was clearly writing for a different reader, a different marketplace—of ideas, values, and philosophy, as well as films. I had understood from an early age that *Variety* was writing for a market—the movie theater proprietors themselves—but Mekas was talking from and to the counterculture, and this was something else altogether.

More startling was the realization that Mekas was writing about some of the same films I'd read about in my favorite monster magazine, *Castle of Frankenstein*. In fact, upon closer scrutiny, it seemed that Mekas and Calvin T. Beck were both writing from and to the growing counterculture—*my* generation of film lovers, rather than prior generations. This suddenly provided a continuum, which stretched back to the older critics whose books filled a shelf in my bedroom closet. Suddenly, the chasm between the monster magazines of my youth and the "real books" collecting critical reviews and essays had a bridge, and my world grew exponentially. Those marvelously concise *Castle* capsule reviews by Bhob Stewart, Joe Dante, Jr., and Calvin T. Beck which spoke so loudly to me were being echoed by this *Village Voice* critic I'd never heard of. Had I stumbled on Susan Sontag's essay on sf and disaster films at this point, I might have lost all my bearings (imagine my surprise when, six years ago, Bhob Stewart told me about inviting Sontag to write for *Castle of Frankenstein*, followed by Bhob mailing me a photocopy of Sontag's letter, politely declining the offer; thank you, Bhob!).

And so, I began writing about the films I'd seen, too. One of my English assignments for junior high school became my own *Movie Guide*, hand-written (lettered, really, in an attempt to match the look of typesetting), earning a B+ and a note from my teacher that I would have gotten an A had I not written about so many horror movies instead of "real movies." Inspired by Mekas, I began to keep my own film journal in high school, paying particular attention to the unclassifiable films I lucked into, as those became more important to me than any others. Once I had my own driver's license, my appetites expanded further, as did my personal movie journals: I could now access the drive-ins, catching triple-bills and dusk-to-dawn shows. I finally began to see the underground films Mekas had written about, thanks to two competing underground film societies that blossomed for a couple of years in the nearest 'big city' of Burlington, VT, and the underground and experimental films shown at the nearby "hippie haven" of Goddard College, which was even more enticing.

My journals became crucial to me, as I was seeing films no one else seemed to be writing about. I remember, for instance, loving a bizarre comedic short film included in one of the underground film festivals in Burlington. It was called *The Secret Cinema*, and upon my return home, I wrote it up while my memory was fresh, embedding the name of its director, Paul Bartel, into my consciousness. Lo and behold, a short time later an ad in the paper for a double-bill at a relatively distant drive-in included the name "Paul Bartel," allowing me to catch Bartel's debut mainstream feature *Private Parts* (sharing the bill with *Don't Look in the Basement*). Thanks to my scribblings, I was now beginning to connect the dots on a new generation of filmmakers, and my own writings took on a renewed value to me that carried me through my college years... but that's another story.

With the beginning of my residency in the Joe Kubert School of Cartoon and Graphic Art in the fall of 1976, and the subsequent launch of my professional career as a cartoonist and illustrator, my movie journals were eclipsed by my sketchbooks, my writing subsumed by my drawing and comics work. Moving from Vermont to New Jersey to attend the Kubert School, I even had to abandon my precious files and scrapbooks, left in my dorm room at Johnson State College (undoubtably to be trashed) when I could find no library, collector, or recipient even vaguely interested.

Still, I never lost the itch, and I jumped at the invitation extended to me in the late 1980s by one Chas Balun, co-founder and editor of the hot new horror fanzine *Deep Red*. Thanks to Chas, I began writing about film again, but this time, my work was being published. Chas welcomed anything and everything horror-oriented that I offered: capsule reviews, longer reviews, articles, interviews with filmmakers.[1] I'll save the particulars of that body of work for the intro to *Gooseflesh*; know, however, that it was Chas Balun who reopened the door for my writing about film, and thus opened the door for my writing professionally, period. Thank you, Chas!

This sideline seemed to my friends, peers, and fellow pros in the comics field an unnecessary and rather childish diversion. It was in fact a lifeline back to something that had always been vital and dear to me, as central to my life as my art and comics had always been. It was part and parcel of who I was, who I am, and as important to me as my comics work, illustrations, and fiction writing. Furthermore, I already had a reputation for stretching and/or missing deadlines with my comics work, but I usually made or beat all my writing deadlines. Writing came easy for me, it wasn't the agonizing struggle that drawing comics (as opposed to single illustrations or sketches) was, became, and remained. So, writing—particularly writing about film—was even more of a pleasure, blighted with none of the depressing personal baggage that drawing comics was increasingly burdened with. Without going into too much detail, suffice to say that as my comics career waned in the late

---

[1] That material will be collected in the near future by Black Coat Press in the multi-volume *Gooseflesh* books series, along with the writings I subsequently completed for other zines like *Magick Theatre*, Tim and Donna Lucas's *Video Watchdog*, Craig Ledbetter's *ETC* (*Euro-Trash Cinema*), Charles Kilgore's *Ecco*, Tony Timpone's *Fangoria* and *Gorezone*, Chris Gore's *Film Threat* and many others.

1990s, coinciding with the implosion of the comicbook Direct Sales Market and a major change in my personal life, my writing became more and more important to my well-being, emotionally and financially.

As necessity led to my easing out of the long, once-lucrative freelance cartooning career I'd enjoyed since the mid-1970s into full-time employment at First Run Video (the local video superstore I'd been an active shareholder in since 1991), I maintained writing rather than drawing as my freelance career of choice. I retired from comics by the end of 1999, a difficult decision made a bit less painful due to the fact I was now writing a weekly video review column for the local newspaper, *The Brattleboro Reformer*. I was also writing reviews and essays on film for the Northampton, MA-based monthly free magazine *VMag* and occasional film pieces for *The Chicopee Herald* and the *Reminder*, along with the occasional review or article for my anchors, *Deep Red* and *The Video Watchdog*. None of this paid much of anything, but it was enormously satisfying, and kept me sane through some momentous life changes.

The weekly column for *The Brattleboro Reformer* grew out of my job at First Run Video (where, at my own insistence, I began as a minimum-wage clerk like everyone else, working my way up to management within a year—hey, it isn't rocket science). First Run Video was and is owned by my friend Alan B. Goldstein, who I'd first met in 1982 when he ran Moondance Comics, at that time the only comicbook shop and mail-order business in southern Vermont. Alan had long since left comics retailing and launched First Run Video as the area's first video superstore in November of 1991. As I said, I was an active shareholder: I had, in fact, pitched in throughout the fall of '91 to categorize First Run's massive initial inventory, and worked as the advertising and promotional manager from 1992-93, during one of the livelier stretches of my comics career.

When Chris Nixon of the *Brattleboro Reformer* approached Alan about First Run possibly providing the paper with a weekly video column for their new weekly *Arts & Entertainment* section (published every Thursday to cover the coming week and weekend), Alan naturally turned to me. He had, after all, typeset two or three issues worth of the writing on dinosaur films and comics I'd done as back-up material for my self-published comics magnum-opus, *S. R. Bissette's Tyrant* (by issue four, I was typesetting that material myself) and was vaguely aware of my writing about horror films for various fanzines, magazines, and books.

So began *Video Views*, my weekly column for the *Reformer*. As it gained momentum, I began to email it every week to a close circle of friends and associates, and their feedback was forever welcome. The fact that they occasionally took the time to respond, along with the face-to-face comments offered by neighbors and the growing body of First Run customers who seemed to enjoy this new feature in the Reformer, made me vitally aware of "my" audience. I was writing for a different market now, a market defined primarily by geography and the parameters of a daily family newspaper.

Thus, unlike my ongoing writing for the horror film fan magazines, I could not presume my readers knew anything about film or filmmakers; there was no communal shorthand I could rely upon. I was writing for an audience that *might* know who Steven Spielberg and George Lucas were, but maybe not. For most *Reformer* readers, only the big movie stars had any name value or instantly identifiable celebrity. So I took it upon myself to remind readers that individuals, artists, indeed made these movies, these videos, that filled the new release wall at First Run Video. I hoped to elevate the interest level in the medium by doing much more than simply write capsule reviews. In doing so, I always had to be sure I provided constant reference points. Thus, I would cite other works by the same filmmakers, other films certain actors had appeared in. In the format of a weekly newspaper column, this wasn't intrusive, but once those columns are collected, the repetition of certain filmographies or references can seem rather dreary. Still, I have decided to run the columns as they were originally published. This may make these collections more useful for younger readers and neophyte film buffs, but I hope this aspect of the columns collected in this series won't prove too exasperating to the knowledgeable film aficionados who deign to dig into these writings.

To write a weekly video column, I was usually screening over four to six films per week. As a diehard veteran film lover, I was also going to the theater whenever possible. As a First Run Video manager and buyer, I was viewing a plethora of films besides (via "screeners," full-length videocassettes of upcoming video releases), if only to know, come pre-order time, what videos we needed to buy and in what quantities. I won't do the math, but suffice to say these columns reflect as many man-hours as any comics series I've ever worked on (a further point of outrage for my comics peers, who would have much rather seen me drawing all those hours rather than watching movies or writing), all jam-packed into a little more than two years of my life.

I must also add that the column took on another dimension for me personally. Having earned a poor reputation for making deadlines in the comics industry, I was determined to run the gauntlet and never miss a weekly deadline for the *Reformer*. That I managed this feat without a misstep is a point of personal accomplishment and honor. I not only made every single (and usually beat the) weekly deadline, I did so for two full years. I managed this feat while pitching additional articles to the A&E editor, writing freelance for other zines, completing a couple of books, writing or drawing my final professional comics work, and working full-time at First Run Video (not to mention raising two teenagers, among other things).

So, it's with some pride that I finally gather together the *Video Views* columns, for posterity and as the vainest of vanity projects. Despite the context I've tried to provide with this introduction, I'm not pretending my weekly columns belong on a bookshelf alongside Agee, Kael, Crist, Simon, Adler and Mekas—whose books still hold a special place in my library, along with many, many others I've since acquired and devoured. But I do hope this collection may have some value for some readers beyond being just a batch of video reviews.

It is also a record of what has been (particularly to my peers in the comics industry) a limbo period in my career, the "lost years" when my comics work came to an end, I disappeared and it was presumed I had simply ceased to be productive in any manner. As I hope the *Blur* volumes demonstrate, I was plenty productive, and hopefully the fruits of those years of labor will still provide some entertainment value and enlightenment to someone, somewhere.

A note on the formats: This collection, to the best of my knowledge, includes every *Video Views* column I wrote between 1999 and 2001. A few of these were articles, but most were the regular weekly column. Supplementing my digital files may, upon occasion, mean including work in later volumes that belonged, chronologically, in earlier volumes; in the end, in any case, *Blur* will indeed encompass my entire body of video review work, with the exception of pieces I choose to reserve for inclusion in *Green Mountain Cinema* (my ongoing book series on Vermont and New England film and video) or the upcoming *Gooseflesh* volumes.

This first volume opens with a sampling of my capsule reviews for *VMag*, edited and published by my friend Stephen Murphy (CroMag Publications, Inc.) from October (cover dated November) of 1997 to spring of 2001 (39 issues)[2]. For its first year of publication, *VMag* published a number of my articles (some of which will be reprinted in *Gooseflesh* and elsewhere), but by 1999 my submissions had narrowed to a trickle of capsule video reviews (as *Vid View*), most of which appear herein. Unlike the *Reformer*, *VMag* did not cater to a family audience, hence the more adult orientation of some of the material written for that zine. Capsule reviewing was a form I was well versed in (my first submissions to *Deep Red* in 1988 had been capsule reviews, written in Chas's then-distinctive, much-imitated *Gore Score* style), but constantly frustrated by: it is too incommunicative a form, offering only the most fleeting of synopsis and most glib (hence useless) of observations and opinions. As had been the case since writing for *Deep Red*, capsule reviews submitted didn't always result in capsule reviews published. For every dozen re-

---

[2] After the demise of *VMag*, Steve launched one more weekly zine in the fall of 2001, *Charm*, subtitled "A New Magazine for Today's Woman" and helmed by Murphy's wife Sonia Pereira. It lasted two issues; Steve retired from publishing.

views completed and submitted, only five or six would ultimately see print.

The time-consuming process of viewing and writing about multiple films, distilling my notes down to short-order capsules that might or might not be published and paid for, was quickly losing what little value it had for me. Still, these *VMag* reviews led to the invite from the *Reformer* and from Alan Goldstein, hence their inclusion here. [3]

The *Reformer* columns began on September 9, 1999, and continued weekly thereafter through October of 2001. Alan initially wanted me to continue writing in the same format—capsule reviews, covering as many of the weekly new releases as possible. I, of course, had other ideas, and thankfully my *Reformer* editor was interested in something more substantial. Before the first month was over, I had abandoned the capsule review format; by the end of October '99, the column had hit its stride and I was beginning to write with confidence.

The dates given cite the original date of publication; on those occasions when unforeseen editorial decisions resulted in a column being "bumped" to the following week or otherwise revised, I have preserved the chronology in which the columns were written (corresponding, by and large, with the respective video release dates), incorporating editorial alterations only when they im-

---

[3] Despite my best efforts, the lack of original digital files and/or a complete set of *VMag* (neither I nor Steve Murphy have yet found a copy of the November 2000 issue) mean a definitive inventory of my *VMag* work was inconclusive at this writing. All references in this volume, however, are complete. If further material surfaces, I will incorporate it into future volumes of *Blur* for the sake of completion.

proved or significantly altered the context of the published review.

Working for the *Reformer* on a weekly basis was a great discipline and venue, and everything I wrote eventually saw print. Initially, it was a relief to stretch beyond the constrictive capsule review format, and that evolution is chronicled in this first volume. I expanded the arena as quickly as possible without setting off alarms, always pushing at the parameters of length and content, though I never once tested the patience of my editors.

The additional "Recent & Recommended" material gave Alan the capsule reviews he longed for, and offered the *Reformer A&E* editor additional material they could play with, to include, exclude, or run the following week as space required or permitted. Longer columns were sometimes run as two-part pieces. As *Video Views* grew and reader response proved favorable, my editors seemed happy to indulge even my wildest schemes.

Also note this collection begins when videocassettes (specifically vhs) were still the dominant format, and DVD was just being introduced into the marketplace. Hence, the occasional references to "also on DVD," tardy DVD releases (sometimes weeks after a title's vhs release), and oddities like *Detroit Rock City* (the first studio title to be released on DVD *before* arriving on vhs; see page 151-152).

Looking back, through the process of compiling and polishing this series of books, I have to say I found many pleasant surprises. I'd forgotten I'd seen, much less written about, many of these movies—hence the title of this book and book series.

Thankfully, it is no longer just a blur, consigned to mouldering boxes of newspapers and magazines in my garage.

Enjoy.

(August 2005; revised November 2006)

1999

April:

ROUTE 9: Solid cast (Kyle MacLachlan, Wade Andrew Williams, Peter Coyote, Amy Locane and Roma Maffia) lend weight to this modest sub-*A Simple Plan* morality tale. Two small-town deputies fleece a drug bust crime scene for $1.5 million, but the thumbscrews tighten on their failing trust, trysts and betrayals. [4]

May:

ANOTHER DAY IN PARADISE: Infamous photographer Larry Clark made his mark as a director with the controversial *Kids*, and moves into Gus Van Sant territory and mainstream narratives with this bleak, confrontational dissection of street lowlifes. Teen junkies Vincent Kartheiser and Natasha Gregson Wagner glide under the wing of mentor hood James Woods and surrogate moll-mom Melanie Griffith, who pluck them out of the gutter to initiate them into a more "rewarding" life of crime. Despite the omnipresent shadow of death, dope and despair, this film packs heat and urgent heart, and dig Lou Diamond Phillips' uncredited cameo as a gay kingpin.

---

[4] *Vmag* publication sources for the April – August "Vid View" reviews are: #18, April 1999, pg. 28; #19, May 1999, pp. 30-31; #20, June/July 1999, pp. 36-37; #21, August 1999, pp. 32-33. There may have been others, submitted but unpublished; if found, they will be published in a future volume.

HAPPINESS: Todd Solondz's insidious successor to his debut feature *Welcome to the Dollhouse* survived its NC-17 rating, limited theatrical release and Blockbuster demands for cuts to earn an 'R' rating (Solondz declined, meaning Big Blue won't carry the title) to emerge intact on home video. 1998's best and bravest American film offers a harrowing, hilarious portrait of three sisters and their orbit of friends, families and fallout. At its core is one of the happily-married sisters' husband, a therapist who happens to be a pedophile (Dylan Baker); Solondz's unflinching depiction of Baker's relationship with his pubescent son is unforgettable. Also starring Lara Flynn Boyle and Jane Adams.

IN DREAMS: Neil Jordan's latest was shot in our own backyard (Quabbin Reservoir, Northampton State Hospital, Brattleboro), adding local interest to this effectively creepy thriller about a woman whose dreams are apparently linked to the mind of a mad killer (Robert Downey, Jr.). It's not up there with Jordan's best (*The Crying Game, Mona Lisa, Michael Collins*), but director and cast bring conviction and imagination to a derivative script, elevating what could have easily been just another creaky suspenser.

ORGAZMO: Genuinely funny satire from *South Park* co-creator Trey Parker targets religion, Hollywood success stories, the porn industry, superheroes and exploitation films in its tale of a Mormon (Parker) sucked into fame and fortune playing triple-X star Orgazmo. Parker's *South Park* confederate Matt Stone provides hilarious support playing a crew member on the porn-film shoot, but Dian Bachar steals the show as "Choda Boy." Big fun!

June:

SHEPHERD (streets June 1) Stars: C. Thomas Howell. High concept, low-budget Roger Corman programmer depicts a religious war in the subterranean dystopia of our future, with Howell (*The Outsiders, Red Dawn, The Hitcher*, and countless direct-to-vid fare) as the hard-boiled mercenary who lights the fuse. Dumb fun.

WAKING NED DEVINE (streets June 1) Stars: Ian Bannen. Slight Irish confection enchanted Stateside audiences, recalling equally delightful minor gems from the 1950s like the Scottish *Tight Little Island* (aka *Whisky Galore*). A tiny island community rallies when a beloved local wins big in the lottery—and is found dead, ticket in hand. As fragile a pleasure as an inexpensive fine wine, so don't raise expectations too high, and you'll thoroughly enjoy yourself.

GODS & MONSTERS (streets June 8) Stars: Ian McKellan, Brendan Fraser, Lynn Redgrave. Brilliant script (based on Christopher Bram's biography of director James Whale, *Father of Frankenstein*), direction, and ensemble cast breathe uncanny life into this portrait of the autumn season of retired director James Whale (*Frankenstein, Bride of Frankenstein, The Invisible Man*, etc.), and his infatuation with a young gardener (Fraser). Introspective, moving, and ultimately devastating, one of the best films of the year. Recommended.

MASTER OF MOSQUITON: THE VAMPIRE (streets June 8) A.D. Vision's latest Japanese anime release tells the tale of a teenage heiress craving immortality who resurrects the deadly bloodsucker Mosquiton. Stylish horror animation bridges London in the 1920s and extraterrestrial terrors with panache. Also look for Central Park's anime classic *Ranma 1/2: Hard Battle Box Set* (12 tapes) streeting on the same date.

PSYCHO (streets June 8) Stars: Anne Heche, Vince Vaughn, William H. Macy. Gus Van Sant's unembarrassed "directed by" credit is a sham: this is the Hitchcock original, save for the shot of a fly in the hotel room, a needlessly explicit masturbation fillip, subliminal flashes during the murder scenes, and a ham-handed last shot. Vaughn is completely miscast as Norman Bates, whose motel murders are pretty damned small potatoes in the wake of Manson, Lucas, Dahmer, and the recent Littleton Massacre, and Heche's fugitive female a complete anachronism in the '90s (who cares if they're not married anymore???). If any genuine thought had been given to this soulless remake, it might have worked: note the Hitchcock's sleek direction of the original is as compellingly contemporary as ever. Film students will find much to enjoy and dissect here, but if you want Van Sant's real juice in the genre, check out *To Die For*; if you want *Psycho*, skip this empty pastiche and rent the real McCoy.

ENEMY OF THE STATE (streets June 15) Stars: Will Smith, Gene Hackman, Jon Voight, Regina King. It took over 20 years, but the Hollywood mainstream finally digested and regurgitated savvy conspiracy-surveillance-paranoia 1970s classics Francis Ford Coppola's *The Conversation* and Alan J. Pakula's *The Parallex View* as a mainstream high-octane blow-'em-up action thriller. *Conversation* star Hackman lends legitimacy and some weight to the pie-eyed scenario, but the cartoony hit men and overkill takes a toll. For a bloated contemporary actioner, there's a few glimmers of intelligence here, but typical of its current breed it skirts the real issues it exploits, and it doesn't hold a candle to its darker (and far less reassuring) precursors—they had enough brains and guts to be *really* terrifying. (Note: *The Parallex View* is re-released at sell-through price on video June 22.)

THE FACULTY (streets June 15) Stars: Elijah Wood, Josh Hartnett, Usher Raymond, Robert Patrick, Piper Laurie. Hotshot pairing of kinetic director Robert Rodriguez (*El Mariachi, Desperado, From Dusk to Dawn*) and overrated but clever screenwriter Kevin Williamson (*Scream, Dawson's Creek*) offers a rousing teen horror flick about an alien invasion beachhead in a small-town high school. Williamson typically pirates his premise from multiple pop classics (*Invasion of the Body Snatchers, The Hidden*, and Robert Heinlein's novel *The Puppet Masters*) with brisk references to his source material, but this confection works pretty well. Great monsters designed by *Swamp Thing* co-creator Berni Wrightson; this would make a fine double feature with last year's sorely underrated *Disturbing Behavior*.

HURLYBURLY (streets June 22) Stars: Sean Penn, Kevin Spacey, Meg Ryan, Chazz Palminteri, Garry Shandling, Anna Paquin, Robin Wright Penn. Screenwriter and playwright David Rabe (*Sticks and Bones, Streamers, Casualties of War*) provides a top-drawer ensemble cast with some cutting-edge moments in this scathing indictment of the L.A. lifestyles of the coked and affluent. Penn is riveting throughout, writhing at the threat of his moral awakening, while Spacey adds yet another memorable face to his reptilian rogue's gallery (*Se7en, Swimming With Sharks, L.A. Confidential*) of amoral citizens, distinguished here by one indelible glimpse of his character agonized by a fleeting confrontation with his own long-buried sense of decency.

A SIMPLE PLAN (streets June 22) Stars: Bill Paxton, Bridget Fonda, Billy Bob Thornton. Whiz-kid director Sam Raimi (*The Evil Dead, Evil Dead II, Army of Darkness, The Quick and the Dead*) comes of age with this gripping, razor-edged parable of corruption, greed, murder, and good people gone bad when they stumble on a downed planeload of big bucks on a remote mountain retreat. Little theatrical play, but this scored two Academy Award nominations, including Best Supporting Actor for Thornton (*Sling Blade*), who reaped four national critics awards for his role. Recommended!

RUSHMORE (streets June 29) Stars: Jason Schwartzman, Bill Murray, Olivia Williams. The lover's triangle relations between ego-eccentric sophomore Max Fischer (newcomer Schwartzman), steel tycoon Blume (Murray in top form), and the teacher they both fall for (Williams) transcends this genre's usual routes to spark some fresh revelations. Truly original take on a tried-and-true tale was one of the year's surprises, marching (as does its hero) to its own quirky, idiosyncratic rhythms. Don't miss it; Recommended!

THE STENDAHL SYNDROME (streets June 29): Slick, sick Italian horror thriller is the latest from director Dario Argento (*Bird With the Crystal Plumage, Suspiria, Deep Red*, etc.), who's past his prime but still capable of staging some genuinely startling and shocking setpieces. His daughter Asia Argento stars as a young artist overcome by "the Stendahl Syndrome" (a psychological disorder in which viewers are overwhelmed by overexposure to art!) who falls prey to a stalking serial killer... and, sadly, unbelievable scripting. There's a college thesis waiting for any feminist student willing to tackle this tangled father-and-daughter lunatic creation. Reportedly, Argento's most brutal sequences were once again scissored by censor-tive US distributors here; you'd think they'd know better by now. Worth a look, but beware of cuts.

July:

A CIVIL ACTION (streets July 13) Stars: John Travolta, Robert Duvall, William Macy, John Lithgow. Low-key, sober chronicle of the true story behind the minor legal firm that tackled the toxic-waste-related deaths of small-town Massachusetts children and found themselves way over their heads. This isn't the unflinching drama the case deserves, but for a Hollywood courtroom melodrama it maintains a clear focus on the issues and detours that derailed the investigation. Uniformly well-played, but Duvall shines as the wily veteran corporate attorney who effortlessly outwits upstart Travolta.

LIFE IS BEAUTIFUL (streets July 13) Jerry Lewis deep-sixed his career in the late 1960s by fumbling with *The Day the Clown Cried*, a vanity project in which he played a clown in a concentration camp. Director and star Roberto Benigni treads similar volatile ground with this tale of Guido Orefice (Benigni), who struggles to charm his family through the atrocities of the Holocaust.

Unlike Lewis, Benigni pulls off his tight-wire act with heart, yielding critical praise, an international audience, and Academy Award recognition. Recommended.[5]

RIKI-OH: THE STORY OF RICKY (July 13) In this uptight era of government and authoritarian alarm over violence in the media, it's refreshing to submit to such a gloriously overblown, mindlessly ultraviolent, massively entertaining diversion. Adapted from the popular *manga* series, this 1991 Hong Kong/Japanese coproduction is one of the most mind-blowingly excessive martial arts fantasies ever concocted. Outrageous gore fest is the ultimate prison movie, and ultimate parody of the genre; *wallow* in it!

WACO: THE RULES OF ENGAGEMENT (July 13) Sober, scathing, and ultimately terrifying documentary chronicles the tragedy at Waco, and is required viewing. You don't have to be a survivalist or conspiracy nut to acknowledge the terrible human toll of gung-ho government agencies out of control. This had only one area theatrical showing at the Real Art Ways in Hartford, CT; don't pass it up on home video. Recommended.

VIRUS (July 20; also on DVD) Stars: Jamie Lee Curtis, William Baldwin, Donald Sutherland. This tanked in theaters and was critically scorned, but it's a fairly lively, inventive variation on the inexplicable 1990s streak of sea-monster movies in which stellar casts wan-

---

[5] *Life is Beautiful*'s scheduled July video release was postponed for the wide Academy Award-related theatrical release of the dubbed version; see November 11 review, pg. 111-113, below.

der seemingly endless dark-and-wet corridors (*Leviathan, Deep Rising*, etc.). Easily the best of the breed, based on an obscure Dark Horse Comics mini-series.

THE GENERAL (July 20; also on DVD) Don't miss this one! Director John Boorman (*Point Blank, Deliverance, Excalibur, The Emerald Forest, Hope and Glory*, etc.) carves a riveting portrait of Irish crime lord and folk hero scoundrel Martin Cahill (who, by the way, once plundered Boorman's flat and stole his gold record award for the *Deliverance* soundtrack, a moment slyly captured here). Brendan Gleeson breathes life into Cahill, and Jon Voight delivers another fine character turn as the Dublin police chief determined to bring Cahill down. One caveat: the theatrical original was in sterling black and white; the video release has been colorized, damn it. Turn off the color on your set when you pop it in, or check it out on DVD, where it remains in its b&w glory. One of the best of 1999, hands down; Highest Recommendation.

OCTOBER SKIES (streets July 27; also on DVD) Stars: Jake Gyllenhaal, Laura Dern, Chris Cooper. Strong sleeper bio of NASA scientist Homer Hickman's Sputnik-era teenage years, looking up from his coal-mining town roots to awaken to the wonder of the stars and kindling of the spark that would fuel his career in space aeronautics. Rare drama that stirs a genuine sense of awe and wonder and charts the heights one person can aspire to as a result. If you were about to write a letter complaining about the *Riki-Oh* recommendation above, shut up and rent this gem, it's the best family film of the year thus far, by far. Highly Recommended.

PAYBACK (streets July 27; also on DVD) Stars: Mel Gibson, James Coburn. Remake of John Boorman's *Point Blank*, sans the galvanizing 1960s angst and metaphysics and stripped down to the marrow. Critics lambasted this lean, explicitly violent, mean-spirited thriller, and it's certainly not everyone's cup of tea. Taut effort evokes the no-nonsense amorality of director Don Siegel's best crime films (like *The Lineup, The Killers, Dirty Harry*, and *Charley Varrick*).

STRANGER IN THE KINGDOM (streets July 27) Stars: Ernie Hudson, David Lansbury, Jean Louisa Kelly, Sean Nelson, Martin Sheen. Director Jay Craven (*Where the Rivers Flow North*) mounts another accomplished regional production based on a book by Howard Mosher, shot in Northern Vermont. The arrival of three strangers to the Kingdom—a black preacher and his son, and a French Canadian mail-order bride—rocks a small town to its core, sparking gossip, scandal, and murder, disinterring its darkest secrets. Solid drama builds to a riveting courtroom final act. (Craven is teaching film again this fall at Marlboro College, and will make a personal appearance at First Run Video in Brattleboro, VT between 6-8 PM on August 7. Be there!) Recommended.

August:

CRUEL INTENTIONS (streets Aug. 3) Stars: Sarah Michelle Gellar, Ryan Phillippe, Reese Witherspoon, Selma Blair. Teen heat remake of *Dangerous Liasons* set amid contemporary NYC high school elite, wherein Gellar and stepbrother Phillippe pop cherries and crush reps for their own entertainment, putting their semi-incestuous lust for one another on the line betting over virgin territory Witherspoon. Lots of posh 'R' turf posing, posturing, profanity, and porking, but its a nasty, glitzy reptile show throughout. Go directly to *Go* (streets Aug. 24, see review below), do not collect $200.

TALE OF THE MUMMY (streets Aug. 3; also on DVD) Aussie director Russell Mulcahy (*Razorback, Highlander, The Shadow*, and many music videos) brings a stylish twist or two to the Mummy mythos in this direct-to-video feature that was swept under the carpet by Universal's *The Mummy* boxoffice bonanza. Worth a look, sporting a heftier dose of horror than the recent theatrical hit, compliments of FX by KNB (*Evil Dead II, From Dusk to Dawn*, etc.), attractive headliners Jason Scott Lee and Louise Lombard, and character turns by Christopher Lee (Hammer's *Dracula* series, etc.), Honor Blackman (*Goldfinger*'s Pussy Galore), and Shelley Duvall (*Popeye*'s Olive Oyl).

CELEBRITY (streets Aug. 10) A fresh spin on the meditation on celebrity that informed *Stardust Memories*, Woody Allen's latest stars Kenneth Branagh as Allen's surrogate at the center of post-Warhol era celebrity frenzies in the Big Apple. As ever, great cast—Judy Davis, Melanie Griffith, Winona Ryder, Joe Montegna, etc.—but greasy-haired brat Leonardo DiCaprio steals the show blazing his underbelly as an arrogant young rocker lapping up (and snorting) all that money can buy (it's as close as we'll ever get to what his turn as Bret Easton Ellis' *American Psycho* might have been).

THE DEEP END OF THE OCEAN (streets Aug. 10; also on DVD) Michelle Pfeiffer, Treat Williams, and Whoopi Goldberg star in this Best-Seller adaptation that comes up a soaper. A family devastated by the disappearance of one of their two sons at a high school reunion finds deeper sorrow when they are reunited during the boy's teen years. Harrowing first third is let down by the water-treading melodrama of the rest, despite rich potential of the cast and premise.

SHAKESPEARE IN LOVE (streets Aug. 10) Stars: Joseph Fiennes, Gwyneth Paltrow, Geoffrey Rush, Colin Firth, Ben Affleck. 1998 Academy Award sweeper (including Best Picture) breezes onto home video in time for summer's end. Literate romantic comedy about Shakespeare (Fiennes) struggling with overdue bills, overdue scripts, and a crisis of the heart culminates in a bracing premiere of *Romeo and Juliet*. It shouldn't work, but it does, brimming with wit, heart, and romance. An irresistible and lavish entertainment, further bejeweled with Judi Dench's Oscar-winning turn as Queen Elizabeth. Highly Recommended.

TRUE CRIME (streets Aug. 10) Director/star Clint Eastwood's latest is another fine piece and rich self-deprecating character study, despite the lukewarm critical and boxoffice reception it received. Eastwood plays a reporter whose career and marriage is on the skids, entrusted in the eleventh hour by editor James Woods to cover a convicted killer's last day on death row. Bucking the odds, he instinctively deconstructs the case against the convict, and begins to suspect an innocent man is unjustly facing execution. Builds with deceptive calm to its taut final act, pausing to reveal the nooks and crannies of the characters (including a mortifying visit to the zoo), crackling when Woods and Eastwood are onscreen. Even when he's catching his breath with efforts like this one, Eastwood is one of the finest filmmakers working today. Recommended.

Y2K: YEAR TO KILL (streets Aug. 10) Scrappy low-budget Spectrum Films beats Roger Corman to the punch with the first unabashed exploitation of the Y2K hysteria. As the shit hits the fan, a gang of young hoodlums loot, pillage, and murder, targeting those who were actually prepared for the Millennium madness. Ray Milland said it all in *Panic in Year Zero* (1961), but we're braced for a new streak of pending-Apocalyptic mayhem—and here's the first volley. Duck!

ANALYZE THIS (streets Aug. 17; also on DVD) Stars: Billy Crystal, Robert DeNiro. *Ghostbuster* Egon-turned-director Harold Ramis (Groundhog Day) crafts another solid Hollywood comedy, anchored by DeNiro's hilarious turn as a crime lord driven to analysis (Crystal, natch). Confection of *Goodfellas* crossed with *What About Bob?* works well, stands as the summer's best mainstream comedy on video. However, note that *National Lampoon's The Don's Analyst* (1997) covered similar comedic turf first.

ED TV (streets Aug. 17) Stars: Matthew McConaughey, Jenna Elfman, Woody Harrelson, Elizabeth Hurley, Martin Landau, Ellen Degeneres, Rob Reiner. Director Ron Howard's latest is essentially a Redneck Americana *Truman Show*, minus the metaphysics. Great cast makes for an amusing evening's entertainment, though it does wear thin.

BEAUTY AND THE BEAST: BELLE'S TALES OF FRIENDSHIP and **HERCULES: ZERO TO HERO**

(both street Aug. 17) Disney Studios latest direct-to-sell-thru video animated featurettes boast the return of the original voice casts (including James Woods reprising his razor-sharp turn from *Hercules*) and the latest from the animation division that gets to play it a little looser than the elite division. Worth a look!

GO (streets Aug. 24, also on DVD) Stars: Katie Holmes, Sarah Polly, Scott Wolf, Jay Mohr. Excellent ensemble cast, delicious story structured to strip its threads and turn back to the source point so as to follow the misadventures of each and every one of its characters to their illogical conclusions—and the culmination of one evening's very frantic activity. First of the post-*Pulp Fiction* generation of films (from the director of *Swingers*) to emulate the potential of that film's ingenious narrative structure (introduced by Stanley Kubrick with *The Killing* back in 1956), rather than copping the mayhem, mock-mojo, and attitude. Great fun, one of the best of the year. Highly Recommended.

THE MOD SQUAD (streets Aug. 24) Stars: Claire Danes, Giovanni Ribisi, Omar Epps. Tepid tea, despite casting that should have lend this some juice. Anachronistic flotsam force-fed to a generation that has no context whatsoever for the word "Mod," and certainly wasn't crying out for another big-budget retread of a forgotten TV series from the late 1960s that sucked back then, too. What Hollywood stooge thought *this* was a good idea? If you must watch it, don't say we didn't warn you.

SPAWN 3: THE ULTIMATE BATTLE (streets Aug. 24) Voices: Keith David, Richard Dysart, Jennifer Jason

Leigh, Eric Roberts. Todd McFarlane's fear-hero franchise continues with this latest animated HBO series installment, fusing the violence and kinetics of horror and *noir anime* with further meandering dialogue and narrative threads (this is not about storytelling, its about merchandising). Sports music videos and a behind-the-scenes short featuring McFarlane and the cast, in case you want to revel in the ego-boo of it all.

THE GREAT MOUSE DETECTIVE (streets Aug. 31) Post-demise-of-Walt, Pre-*Little Mermaid* Disney animated feature isn't usually ranked with the studio's real classics, but (like *The Fox and the Hound*, a gem from this same limbo Disney era) this period rodent pastiche of Conan Doyle's *Sherlock Holmes* archetype has many charms. Primary among them is Vincent Price's vocal performance as the villain, kidnapping a toymaker whose daughter engages the services of Baker Street's finest. Don't overlook this jewel. Recommended.

THE JACK BULL (streets on Aug. 31; also on DVD) John Cusack stars and produces what was clearly a labor of love (scripted by Dick Cusack), the powerful tale of horse rancher Myrl Redding (Cusack) whose personal integrity (and support for Wyoming's pending bid for statehood) pisses off wealthy land baron Henry Ballard (vet character actor L.Q. Jones in excellent form), sparking a conflict that leads to vigilante action, a manhunt, and trial, devastating Redding's family and scorching the entire territory. Grounded in the land, ethics, and grass roots people of its narrative, this is without a doubt the finest American Western since Clint Eastwood's *The Unforgiven*, deeply moral and absolutely relevant to today's issues and abuses of power. Evocative of the best work of genre masters like John Ford and Anthony Mann, it's also the best picture director John Badham (*Saturday Night Fever, War Games*, etc.) has helmed in over a decade, though it's Cusack's show first and foremost. Fine casting throughout, with John Goodman delivering a memorable turn as the judge entrusted with dispensing ultimate justice. One of the best of the year; Highly recommended.

September 9:

CELEBRATION (1998): Engaging foreign film, in which a celebratory family gathering spirals into increasing chaos after the grown son toasts his father by announcing to one and all that dear ol' Dad molested him as a child. Angry contemporary dissection of "family values" stands as one of the premiere entries from the "Dogma '95" school of filmmaking, insisting on 'real time' cinema shorn of any manipulative editing, musical scoring, or special effects. *(This is an adult drama, spiced with strong language and sexual situations.)*

DEAR JESSE (1998): Semi-autobiographical documentary from young director Tim Kirkman, who returns to his hometown to interview family, friends, and townspeople about a fellow native, Senator Jesse Helms. Thought-provoking, insightful probe of Kirkman's personal roots successfully addresses broader social and political issues, driving its point home with an offhandedly poignant coda. *(Helms supporters are the only ones who may find anything offensive here, though the strongest language onscreen comes from homophobic politician Helms himself.)*

EAT YOUR HEART OUT (1999): Contemporary romance simmers as a handsome live TV cooking-show chef (Christian Oliver) is caught up in the whirlwind of celebrity stirred by his saucy new agent (Laura San Giacomo), which quickly spills into his personal life, alienating his roommate and arousing his best friend (Pamela Segall). An appealing cast brightens this frothy confection, perfect for staving off the September blues. *(Sexual situations.)*

HOME IMPROVEMENT: THE SERIES FINALE (1999): The final two episodes of the popular Tim Allen situation comedy TV series are sweetened on video with a concluding documentary featuring interviews with the cast and crew, bloopers, outtakes, and clips from the show's highlights. *(Suitable for all ages.)*

IDLE HANDS (Columbia) Sick, reckless teen black comedy was essentially pulled from the boxoffice, and it's sure to rattle unwary adults who stumble into the room in their post-Columbine haze. Its target audience, however, will find much to enjoy in this wise-ass send up of slacker and splatter stereotypes. *Teenbeat* meat Devon Sawa (*Casper, Wild America*, etc.) savors his role's retread of Bruce Campbell's "possessed hand" slapschtick routines from *Evil Dead II*, Seth Green delivers another amusing supporting character performance, and Viveca A. Fox is the fox at the heart of the beast. It isn't as funny as it wants to be, but there are a couple of howlers (undead Green's reason for not going "into the light" still cracks me up) and my teenagers ate it up, so what do I know? *(Rated 'R' for violence, gore, sexual situations, strong language, blasphemy.)* [6]

THE OTHER SISTER (1998): Director Garry Marshall (*Pretty Woman*) plucks your heartstrings again with this romantic comedy in which mentally-challenged young Carla (Juliette Lewis of *What's Eating Gilbert Grape?*) struggles with her caring but nervous mother (Diane Keaton) for independence. When Carla falls head-over-heels in love (with Giovanni Ribisi of *Saving Private Ryan, The Mod Squad*, etc.), her yearning for freedom only intensifies as their romance blossoms. *(Rated 'PG-13' for language, suggestive situations.)*

SOMETIMES THEY COME BACK... FOR MORE (1999): Sometimes... they don't. Fourth installment of the direct-to-video horror series inspired by the Stephen King short story abandons the small-town settings of prior entries to borrow elements from *The Thing*. An investigation team encounters the latest demonic infestation in a remote Antarctica research installation. Yawn. *(Rated 'R' for violence, some strong language.)*

SOUTHIE (1999): Donnie Wahlberg (formerly of New Kids on the Block, recently registering as the traumatized bedroom intruder in the opening scene of *The Sixth Sense*) finds you can't go home again—especially when home is the underbelly of South Boston, and your family (including sister Rose McGowan) is intent on pulling

---

[6] The *Video Views* reviews (or abridgements) for *Cookie's Fortune, Idle Hands, The Matrix, Naked Man, Ravenous, Twin Dragons* and *Yellow Submarine* also appeared in "Vid View" in *VMag* #22, September 1999, pp. 40, 42.

you down with them. Harrowing urban drama directed by John Shea scored at numerous independent film festivals, and is well worth a look. *(Unrated, but would have earned an 'R' for strong language, street violence and gunplay.)*

TWIN DRAGONS (1991) Jackie Chan stars as twin brothers separated at birth in this spry, comical contemporary kung-fu reinvention of the venerable *The Corsican Brothers*. One had grown up to be a celebrated classical musician, the other a kung-fu-wielding gangster, and sparks fly in the subsequent culture clash and confused identities. Co-directed by Hong Kong action masters Tsui Hark and Ringo Lam, who keep the kettle at a high boil throughout and coax one (two?) of Chan's most ingratiating performances among the jaw-dropping barrage of stunt work, making this one of Chan's most accessible films. Great fun for all, especially Chan fans who've been waiting to see a decent version of this decade-old gem (prior video releases were washed-out and poorly-dubbed), and a much more entertaining intro to Jackie's charms than *Mr. Nice Guy*. Once again New Line has tampered with the original film for the Americanized version. Leave 'em alone! *(Rated 'PG-13' for martial arts action, but like all Jackie Chan movies, this is a playful film, and never mean-spirited.)*

URBAN MENACE (1999): Gritty urban actioner stars Snoop Dogg as a lunatic preacher out to settle a score with a nasty church-burning, family-killing crime syndicate (led by Big Pun and Fat Joe). This hyper-violent shoot-'em-up and action fest from vet action director Albert Pyun (who made mark with *The Sword and the Sorcerer* in the early 1980s) boasts an edgy rap and hip-hop cast (also including Ice-T and Big Punisher), score, and attitude, but that doesn't really put much meat on these bones. *(Rated a strong 'R' for language, gunplay, and relentless violence.)*

September 16:

COOKIE'S FORTUNE (1999): Lively Southern Gothic confection from veteran director Robert Altman (*M*A*S*H, McCabe and Mrs. Miller, Nashville, The Player, Short Cuts*, etc.) enlivens a spare melodramatic comedy-of-ill-manners with a great ensemble cast (including Liv Tyler, Julianne Moore, Charles S. Dutton, Chris O'Donnell, Ned Beatty, and more). An entertaining gumbo of trouble is bubbling way down south in Holly Springs, Mississippi. A rich widow's suicide leaves her grieving friends reeling—and dealing with the chaos and accusations prompted by greedy relatives scrabbling for her fortune by making it look like the old belle was murdered. Glenn Close soars like a vulture throughout, trying to steal the show as the greediest of the lot, but the more laid-back performers wisely hold his or her own against the scenery-chewing. Altman and company evidently enjoyed themselves, and the fun is infectious. Too bad there's no good catfish enchilada takeout in the area... Lesser Altman, but rewarding fun for discriminating viewers. Recommended! *(Rated 'PG-13' for strong language and sexual situations.)*

THE CORRUPTOR (1999): Underrated director James Foley (*At Close Range, Fear*) delivers the gritty goods in this somber adult thriller that boasts Chow Yun-Fat's breakthrough performance in an American film. Chow Yun-Fat has enjoyed stellar stardom in Hong Kong and

Asia for well over a decade, scoring international success as the lead in classic urban shoot-'em-ups like Ringo Lam's *City on Fire* (which provided the blueprint for Quentin Tarantino's *Reservoir Dogs*) and John Woo's exhilarating *A Better Tomorrow I* and *II*, *The Killer*, and *Hard-Boiled* before making his leap to Hollywood with last year's *Replacement Killers*. Director Foley coaxes absorbing, sharp character studies out of Chow Yun-Fat and co-star Mark Wahlberg (*The Basketball Diaries, Fear, Boogie Nights, The Big Hit*), and at its best this sleeper is evocative of director Sidney Lumet's introspective policers (*The Offence, Serpico, Prince of the City, Q&A*). *(Rated 'R' for strong language, gunplay and violence, and sexual situations.)*

CURSE OF THE BLAIR WITCH (1999): Frightening "mockumentary" companion piece to the record-breaking summer horror chiller *The Blair Witch Project* [see pp. 79-88], the most profitable independent film ever made. No, it's *not* a true story; it's an ingenious and convincing concoction, a pop-cultural urban legend contrived by two hungry filmmakers eager to make their mark. This featurette blends interviews, archival footage (some real, lifted from older horror films like *Horror Hotel*, 1960, but the rest of it is expertly faked), and excerpts from the feature to document the invented "backstory" of the Blair Witch, the case histories of area disappearances and hauntings associated with her legacy, and the lives of the three students whose fate was chronicled in the feature (which, by the way, hits video stores October 22 (see review, below)). Clever and chilling. *(Unrated; Like the feature, there's nothing explicit shown here, but it's pretty creepy stuff, not intended for children or overly gullible viewers.)*

FORCES OF NATURE (1999): En route to his wedding in Georgia, Ben Affleck is stranded in New York and desperately hits the road hitchhiking with Sandra Bullock, silly fellow. He of course finds his life spiraling madly out of control, swept up in a whirlwind romance. Affleck and Bullock lend their questionable charisma to this lame, hyperactive comedy-of-bad-manners from DreamWorks, calculated to heat up the coolest September nights—if you're among the susceptible. *(Rated 'PG-13' for language and sexual situations.)*

GOD SAID HA! (1998): Exceptional, confrontational one-woman stage show by comedienne extraordinaire Julia Sweeney (of *Saturday Night Live* fame and *It's Pat!* infamy) intimately dissects the roller coaster ride of her past few years. Suddenly single and aching for privacy in her new home, Julia's life was turned inside-out by her brother's terminal illness: thrust into the role of primary care giver, her privacy shattered by brother, mother, and father moving in with her, and her career nose diving in the wake of the calamity, she discovered she, too, had cancer. Well, yes, it's a bummer, but Julia's extended monologue detailing this harrowing rite-of-passage is both surprisingly hilarious and ultimately heartbreaking, and a testimonial to the remarkable life-saving device humor provided in coping with the tragedy and absurdity of all she and her family endured. A rare theatrical event, thankfully committed to video and highly recommended. *(Rated 'PG-13' for strong language.)*

PRINCE OF EGYPT (1998): DreamWorks honcho Jeffrey Katzenberg was the studio bigwig behind the resurrection of Disney animation back over a decade ago, scoring big with his revamp of the animation unit and productions like *The Little Mermaid, Beauty and the Beast*, and *The Lion King*, which broke boxoffice records around the world. This is Katzenberg's first creative (as opposed to legal) salvo at the Disney empire from his DreamWorks kingdom, and it is an often breathtaking animated epic. Eschewing the fairy tale source material Disney and its imitators depend upon, *Prince of Egypt* boldly draws from the Biblical Old Testament to chronicle the life of young Moses, his coming of age, and awakening to the will of God and role as leader of the chosen people. Expansive, exciting, and visually magnificent, this is much more than just a cartoon remake of *The Ten Commandments. (Rated 'PG' for mild violence, Old Testament "blood and thunder"; some imagery may frighten very young viewers.)*

YELLOW SUBMARINE (1968): Long out of print on video and richly deserving of this overdue restoration and re-release, *Yellow Submarine* was the premiere psychedelic-era cartoon feature of the 1960s that proved Walt Disney's reign over theatrical feature animation could be usurped—"All you need is love!" This magnificent restored version (with the original monaural soundtrack supplanted by a full stereo Dolby Digital remaster) has enjoyed limited theatrical showings across the US this month; sadly, the closest shot we had was the recent engagement in Boston. Animator/cartoonist Scott Shaw caught it (three times!) last week in Los Angeles, and reports online: "We just got back from seeing *Yellow Submarine*... The sound is great; not only did the Beatles' songs sound like they'd been rearranged, but George Martin's score was much richer and more evident in general.... The *big* news is that the "Hey, Bulldog" sequence is included in this new version, but *not* where I expected to see it! ...in my opinion, *Yellow Submarine* definitely still holds its own against the slicker modern animated competition" (which, as Scott points out, includes this year's Disney's *Tarzan*, Warner's excellent *The Iron Giant*, and the impending Disney theatrical release of the *anime* classic *Princess Mononoke*). It took four writers (including Erich Segal, hot off the staggering best-seller success of his novel *Love Story*) to concoct the nonsensical plot, sending the Beatles aboard the Yellow Submarine (borrowed from their joyous song) to brave the Sea of Time, the Sea of Monsters, the Sea of Holes, and more to save Pepperland from the ravages of the invading Blue Meanies. Still as ravishing, playful, and eye-popping as ever, peppered from stem to stern with now-vintage Beatles songs and the animated Fab Foursome themselves (who, sadly, did not provide the voice performances, though they do make a live-action cameo appearance at the end). There's also Jeremy Hilary Boob Phud (PhD), Lord Admiral Fred, the venerable Mayor of Pepperland, but best of all are the Blue Meanies, including the corps of giant Apple Bonkers, the Snapping-Turtle Turks, the Butterfly Stompers, Countdown Clowns, Max, and the Chief Blue Meanie ("Bring me my GLOVE!"). Heinz Edelman's incredible design work borrowed elements from artist Peter Max and other artifacts of the era, synthesizing them into an inventive imaginary landscape with its own very distinctive identity; Beatles producer George Martin provided a lovely orchestral score seamlessly weaving between the Beatles numbers, and British animation director George Dunning brought it all to the screen with wit and vision. What are you waiting for, then? "All Together Now..." This sell-through video re-release also sports delectable extras, including previously unseen sequences restored to their proper place in the narrative, the song cut from the original theatrical version of the film ("Hey, Bulldog"), and a very cool documentary chronicling the making of the film. It's even better on DVD, with many more extras, including commentary, storyboards (including sequences that were never completed), full Dolby Digital 5.1 soundtrack and a lavish booklet detailing the film's production and history. *(Rated 'G', suitable for All Ages.)*

Recent & Recommended: Children of Heaven (1998, charming Iranian tale of young brother and sister trying to hide the loss of the little girl's shoes, nominated for an Academy Award as Best Foreign Film); ***Deep Crimson*** (1997, wicked masterpiece from Spain based on the true-life "Lonely Hearts Murders" previously filmed as the cult gem *The Honeymoon Killers*); ***Jack Kerouac's Road*** (1996, fine documentary from the National Film Board of Canada detailing the life, times, and bohemian artistry of the King of the Beats); and ***Razorblade Smile*** (1998, an interesting British urban blend of the female vampire genre and *La Femme Nikita* action).

September 23:

THE MATRIX (1999): The Wachowski Brothers wrote and directed this remarkable followup to their previous thriller *Bound* (1996, also highly recommended), flexing considerable storytelling muscle and mobilizing big-budget studio backing and state-of-the-art effects work. Keanu Reeves (who cuts his teeth for this role in his first cyberpunk outing as *Johnny Mneumonic*, 1995) finds the equivalent to the rabbit hole of *Alice in Wonderland* in all those little holes in your telephone mouthpiece—which, in this delirious dystopian thriller, doubles as a teleporter for a desperate group of fugitive rebels who think Reeves is their promised Messiah. Deservedly one of the surprise boxoffice smashes of the year, this ingenious science-fiction tale of "us" (the last sentient human beings) vs. "them" (the nastiest tyrannical non-human entities in recent cinematic memory, disguised as omnipotent "men-in-black") in the virtual lane calculatedly pulls the rug out from under your feet at every turn on first viewing. Stay with it, though—it all makes perfect sense in the end. This hyper-kinetic crazy-quilt of futuristic science-fiction archetypes, Hong Kong martial-arts films, Lewis Carroll references, and drop-dead action sequences works up quite a head of steam and coalesces into one of the decade's best sf epics. Pop cultural cross-references abound, but comics-and-comix-illiterate critics completely missed the considerable debt due to Last Gasp's underground comix title *Slow Death* of the early 1970s (owing a particular debt to Richard Corben's chilling comix story "How Howie Made It In The Real World," in which 'Howie' wakes up to find the illusory utopia he savors cloaks a horrific dystopian reality, and Charles Dallas' horrific "The Book of Zee," in which what's left of the human race is subjugated by a subterranean insect-like dominant species and bred to be their food), and the fact that this is essentially a super-hero movie. Forget about *Superman, Batman*, and *The Mystery Men*—*The Matrix* is the best super-hero movie ever made, period. The DVD is one of the best DVD bargains to hit the shelves, chock-full of commentary, documentaries, and extras, including jaw-dropping analysis of the unprecedented special effects miracles throughout. If you've never tried DVD in your own home, make this the trial run. Recommended! *(Rated 'R' for sometimes strong violence, martial arts action, gunplay, and strong language.)*

MY FAVORITE MARTIAN (1999): Believe it or not, it all began with a one-shot 1958 television play by none other than Gore Vidal entitled *Visit to a Small Planet*, which lost its most topical satirical elements when adapted to the big screen as a Jerry Lewis theatrical feature in 1960. Nevertheless, *Visit to a Small Planet* was successful enough to spawn the sitcom *My Favorite Martian* (Sept. 1963 - Sept. 1966), in which excitable newspaper reporter Tim O'Hara (Bill Bixby) sheltered a benevolent extraterrestrial castaway, claiming he was his own Uncle Martin (Ray Walston). This Disney Studios remake of the venerable CBS-TV series appropriately recasts Jeff Daniels in Bixby's role, Christopher Lloyd in top geek-form as Uncle Martin, and spices the inevitable sitcom romance with Darryl Hannah (and, in a nod to the source material, Ray Walston as a government agent with a secret). In the spirit of their recent Robin Williams fantasy *Flubber* (which was, in turn, a remake of Disney's own 1961 *The Absent-Minded Professor*), inventive CGI (Computer-Generated Imagery) special effects liven up the slapstick from beginning to end, spicing the original TV series' low-tech antics (Uncle Martin's antennae, finger-pointing telekinesis, etc.) with dazzling, cutting-edge high-tech creations (primary among them Zoot, Uncle Martin's talkative, shape-shifting polymorphic space suit). Needless to say, Gore Vidal it's not, but the kids will love it, and Lloyd and Daniels are in good form. No doubt, a *Mr. Ed* or (shudder!) *My Mother the Car* remake is already in the works.

(Rated 'PG'—as in Disney Studios' recent Eddie Murphy Doctor Dolittle *remake, many of the gags are suggestive and somewhat scatological, though on third-grade playground level.)*

THE NAKED MAN (1998): Don't be fooled by the ballyhoo playing up Ethan Coen's creative role in this mess. And it *is* a mess. Ethan only co-wrote the screenplay; the film itself was co-authored and solo-directed by J. Todd Anderson, marginalizing Coen's effort. And don't forget that while the Coen Brothers have carved a unique niche for their own idiosyncratic brand of bizarro comedy, the charms of *Raising Arizona* and *The Big Lebowski* go hand-in-hand with the misfires of *Barton Fink* and their association with Sam Raimi's sophomore debacle *Crimewave* (both films I happen to love, but they are misfires). *The Naked Man* (no relation to Randy Newman's classic song) chronicles the maturation, mental collapse, and resurrection of one chiropractor extraordinaire named Ed (Michael Rapaport) who moonlights as "The Naked Man," a wrestler adorned in a "visible man" leotard externalizing the internal organs of the human body. This contrived, off-kilter deadpan parody opens with a promisingly engaging first act that loses its footing after the traumatic event that causes Ed to lose his mind and memory, never to regain its balance. It quickly degenerates into an increasingly unpleasant and unamusing mishmash of disparate elements (including a villainous mock-Elvis, bikers, a scheming paraplegic pharmaceutical-chain mogul, and a ludicrously graphic death-by-plane-propeller finale). Produced by Ben Barenholtz, one of the pioneers of the Midnight Movie phenomenon of the 1970s (including the release of David Lynch's *Eraserhead*), evidently still in search of cinematic oddities worthy of attention, but pedigree and good intentions do not a cult movie make. "Feel the marshmallow," indeed. *(Rated 'R' for language, violence, and sundry unpleasantries.)*

OPEN YOUR EYES (ABRE LOS OJOS, 1997): Compelling, convoluted subtitled Spanish psychological suspenser blurs romance, reality, dreams, nightmares, and waking visions as it tells the tale of handsome young heartbreaker Cesar (Eduardo Noriega). Cesar is a beguiling fellow who has inherited a fortune and lives in sterile luxury, repeatedly stealing his best friend's dates, squirming under the obsessive pursuit of a woman he bedded and desperately wants to abandon, and believing he is finally, honest-to-God falling in love with another of his best friend's dates (ravishing Penelope Cruz, who co-starred in the underrated western drama *The Hi-Lo Country*). His affairs are further complicated by the fact that he may or may not have been hideously disfigured in an auto accident, or that his features may or may not have been surgically reconstructed, or that the love of his life may or may not be—ah, but that would be telling. This haunting, erotic mystery twists and turns through many detours, blind alleys, and narrative surprises, and will keep you guessing to the last second. *(Rated 'R' for strong language, sexual situations, and violence.)*

THE OUT-OF-TOWNERS (1999): My fellow Vermonters, native or transplanted, will find plenty of nightmare material in Neil Simon's black comedy about a cranky, affluent, and excruciatingly stupid married couple stranded in an increasingly hostile New York City purgatory. This was originally filmed in 1970 with Jack Lemmon and Sandy Dennis as the cosmopolitan castaways. This time around the block, Steve Martin and Goldie Hawn star as the hapless duo; they are put through their paces en route to a badly needed job interview. *Monty Python* vet John Cleese (recreating his legendary *Fawlty Towers* role) spices the Neil Simon stew as the manager of the posh NYC hotel Martin and Hawn repeatedly seek shelter in, though lack of cash or a valid credit card is soon the least of their troubles. Martin Scorsese recognized that this scenario is really a horror movie in disguise, offering his own unofficial remake back in 1985 under the title *After Hours*. *(Rated 'PG-13' for language, sexual situations.)*

RAVENOUS (1999): A discredited soldier (Guy Pearce of *L.A. Confidential* and *Priscilla, Queen of the Desert*) is exiled to a remote military compound in the wintry mountains of the Northwest, he encounters a crazed cannibal (Robert Carlyle of *Trainspotting, The Full Monty, Go Now*, etc., in a razor-sharp performance). The ensuing terrors leave him stranded, alone and wounded, wrestling with his own awakening thirst for blood, until he makes his way back to the fort, where he finds himself out of the frying pan and into the fire. This unique blend of genres isn't for all tastes, and definitely not for the squeamish, but adventurous viewers will find much to savor in this harrowing tale distilled from the notorious true-life accounts of the Donner Party and Alferd Packer. In the tradition of filmmakers like Kathryn Bigelow (*Near Dark*), Mary Lambert (*Pet Semetary, Siesta*) and Katt Shea (*Poison Ivy, The Rage: Carrie 2* [see review, pg. 69]), director Antonia Bird (who made her mark with the controversial 1994 Miramax title *Priest*) proves she can leave the timid Hollywood men's club in the dirt when she wants to disturb and terrify an audience, slyly incorporating many primal folklore demons, including lycanthropy, vampires (note Carlyle's startling evocation of the real-life Vlad the Impaler, historical inspiration for Bram Stoker's *Dracula*), and the Wendigo. Bird's stature and the top-drawer cast only added to the woes of 20th Century Fox's marketing department when they tried peddling this decidedly odd, utterly original horror-western curio to the public. No surprise it stiffed at the boxoffice, but it's ripe for rediscovery on video. *(Rated 'R' for strong violence.)*

September 30:

DESERT HEAT (1999): Action star Jean-Claude Van Damme has lost some of his stellar luster of late, but this modest actioner set in the modern west finds Van Damme in fine form, executive-producing as well as starring and wisely surrounding himself with a solid cast of veteran character actors (including Pat Morita, Danny Trejo, Larry Drake, and Vincent Schiavelli). Lone drifter Eddie Lomax (Van Damme) is left for dead in the desert, and in his own good time gets back on his feet to exact revenge for his agonies... but Eddie isn't your typical angry, soulless, teeth-gritting killing machine. Identified throughout with the coyote as his "familiar," Van Damme doesn't take himself too seriously this outing, delivering an amusing lead performance which lends considerable playful energy to the usual shoot-'em-up genre exercise. *(Rated 'R' for language, one sex scene, gunplay, a little martial arts action, and violence.)*

JERRY SEINFELD, LIVE ON BROADWAY: "I'M TELLING YOU FOR THE LAST TIME" (1998): In the wake of the series finale of his popular primetime sitcom series Seinfeld, an international tour of Jerry Seinfeld's stand-up comedy routines concluded with this performance at New York City's Broadhurst Theater on Broadway. It's an ideal synthesis of the material that landed Seinfeld a series in the first place. From his verbal snapshots of taxi drivers, horse races (from the horse's point of view), dry cleaners, airport security, questionable Olympic events, and late-night TV "infomercials," to his memorable characterization of those nasty wet hairs that cling to the walls when you shower, Seinfeld's assured delivery and breezy, often hilarious stream-of-consciousness style jaunts through a seemingly endless variety of topics, casually linking the unlinkable. At times, however, you can't help but note how far success distanced the comedian from the source of his original routines; when Jerry commiserates about the agonies of flying coach, one inevitably wonders how long it's been since Jerry saw the other side of the first-class curtain on a jumbo jet. Still, the man was in top form this particular night, and we're thankful for the parting shot. The opener, fantasizing a gathering of Seinfeld's precursors and peers (from Alan King to George Carlin, all playing themselves) sobbing over a funeral service for Seinfeld's classic stand-up material, is a corker. *(Unrated; Suitable for all ages.)*

JOAN OF ARC (1999): Leelee Sobieski delivers a galvanizing performance as Joan of Arc, the teenage girl moved by visions of her patron saint and dialogue with God to become a warrior and forge a free and united France—only to be burned at the stake as a heretic at the age of nineteen. Sobieski soars, but the older members of the stellar cast deliver the goods, too, with Peter Strauss, Powers Boothe, Shirley MacLaine, and particularly Peter O'Toole (as the Bishop Cauchon) filling their roles with veteran prowess. Those who grew up with TV's *Doogie Howser*, however, may not be able to suppress a chuckle or two at Neil Patrick Harris' turn as the crowned King of France. This is at least the fifth major film adaptation of the Joan of Arc legend; Ingrid Bergman (*Joan of Arc*, 1948), Jean Seberg (*Saint Joan*, 1957), and others made their mark on the role, but Maria Falconetti remains the most radiant of all in Carl Dreyer's 1928 silent classic *The Passion of Joan of Arc* (coming to video later in October in a remastered, rescored edition, which is *highly* recommended). This contemporary production is the best in the recent run of made-for-TV spectacles, undoubtably the finest since *Gulliver's Travels* and bringing a far more sober and appropriately reverent approach to its religious subject matter than the misconceived epic *Noah's Arc* (1999). Canadian director Christian Duguay helms with assurance and dignity (having come a long way from his debut in 1991-92 with two cheapjack sequels to David Cronenberg's telekinetic horror film *Scanners*), mounting a handsome period atmosphere rich in color, costume, and pageantry while capturing the agonies of poverty, repression, and war. The musical score is lavish, too, embellished by the vocals of young Charlotte Church. Recommended. *(This made-for-television production was not rated by the MPAA. It is suitable for all but the very young and impressionable; older children, however, may find be inspired by the film. The scenes of battle are occasionally graphic, and the film is emotionally harrowing, but the film does not unduly linger over the violence of battle or Joan's torture.)*

A LESSON BEFORE DYING (1999): Winner of this year's Emmy Award for best made-for-TV feature, this moving adaptation of Ernest J. Gaines' best-selling novel boasts fine performances from its top-drawer cast, led by Don Cheadle, Cicely Tyson, and Mekhi Phifer. A young man (Phifer, who first starred in Spike Lee's *Clockers*) caught in the wrong place at the wrong time is found guilty of a murder he did not commit and sentenced to death, and is further agonized by his racist defense attorney's dismissal of him as being no more than an animal. Goaded by family and friends, the village schoolteacher (Cheadle) reluctantly engages with the prisoner, and together they struggle to come to terms and seek some kind of peace with the monstrous injustice of the verdict, and the world they grew up in. Don Cheadle is a remarkable actor, and this is the latest in an unbroken run of fine, surprisingly diverse performances (he previously appeared in *Devil in the Blue Dress, Boogie Nights, The Rat Pack*, and others; check 'em out!). Recommended. *(Rated 'PG-13' for language, violence, and emotional intensity.)*

THE MUMMY (1999): Populist director Stephen Sommers cut his teeth with a trio of Disney live-action family films (*The Adventures of Huckleberry Finn, Tom and Huck*, and *The Jungle Book*) and blended science-fiction monsters and high-seas heist action in his previous effort, *Deep Rising* (1998). Much as I loathed *Deep Rising*, Sommers hit it big time with this clever, audience-pleasing reworking of the Universal *Mummy* archetypes, and have to admit I fell for it, too. Forget about Boris Karloff's brittle, lovelorn Im-Ho-Tep in the original 1932 classic *The Mummy*; western star Tom Tyler's turn as the resurrected Kharis in *The Mummy's Hand*

(1940); Lon Chaney Jr.'s memorable foot-dragging through the rest of the 1940s sequels; or Christopher Lee's athletic revamp of the character for the first full-color *Mummy* (complements of the British Hammer Studio in 1959). Sommers retools the dusty archetype as an exotic post-*Indiana Jones* action-adventure epic, and the pleasure is all yours. There are a few chilling moments, a little grue, and a plethora of dazzling computer-generated wonders, but atmospheric horror takes a backseat to romantic comedy-action hijinks and sprawling fantasy imagery as Brendan Fraser and Rachel Weisz struggle against the mounting supernatural might of Arnold Vosloo's omnipotent Im-Ho-Tep, who whips up sandstorms, hordes of flesh-eating scarabs, and a small army of fellow mummies with malevolent abandon. Imaginative, rousing fun and aggressively American from beginning to end, suitable for all but the youngest and most impressionable viewers. *(Rated 'PG-13' for violence and horrific imagery; some viewers may find the Hollywood Arab stereotypes offensive.)*

THREE SEASONS (BA MUA, 1999): Vietnamese filmmaker Tony Bui returned to his native country to shoot this compelling, carefully crafted, visually splendid portrait of four citizens of "the New Vietnam," finding their way in modern Saigon. Director Bui engages all our senses as he steeps the viewer in the people and the landscape, from the oven of the inner city at high noon (where a cyclo-driver ekes out a living and aches for an evening alone with a prostitute he is smitten with; and a young street urchin's suitcase is stolen, driving him to seek out the American G.I. he believes is the thief) to the intoxicating waters where the white-lotus harvest blooms (and a young woman labors for a reclusive poet, in whom she awakens a spark which prompts him to write again). Harvey Keitel co-financed, executive-produced, and co-stars (as the Marine returning to Saigon to find the child he left behind). A heartfelt labor of love, which conveys the beauty, menace, poetry, underbelly, scars, spirit, heart, and voice of a country few of us will ever otherwise experience. Filmed in Vietnamese (subtitled in English) and English, and most highly recommended—this is the week's best film, without a doubt. *(Rated 'PG-13' for language, adult and sexual situations.)*

October 7:

DETOUR (1999): John Travolta's brother Joey directed this low-key rural thriller. A thief on the skids (Jeff Fahey) is set up by a local mobster (Gary Busey) to rob the mob boss' business front—after Busey has already cleaned out the safe. Fahey is on the run, squeezed between the mob, the hometown sheriff (Michael Madsen) who also happens to be his brother-in-law, and his partners itching for one more score, all while tending to a family legacy that includes a daughter he didn't know he had and the ball-and-chain of a diary farm. Like Fahey's character, this film frantically straddles gritty shoot-'em-up violence and homespun sentimentality, but it's a pleasant evening entertainment for thriller fans. *(Rated 'R' for language, violence, gunplay, nudity, and sexual situations.)* [7]

---

[7] The *Video Views* reviews (or abridgements) for *Detour, eXistenZ, Pirates of Silicon Valley, Pushing Tin* and *The Rage: Carrie 2* also appeared in *VMag* #23, October 1999, pp. 36-37.

HANDS ON A HARD BODY (1998): That's "Hard Body" as in *truck*, pardner. Winner of the American Film Institute's Audience Award, this surprisingly engaging documentary chronicles an annual endurance contest sponsored by a Nissan dealership in Longview, Texas. The contest is simple: whoever can stand awake and upright with his or her hand on the prize brand-new "Hard Body" pickup truck the longest gets to drive the truck home, free of charge, no strings attached. The action—or inaction, I should say—is confined to one parking lot and an ever-dwindling group of contestants, but filmmaker S.R. Bindler captures it all on video with clarity and heart. Bindler doesn't mock the participants, or inflate their self-imposed purgatory into an attack on our consumer culture—he just captures their struggle for all to see. We recognize them as our friends, neighbors, family, and ourselves, with needs and desires we all share. Neil Kassanoff's laconic musical score and Guy Forsyth's steel guitar tie it all together; note that Texan actor Matthew McConaughey and *The Mummy* star Arnold Vosloo helped finance the production. Absurd as it may sound, this is a fine little movie, highly recommended. Where do we sign up? *(Rated 'PG' for a flurry of strong language from one unhappy contestant who dropped out, this is otherwise suitable for all ages.)*

LOST AND FOUND (1999): Fans of *Saturday Night Live*'s David Spade won't want to miss this latest outing, in which Spade's usual slippery-sleazeball character falls for the ravishing cellist next door (Sophie Marceau) and schemes to woo and win her by imprisoning her little pet terrier in his apartment until the time is right to contrive a faked rescue. However—as is the case with other contemporary comedy stars (like Adam Sandler), if you're not a fan, this may not be your cup of tea. Spade's comedy is intentionally grating, and the little dog routine echoes *As Good As It Gets* and *There's Something About Mary*, which were much better films. *Lost and Found* doesn't satirize romantic comedy clichés; it embraces them, which doesn't jive with Spade's schtick or persona, undermining the whole enterprise. If you like Spade, though, you'll find some belly-laughs here. *(Also on DVD; rated 'PG-13' for language, sexual situations, and scatological gags: lots of dog-doo jokes here, folks.)*[8]

PUSHING TIN (1999): Just in time for those of you booking flights for the upcoming holiday season, here's a flick calculated to fray the nerves of those already nervous about "flying the friendly skies." It's a rocky plane ride with a bumpy landing, but the top-drawer cast

---

[8] For the record, here's my unpublished review of the same title written for *Vmag*: **LOST AND FOUND** (Warner): *SNL*'s David Spader has his fans, and they will undoubtably enjoy this "romantic comedy," in which Spader plays an utter asshole who uses everyone around him in such an offhand way that he's supposed to still come off as likable (the comedian's schtick, y'understand), while conniving to keep the pet dog of the hot babe next door imprisoned in his apartment long enough to score with her. What a fucking weasel—which is, of course, the joke—ha. ha. The little dog routine was better used and abused in *As Good As It Gets* and *There's Something About Mary*; we're supposed to laugh at the conceit that Spader's brain dead cronies will even manhandle dog shit for him, but not a spot of dung rubs off on our hero, robbing viewers like me who are tired of Spader's comedy persona of whatever potential payoff this confection might have once harbored.

(John Cusack, Billy Bob Thornton, Cate Blanchett, and Angelina Jolie, among others) elbow their way through a quirky mix of cutting-edge black comedy and increasingly annoying soap opera hysterics (the fallow and frayed home life with ignored, bored, restless, and understandably fed-up spouses and sexual partners), elevating the material throughout as best they can. *Pushing Tin* is a skewed *Airport* for the 1990s based on an article by journalist Darcy Frey, whose main points (air controller working conditions and lifestyles can be deadly) are diluted by the Hollywood formulas imposed on this lethal concoction; oh, it's a mess, but it sure has its moments. The control room sequences are mesmerizing, as overworked air controllers struggle to maintain their professional edge and occasionally gamble with plane routes and the lives of thousands. When the sparks fly, the film sizzles—particularly when it focuses on the escalating macho one-upsmanship fever Cusack mounts against hotshot newcomer Thornton, whose landing-strip "therapy" treatment is a real howler. *(Also on DVD; Rated 'R' for language, partial nudity, and sexual situations.)* Note that John Cusack also stars in another brand-new release *This is My Father* (1999, rated 'R'), a moving, critically-acclaimed drama co-starring Aidan Quinn, Stephen Rea (of *The Crying Game*), and James Caan (in his best role since *Misery*), which I heartily recommend.

THE THIRTEENTH FLOOR (1999): This compelling science-fiction mystery-thriller was overshadowed at the boxoffice by the somewhat similar trappings of *The Matrix*, but it's well worth catching up with on video. Convoluted, intricately-plotted tale of experimental simulated time-travel via "thought transference" from the present-day Los Angeles to L.A. circa 1937 is evocative of *Blade Runner* and *Dark City*; this time, the retro-*noir* atmospherics are absolutely anchored to the narrative itself. When the billionaire genius behind the secret project (Armin Mueller-Stahl of *Shine*) is murdered, his partner (Craig Berke) is the prime suspect, prompting him to cross back and forth between the parallel eras to unravel the truth about the crime and the project—and his own existence. Vincent D'Onofrio and Gretchen Mol deliver the goods in their doppelganger roles; stylish, cunning, and engrossing throughout. Recommended. *(Also on DVD; rated 'R' for language, gunplay, and violence.)*

Recent & Recommended:

Two vintage thrillers are new to the shelves this week, and both are highly recommended. Young and old will savor William Castle's deliciously creaky **House on Haunted Hill** (1958), starring the master of menace Vincent Price. This was originally released with one of Castle's renowned gimmicks, "Emergo!", which you can recreate in your own home by flying an inflatable skeleton on a clothesline over your TV and zinging it across the room toward the couch when the on-screen skeleton emerges from the acid-bath. Catch it before the big-budget remake hits the theaters! The second title, though, requires a warning: Michael Powell's terrifying **Peeping Tom** (1960) is decidedly for mature viewers, and cuts much, much deeper than most horror films ever aspire to with its unflinching portrait of a scopophilic serial killer (Carl Boehm). Mind you, there's no explicit sex or graphic violence (the film seems tame by 1990s standards), but *Peeping Tom* remains profoundly disturbing; it also introduced the concept of 'snuff films.' In

1960, the film was so critically reviled that it barely played theatrically, and it ended the career of one of Britain's most renowned directors, Michael Powell (*The Red Shoes, Black Narcissus*, etc.). None other than Martin Scorsese sponsored the restoration for this special letterboxed edition.

Also recommended: the remastered letterboxed re-release of ***The Element of Crime***, the debut film from Danish director Lars Von Trier (*Breaking the Waves*); the one-of-a-kind documentary ***Freaks Uncensored!***, featuring rare archival film footage to trace the history of the human oddity "industry" from the Middle Ages to the 1990s; don't miss Rip Torn's electrifying screen debut as the self-destructive musician awaiting ***Payday***, finally available on video; and Steve McQueen and Faye Dunaway in the remastered original 1968 caper classic ***The Thomas Crown Affair*** (not to be confused with the 1999 remake [see review on pp. 168-170]).

October 14:

GOODBYE LOVER (1999): A gigolo for all ages since he hit Hollywood in the late 1960s, Don Johnson stars as a political public-relations pro having a hot and heavy affair with his brother's upscale real-estate broker wife (Patricia Arquette, the 1990s *femme fatale* of choice from *True Romance, Lost Highway*, and others). When he wants out, she gets vicious, sending careers into tailspins, bodies over balconies, and heads rolling amid the elegance and chic of high-rise big business and the homes of the *nouveau* rich. Far, far from helming *The Killing Fields* and *The Mission*, filmmaker Roland Joffe's direction is slick, sleek, but hardly slumming, playing the constant coupling, scheming, and opportunistic double-and-triple-crossing for cool, coy black comedy entertainment throughout. This calculatedly irreverent, utterly mean-spirited adult amusement also boasts Dermot Mulroney as the cuckold brother, Mary-Louise Parker as the office lover, Ellen DeGeneres as the cynical detective who's seen it all and had her fill ("I don't trust anyone over ten who listens to *The Sound of Music*"), and a co-scripting credit from Joel Coen (of *Fargo* fame). *(Rated 'R' for nudity, sexual activity and situations, and a smattering of on-screen mayhem.)*

PIRATES OF SILICON VALLEY (1999): American movies rarely capture the intricacies or interpersonal nature of business—much less "Big Business"—with any substance or urgency. This is the notable exception, and as such ranks among the best films of the year. Here's an engaging, ultimately devastating chronicle of the rise and rise of Bill Gates (played by former bratpacker Anthony Michael-Hall, delivering the best performance of his adult career) and the rise and corporate consumption of Steve Jobs (*E.R.*'s Noah Wyle, beguiling and riveting throughout as he blithely sells everyone dear to him down the river). Given the constraints of the medium and prescribed running time this made-for-cable docudrama labored within, *Pirates of Silicon Valley* emerges as a meticulously crafted and surprisingly lucid dissection of the personalities and power struggles relevant to the explosive emergence of the personal computer technologies, tracing their respective bids for success, grassroots reinvention of the computer language and technology, and (most importantly) the toll it exacted in human terms from those involved behind closed doors. Power corrupts, but writer-director Martyn Burke (adapting the book by Paul Freiberger) persuasively argues that the seeds of success and tragedy were visible long before either Gates or Jobs became public figures, tracing their intertwined fates from their threadbare roots in the college dorms to the high-tech piracy and power-brokering that made their fortunes. *Pirates* doesn't sweep the real issues under the carpet to play it safe or keep things simple, scoring with wit, clarity, and gripping immediacy. Highly recommended! *(As a made-for-TV feature, this film has not been rated by the MPAA; there is little objectionable material, but note there is occasional strong language, along with depictions of campus riots, counter-cultural sexual values and gender issues, and recreational drug use necessary to biographical recreations of these characters and events.)*

THE RAGE: CARRIE 2 (1999): Just another teen carnage epic, right? Wrong. *The Rage* did well in theaters despite the critical pasting it received for its derivation from King's classic debut novel and Brian De Palma's successful film adaptation (which, by the way, deservedly netted an Academy Award nomination for its star Sissy Spacek) and its unfortunate proximity to the tragic Columbine massacre. It scored at the box office because it's a pretty good little shocker, not just a retread of its namesake, and it has some meat on its bones. Emily Bergl stars as Rachel, the teen with the latent, potentially lethal telekinetic powers, who finds herself unwillingly pitched against the increasing malice of her high school senior classmates (including some familiar faces, like *Dazed and Confused*'s Jason London and *Home Improvement*'s Zachary Ty Bryan); Amy Irving provides the overt link to the original *Carrie*. Director Katt Shea (formerly Katt Shea Rubin) takes the material seriously and on its own terms. She coaxes strong performances from the cast in archetypal roles all concerned could have stumbled through; orchestrates potent setpieces that use the language of its genre to confront genuine issues of teenage and gender anxiety, confusion, and anger; and builds upon documented case histories of communities tolerating (even encouraging) high school sports star "date rapes" of their female classmates, questioning societal misperceptions of the piranha-pit pressure-cookers all too many school environments have become. Though ignored by most critics and feminist cineastes, director Rubin is an exploitation filmmaker deserving of more attention. She went from the grind of acting in a couple Roger Corman T&A fantasy potboilers to directing Corman T&A programmers (*Stripped to Kill 1* and *2*, *Dance of the Damned*, etc.), graduating to the majors with the steamy Drew Barrymore vehicle *Poison Ivy*. Like director Kathryn Bigelow (*Near Dark, Blue Steel, Point Break, Strange Days*, etc.), Rubin seems to prefer working in tried-and-true genres, embracing their pop-cultural shorthand and expressive power. *(Rated 'R' for harsh language, violence, gore, drug and alcohol abuse, nudity, and sexual situations.)*

SLC PUNK (1999): Carrie and Rachel had it rough, but things weren't much easier in the 1980s, particularly if you were a punk rocker trapped in the Mormon paradise of Salt Lake City. Writer/director James Merendino's semi-autobiographical portrait of the trials and tribs of being a hard-core punk college grad slumming it in SLC is a bracing testimonial to a prior generation's struggle to define one's identity and maintain those ideals against the encroaching odds of either snuffing it or joining the Reagan-era rank-and-file—even if those ideals happen to embrace "No Future" and utter despair. Matthew Lillard (who first caught my eye in John Waters' *Serial Mom*, and went on to score in *Scream, She's All That*, and *The Curve*) stars as Stevo, the film's reckless, fearless narrator and protagonist, who sums up his here and now vs. the inevitable compromises down the road by declaring, "If the guy I was then met the guy I am now, he'd beat the **** out of me. Those are the facts." Unflinchingly direct, by turns hilarious and heart breaking, with excellent support from Michael Goorjian, Annabeth Gish, Adam Pascal, and Devon Sawa (the former teen heartthrob of *Casper* and *Wild America* who's lately embracing teen burn-out roles in *Idle Hands* and his sobering turn here as an acid-casualty derelict). Not for all tastes, but nevertheless heartily recommended if you lived through it yourself or are otherwise curious about the period or punk movement. *(Rated 'R' for strong language, sexual activity and situations, drug and alcohol abuse, and violence.)*

10 THINGS I HATE ABOUT YOU (1999): Like *The Rage: Carrie 2* and *SLC Punk*, this teen pic is ultimately concerned with the often harrowing friction between class castes and the risks of stepping beyond one's prescribed boundaries, but it tackles these issues in the language of its preferred genre: the teenage romantic comedy, in which the rewards are usually worth the risks. In fact, *10 Things...* goes back to one of the grandfathers of the entire genre—William Shakespeare's venerable romantic-comedy *The Taming of the Shrew* —to translate the Bard's playful mismatching of couples and entanglements of the heart to a 1990s urban high-school with surprising success. Julia Stiles is Kat (the Shrew), promising Aussie newcomer Heath Ledger is the tamer, Joseph Gordon-Levitt (of TV's *3rd Rock from the Sun*, long locks shorn) is the lovesick beau, and Larisa Oleynik the object of his affection, with nice turns from Andrew Keegan as the arrogant hunk and Larry Miller as the schemer. The youthful cast is appropriately brash and attractive, the dialogue hardly Shakespearean ("What it is with this chick, does she have beer-flavored nipples?"), and the pop tunes play from wall-to-wall in synch with the onscreen antics, but this melding of classical and contemporary formulas manages to come across with its own voice and energy. In the end, all's well that ends well, staying true to its revamped source material, and absolutely in tune with its teen-flick precursors (*Pretty in Pink, Some Kind of Wonderful*) and peers (*She's All That*), proving once again that what goes around, comes around. *(Rated 'PG-13' for suggestive language and sexual situations.)*

Recent & Recommended:

The Chambermaid on the Titanic, the latest, lavish erotic delight from Spanish director Bigas Luna (in Spanish, with English subtitles); ***The Crazy Stranger*** (***Gadjo Dilo***, 1997) once again captures the raw, emotional tapestry of life among the gypsies through the eyes of Tony Gatlif, the director of *Latcho Drom* (highly recommended; subtitled); the 30th Anniversary Edition of Dennis Hopper and Peter Fonda's seminal threnody of the 1960s counterculture, ***Easy Rider***, which ushered in a new era of independent filmmaking and is well worth another viewing if only to savor Jack Nicholson's star-making turn as a reckless alcoholic attorney who joins the bikers in their "search for America."

October 21:

Halloween may be around the corner, but a trio of romances dominates this week's overabundance of new video releases. All three are surprisingly good, and all involve the family arena. Their adult flirtations with tragedy are prompted by yearnings for love lost and love found; the craving for intimacy and the fear of abandonment; the banality of the familiar, the temptation of alternatives, and remorse over roads not taken. All three boast fine performances, well-crafted scripts and direction, and offer engaging mature entertainment for those seeking a little warmth during the season of the Blair Witch.

The first, **A WALK ON THE MOON** (1999), focuses on a wife's emotional sojourn. Diane Lane stars as Pearl, a conservative middle-class 1960s mom feeling trapped in her marriage to Marty (Liev Schreiber), who were wed as teenagers with the birth of their first child, Alison (Anna Paquin, of *The Piano*). Left to her own devices at a an upper-New York State family summer camp, she finds herself irresistibly drawn to the young, long-haired camp blouse salesman Walker (Viggo Mortensen) and his countercultural lifestyle. Mother and daughter's respective sexual awakenings amid the summer of Woodstock and the moon landing set the stage for this involving confrontation with the promise and pain of life changes. Despite the Hollywood gloss and familiar material, it all works thanks to the excellent cast, fine-tuned script (by Pamela Gray), and skillful direction (by actor Tony Goldwyn, still best-remembered as the villainous Lothario of *Ghost*, though he's starred in plenty of films since).

The second, the British production **METROLAND** (1998), casts another sobering, longing look back at the free love legacy of the '60s from the male perspective of an arrested adolescent who still has some growing up to do. Provoked by the visit of his hedonistic childhood friend Toni (Lee Ross), comfortably middle-class London husband and father Chris (Christian Bale) becomes restless in his marriage with Marion (Emily Watson, anchored from the extremes of her startling performance in *Breaking the Waves*). Increasingly consumed by memories and reveries of his bohemian life and love in Paris almost a decade before, Chris is tempted by the freedom and titillation Toni's lifestyle promises. In its engagingly modest way, *Metroland* essentially covers the same ground as this summer's controversial *Eyes Wide Shut*, albeit in more believably human terms and with considerable heart, sans the *nouveau* rich trappings, cabalistic orgies, and Kubrickian sterility.

More magical is the Spanish film **LOVERS OF THE ARCTIC CIRCLE (LOS AMANTES DEL CIRCULO POLAR**, 1997), casting its spell with mystical guile by interweaving the female and male perspectives of its star-crossed partners. The sensual tale of Otto (Fele Martinez, recently seen in *Open Your Eyes*) and Ana (Najwa Nimri) stretches from their first childhood rendezvous through their troubled adolescence, unrelated but living as brother and sister and secret lovers. Separated as adults when the web of synchronicity that binds them seems to break, Ana prematurely says, "There are no good coincidences any more... I used them up too early," though the most extraordinary events lay ahead in the land of the Midnight Sun. If you enjoyed Vincent Ward's *Map of the Human Heart* (1993), this is for you—a marvelous, lyrical film, and highly recommended. Be sure to watch it in one sitting.

There's nothing romantic about **ELECTION** (1999)—which is, really, another of the year's high-school horror films, disguised as a Matthew Broderick comedy—though it too focuses on misunderstood, lovelorn husbands seeking comfort and love in forbidden *Lolita* territory, where angels fear to tred. This relentless, rib-tickling, MTV-produced black comedy from director Alexander Payne (who co-adapted Tom Perrotta's novel) finds galvanizing intrigue amid the banalities of high school student office elections. On the way down (and we do mean "down"—this is a descent into hell) the campaign trail, teacher Matthew Broderick squirms and Payne scores bullseyes targeting teacher-student seductions, opportunistic ethics, questionable role models, the meaning of "success," and the legacy of Reagan era politics which spawns ambitious monsters like Reese Witherspoon's lead character, who will do anything to win because, well, she deserves to win, damn it! You won't be able to take your eyes off the screen; terrifying, sad, utterly hilarious, and highly recommended. *(All four of the films discussed above are rated 'R' for strong language, nudity, sexual activity and situations, and adult themes.)*

Also on the video shelves this week is **LIFE** (1999), Eddie Murphy and Martin Lawrence's first team effort. The film is ambitious, covering a wide canvas of time—chronicling the entire adult lives and uneasy bond between Ray (Eddie Murphy) and Claude (Martin Lawrence)—bound by the emotionally narrow confines of their relationship and the life sentences they serve in a Southern prison for a crime they did not commit. By soft-pedaling the real horrors of the notorious Jim Crow era prison camps (which indeed lasted in the 1970s, and were used to break the spirit of many black civil rights activists)—subject matter that may have initially inspired and attracted the considerable talent evident on this project—the film downplays tragedy for comforting laughs and pathos, and the characters (including Ray and Claude) soon fade from memory just as the supporting players fade from the narrative to mark the passing of time. Still, there's much to enjoy here, particularly Bakeem Woodbine (of *Freeway, Dead Presidents, The Rock*, and *The Big Hit*) as Can't Get Right, a slow-witted mute who unfailingly nails home-runs for the prison team and has a sweet touch with the white ladies. *(Rated 'R' for strong language and some violence.)*

As for Halloween fare, **THE BLAIR WITCH PROJECT** is without a doubt the week's hottest Halloween title—hitting the shelves tomorrow! (see separate article in this section [pg. 79])-- but there's plenty other chilling new titles worth staying up late for.

The biggest surprise is—I kid you not!—**CHILDREN OF THE CORN 666: ISAAC'S RETURN** (1999), the best of a series which I have no doubt Stephen King (whose short story was the source) wished away long, long ago. This latest entry rewarded two viewings, which is more than I can say for any prior offspring. No need to have seen the rest, though the creepy child-man of the original John Franklin returns as lead actor (and co-scripter), playing still-creepy man-child Isaac. All hell breaks loose with the prophetized return of Hannah (Natalie Ramsey), the "first daughter" of "the children of the children" who still worship He Who Walks Behind the Rows. This solid little shocker offers ample twists and turns as Hannah finds herself caught between rival cult factions, and for a change the blood-spilling is chilling. Vets Stacy Keach and Nancy Allen deliver fine supporting roles, and young Paul Popowich is particularly good as the alluring Gabriel. Don't pass this one by, despite the title and deserved bad rep of its corny precursors; it's the best direct-to-video horror film of the Halloween season. *(Rated 'R' for strong language, nudity, sexual activity, violence, gore, and paganistic religious content some might consider blasphemous.)*

Stranger still is **MODERN VAMPIRES** (1999), offering fresh blood to an old vein. Casper Van Dien (*Starship Troopers*) stars as the fanged prodigal son who returns to Los Angeles, infuriating the regional ruling vampire (Dracula himself) and rekindling an age-old feud with vampire-hunter Van Helsing (Rod Steiger, chewing the scenery). The irreverent humor, dialogue, sex, riffs on racist stereotypes, and patently fake gory violence is characteristic of screenplay writer Matthew Bright (*Freeway, Dark Angel: The Ascent, Guncrazy*) and director Richard Elfman (*Forbidden Zone, Shrunken Heads*), brother to Danny Elfman (who scored *Batman, Nightmare Before Christmas*, etc., and provides the title track here). The Elfmans helmed L.A. punk/new wave band Oingo Boingo in the '80s, and Richard directed their giddy midnight movie *Forbidden Zone* (a highly recommended cult curio), co-starring Bright and Danny. *Modern Vampires* will infuriate those who prefer their blood drinking straight up, but if you're in a playful mood, this is delightful. *(Rated 'R' for strong language, sexual activity and situations, violence, and gore.)*

Weirdest of the week's offbeat offerings is David Cronenberg's **EXISTENZ** (1999), starring Jennifer Jason Leigh as Allegra Geller, a world-renowned video game designer whose latest invention literally plugs the player into a deadly virtual reality experience (using a fleshy umbilical cord jacking into a "bioport" drilled into the base of the player's spine). Co-star Jude Law is Geller's protector and fellow player, eluding an apparent competing corporate power's bid to destroy Geller and her new game, "eXistenZ," before it reaches the market. Fans of director Cronenberg (*Scanners, The Fly, Videodrome, Dead Ringers, Naked Lunch, Crash*) have been down this road before and will recognize the familiar turf, from the imagery of pulsing biomechanical devices and flesh-guns to the constantly shifting planes of perceived reality. For the uninitiated, however, this is decidedly different fare, uncompromisingly audience-unfriendly as it calculatedly disorients the viewer, providing a spellbinding, mind-bending roller coaster ride that provides an ideal intro to Cronenberg's inventive, obsessive cinematic universe. Sadly, *eXistenZ*'s limited theatrical run paled in the boxoffice wake of similar "virtual reality" fare like *The Matrix, Dark City* and *The Thirteenth Floor*; catch it now on video and DVD. *(Rated 'R' for violence, gore, and very strange, suggestive imagery involving bioports, umbilical cords, and wet, fleshy objects.)*

Recent & Recommended:

Joan Chen's (of *Twin Peaks*) remarkable directorial debut feature ***Xiu Xiu: The Sent Down Girl*** (1997), which she also stars in and which was banned in her native country China, where it was filmed; Marlon Brando's return to the screen in the low-budget but hilarious redneck black comedy ***Free Money***; the original foreign gem ***Jacob the Liar***, recently revamped by Hollywood for Robin Williams—see the original!—along with two fellow German masterpieces: ***The Ogre***, from *The Tin Drum* director Volker Schlondorff, starring John Malkovich and Armin Mueller-Stahl (*Shine*) and blessed with a remarkable musical score by Michael Nyman (*The Piano*), and the terrifying ***Tenderness of the Wolves***, based on the true case of post-World War 1 cannibal-killer Fritz Haarman (Kurt Raab). And don't overlook the long-awaited return of the wickedest witch of them all in the remastered re-release of the family fantasy classic ***The Wizard of Oz***!

October 21:

Babes in the Woods: THE BLAIR WITCH PROJECT [9]

If you lived through the summer of '99—and if you're reading this, you must have—you've at least heard of ***The Blair Witch Project***. If you're 25 years of age or younger, it was the only "must-see" movie of the year, beckoning long after the memory of *Star Wars: The Phantom Menace* had faded, earning an astounding $109 million plus at the boxoffice. As such, it stands as the most profitable independent film ever made. Springboarding from its considerable summer buzz, *The Blair Witch Project* hits video stores across the nation tomorrow, enticing an even wider audience to invite the witch, for at least one evening, into their own homes.

Love it or loathe it, *Blair Witch* was the event film of 1999, made by and for its own generation, leaving its

---

[9] An abridged version of this article was published in *VMag* #23, October 1999, pg. 38, as "Good Witch/Bad Witch: *The Blair Witch Project*: Two Views"; my review ran as "Good Witch," Brooks Robards wrote "Bad (Bleah) Witch."

mark in the collective imagination as it confounded Hollywood executives and its detractors by breaking all the rules governing what a horror film and boxoffice hit "should" be. What *is* it with this movie? How did a feisty, cheapjack (reportedly made for less than $60,000) independent film with a minimalist plot lacking any name actors, special effects, or Hollywood muscle so completely capture the public eye and imagination? To understand *The Blair Witch Project*—the film, the buzz, and the phenomenon—you must accept one irrefutable fact: There is nothing rational about it.

In all media, from literature to painting, from music to film, the horror genre defies logic. By definition, what we call "horror" is an irrational genre, forever tapping the raw and instinctive realms we work so hard to avoid or suppress in our real lives: fear, dread, dis-ease, along with wonder and awe. Mind you, the best contributions to the genre adhere quite passionately to their own respective internal logic and rhythms, but it is the logic, or illogic, of dreams and nightmares, a primal, atavistic, and utterly emotional terrain.

In the history of cinema, we find that each generation embraces a low-budget independent horror film as its choice collective nightmare, to be terrified by or reviled, with no middle ground possible between these emotional polar-opposite reactions. Critics and detractors lambaste the nightmare as irrational, senseless, repulsive, offensive, and pointless, while those unable to shake its impact spread the word, building the buzz and a cult following. From *The Cabinet of Dr. Caligari* (1919) to *The Evil Dead* (1982), these films seem to literally crawl out of the woodwork, unbidden by the Hollywood powers-that-be. In the 1940s, it was Val Lewton's horror-by-suggestion gems like *The Cat People*; in the 1950s, *I Was a Teenage Werewolf* and *Invasion of the Body Snatchers*. In the early 1960s, it was *Psycho* (yes, it's Alfred Hitchcock, but it was refused by his home studio, Universal, produced via Hitchcock's TV unit in black and white and picked up by a rival studio, Paramount, who laughed all the way to the bank). For my generation, it was George Romero's *Night of the Living Dead* (1968), which broke all the rules. I caught *Night of the Living Dead* with my high-school sweetheart and a close friend who provided the wheels to get us there; halfway through the film, my friend providing the ride stormed out, furious at the movie, threatening to abandon us at the theater. During the climax, my overwhelmed girlfriend was in tears and I escorted her out to the lobby, where I had to beg them both to stay put so I could watch the last few minutes. It was a miserable ride home, but I had never been so scared by a movie in my life. For the 1970s, it was *The Texas Chainsaw Massacre, Eraserhead*, and *Halloween*; for the 1980s, *Friday the 13th, The Evil Dead*, and *Henry: Portrait of a Serial Killer*. We were due for fresh blood, and it just arrived.

Clearly, *The Blair Witch Project* is the collective nightmare of the moment, eschewing the explicit horrors of recent fare to embrace the less-is-more aesthetic of the Val Lewton films of the 1940s (*The Cat People, I Walked With a Zombie*, etc.). It's what you don't see, what you *can't* see, that scares you (the same aesthetic that drove the recent *The Sixth Sense*). The story, such as it is, is simple: three young filmmaking students hike into a stretch of Maryland woodlands to make a documentary about a local witch legend only to become disoriented, lost, and succumb to either their collective madness or the malign supernatural forces they fear.

The Blair Witch Project was the product of young filmmakers working with the available technology and means within reach, clearly addressing many of their generation's fears in their own terms. The shorthand of its chosen genre allows the film to dissect that communal dread with disarming candor. The film calculatingly taps many ancient phobias—of abandonment, of being hunted, of the wilderness, witchcraft, empty houses, and the echoes of the past. But its most unflinching gaze is literally turned back upon the obsessive, narcissistic, emotional scopophilia of a generation raised with "reality TV," a media they wish to capture and claim as surely as it has claimed them. We never see the titular Blair Witch: the screen is dominated throughout by Heather (Heather Donaghue), whose Ahab-like determination to capture the witch on film justifies her craving to capture their every move on video down to their final moments. It's the underbelly of *The Real World* captured with the urgent hand-held camera *verite* of *Cops*, evoking a fate worse than any ever seen on Fox TV's atrocity specials or the notorious *Faces of Death* series. It is all the more terrible because it *cannot* be seen; falling outside the narrow "reality" defined by the camera lens, it is unseeable, unknowable, and incomprehensible.

The film creates a new urban legend grounded in historical fiction. This is part of its allure, enhanced (and hyped) by the inventive subtextual environment crafted online and in its companion "mockumentary" featurette, *Curse of the Blair Witch* (recommended as a companion piece). This conceit is so seductive that many have come to believe the Blair Witch is "real," but rest assured, it's all part of the web the filmmakers are weaving.

This isn't as original a conceit as fans of the film would argue. Orson Welles paralyzed America in 1938 with his "you-are-there" radio broadcast of *The War of the Worlds*, which convinced many panicked listeners that the Martians were indeed coming. In cinema, the "mockumentary" (fake documentary) has been a viable vehicle for almost every genre, from satire (*This is Spinal Tap*) to war films (*13 Charlie Mopic*). The seductive verisimilitude of the form lent potent gravity to two genuinely terrifying TV movies, Peter Watkins' *The War Game* (1967, banned by the BBC for its all-too-believable portrait of England devastated by nuclear war) and Edward Zwick's *Special Bulletin* (1982, in which a faked news broadcasts chronicle America's first nuclear terrorist attack). The BBC terrified UK viewers so badly with the ghost-and-possession 'live TV event' *Ghostwatch* (1992) that it was roundly blasted in the press and the teleplay was never broadcast again. Italian director Ruggero Deodato's horrifyingly explicit "found-footage mockumentary" *Cannibal Holocaust* (1981) was so convincing that the director was brought to trial in Italy for the faked deaths. Closer to home, the independent feature *The Last Broadcast* (1998) preceded *Blair Witch* by over a year, chronicling the dire fate of a young TV film crew filming a segment on the Jersey Devil, leading many to claim *Blair Witch* "borrowed" its premise and approach (you can find out for yourself when *The Last Broadcast* finally comes to video on November 30th [see pg. 136]). There's no doubt, however, the celebrated *Blair Witch* online marketing coup was lifted almost verbatim from *The Last Broadcast*'s own site, which consciously fictionalized the look, feel, and techniques of the site for the genuine documentary *Paradise Lost: The Child Murders at Robin Hood Hills* (1996). Furthermore, *Blair Witch*'s illusory "you are there" film reality adopts the aesthetic of the contemporary European Dogme 95 school (*Celebration, The Idiots*, etc.).

True to form, *Blair Witch* invites the derision of those who (for whatever reason) do not fall under its spell. Yes, the film feeds upon and induces an irrational fear of the wilderness: so did *Deliverance, The Texas Chainsaw Massacre* (Texas BBQ, anyone?), *The Hills Have Eyes*, and most classics of the backwoods horror genre. Agreed, the trio of students act like idiots (no boy scouts in this bunch: follow the damned stream, you boneheads!) and they sure have healthy camera batteries when food seems wanting. But for the duration of its running time, I fell under its spell. *The Blair Witch Project* worked for me, and still does. When the final image sent a genuine chill up my spine, I became a believer.

There's no arguing the point: *The Blair Witch Project* either scares you or it doesn't, and there are no rational explanations or arguments that will sway either camp. It is, by definition, an irrational, emotional experience, a "weird tale" in the classic sense. Just for the evening, put out all the lights. Unplug the phone. Hide the remote and don't look away. If you fall under her spell, I dare say you'll become a believer, too.

A final warning: many viewers suffered the symptoms of motion sickness (headaches, nausea) brought on by the relentless hand-held cinematography. It shouldn't be as problematic on video, but beware.

The following review was written in April 2001, but never published. It is included here as an addendum to The Blair Witch Project *review:* [10]

Artisan's recent related *The Blair Witch Project* video sequel, **THE MASSACRE OF THE BUR-KITTSVILLE 7: THE BLAIR WITCH LEGACY**, features **SHADOW OF THE BLAIR WITCH** and **THE BURKITTSVILLE 7** (both 2000) on a single videocassette, both by writer/director Ben Rock. The first of these proffers that the feature sequel *Book of Shadows: Blair Witch 2* (2000) was actually based upon the September 22nd, 1999 murders attributed to Burkittsville youth Jeff Patterson (Andre Brooks).

The original faux-documentary companion to *The Blair Witch Project* was *Curse of the Blair Witch* (1999, released individually on video and as an 'extra' on the original *Blair Witch Project* DVD), an ingenious concoction which blended interviews, archival footage (some lifted from older horror films like *Horror Hotel*, the rest of it expertly faked) and excerpts from the feature to document the invented backstory of the Blair Witch. These included case histories of disappearances and hauntings associated with her legacy, and details of

---

[10] This material—along with the *Curse of the Blair Witch* review (page 47), coverage of *The Last Broadcast* (see pages 136-138, and pages 176-182), mention of Paula Goldberg's *The Blair Princess Project* (1999; see page 132-133), and the review of *Book of Shadows: Blair Witch 2* (reviewed February 22, 2001, to be reprinted in *S.R. Bissette's Blur, Volume 2*)—archives pretty much all I had to say on the film, its phenomenal success, its spinoffs, and the subsequent backlash.

the lives of the three students whose fate was chronicled in the feature. Originally shown as a promotional piece on the Sci-Fi Channel, *Curse of the Blair Witch* was unexpectedly clever and chilling. Note that there was also a shorter featurette, *Sticks and Stones: Investigating the Blair Witch* (1999), prepared as a Blockbuster Video chain store 'exclusive'; comprised primarily of excerpts and outtakes from both *Curse of...* and *The Blair Witch Project*, it was a much less substantial offering.

Building on that bedrock, writer/director Rock emulates the video and audio textures of multiple media sources (e.g., video, film, 'found' archival footage, etc.), intercut with actual news clips of notorious convicted killers like Charles Manson, Ted Bundy, and David Berkowitz ('Son of Sam') for verisimilitude. Unfortunately, Rock's almost interminable presentation of the supposed 'facts' of Patterson's crimes, arrest, and conviction betray more than ever before the entire series' debt to—indeed, theft of—primary elements from the documentary *Paradise Lost: The Child Murders at Robin Hood Hills* (1996) and Stefan Avalos and Lance Weiler's *The Last Broadcast* (1998). In fact, *Shadow of the Blair Witch* is almost a remake of the latter feature, adding insult to the many slights and injury already perpetrated by the original *Blair Witch* media frenzy. (According to some sources, *Shadow of the Blair Witch* is comprised of outtakes from an earlier edit of *The Blair Witch Project*, removed prior to the film's historic Sundance premiere in order to minimize its resemblance to *The Last Broadcast*, but that could not be verified at the time of this writing; this claim seems dubious given the cohesive text and length of the original *Blair Witch Project*, which would have been a quite different—and longer—feature had this material been included.)

Rock's *The Burkittsville 7* is the more compelling of the two featurettes. Originally produced for Showtime, this constructs an involved 'mockumentary' scenario in which amateur sleuth and film archivist Chris Carrazco (John Maynard) argues his theories concerning the notorious murder case in which seven children fell victim to recluse Rustin Parr, supposedly under the malignant influence of the Blair Witch. Parr's faux 'true crime' was central to the original *Blair Witch Project*'s narrative and attendant multi-media companions (e.g., the website, books, *Curse of the Blair Witch*, etc.), and the 'found footage' of that fictitious 'case' still carries a resonant power when rerun here, a still-effective echo of the first film's power in the summer of '99.

Fictional sleuth Carrazco's claim is that the convicted and executed killer of the seven children, Rustin Parr, was innocent; rather, it was the sole child survivor of the atrocity, Kyle Brody (played by two actors, David Grammer and Tom Horan, to simulate two distinct phases in Brody's life) who was responsible for the butchery. In documenting these claims, writer/director Rock proffers yet another fake documentary, showing us clips from a film entitled *White Enamel* by one David Hooper (played by Robert David Hall), in which we see the adult Brody endure miserable conditions in the state asylum he was eventually consigned to. This footage is persuasively convincing, lending unexpected gravity to *Burkittsville 7*'s flimsy proceedings.

Rock aggravates his *own* crimes, however, by overtly restaging specific sequences in *White Enamel* (particularly the force-feeding of a patient who refuses to eat) from Frederick Wiseman's notorious documentary *Titicut Follies* (1967), a further act of cinematic piracy that would no doubt infuriate Wiseman, who has yet to permit video releases of any of his films and would surely disapprove of such wholesale appropriation of the genuine human agonies he filmed for an exploitative, ephemeral entertainment such as this. *Titicut Follies* is among the most harrowing documentaries ever made, its notoriety furthered by the State of Massachusetts' legal proceedings and subsequent effective banning of the film (permitting it to only be shown to medical and psychiatric professionals) for over two decades. Though that ban was lifted in the early 1990s, *Titicut Follies* is still a rarely-screened masterpiece known primarily for its reputation than via first-hand viewing experience. While one must acknowledge the cleverness of Rock's cinematic sleight-of-hand, this only further compromises the *Blair Witch* legacy of creative misappropriation (some would indeed call it 'theft') of the particulars and substance of other creative works.

This growing shadow over the entire dubious franchise probably isn't the sort of 'Blair Witch Curse' the producers would care to have their fan base aware of, but which true film lovers can only further question and revile. Equally abrasive is Sasha Bogdanowitsch's interminable musical score to *The Burkittsville 7*, a reductive consolidation of the prior *Blair Witch* 'mockumentary' audio atmospherics into a grating, overloud, and utterly maladroit blend of ominous whispers, scrapings, chants, and noisy clutter. It hinders, rather than enhances, the few virtues Ben Rock's 'mockumentary' offers.

October 28:

Can you believe it? Halloween week and there's not one new horror title hitting the racks! With last week's release of *The Blair Witch Project* blowing all remaining genre competitors into November, it's no surprise, really. Still, there are plenty of great new titles waiting for you, showcasing a trio of bracing performances from three of the finest actresses working today.

Who needs seasonal bogeymen when right-wing terrorists move in across the street? Jeff Bridges and Tim Robbins lock horns in the paranoid thriller **ARLINGTON ROAD** (1999), which remains the year's most nerve-fraying non-supernatural roller-coaster ride. The jarring opening upsets the apparent tranquility of American suburbia with blunt urgency, inadvertently introducing widowed college professor (Bridges) and his son to their new next-door neighbors (Robbins and Joan Cusack). Bridges' growing suspicions of their true nature and possible terrorist activities soon sends their lives into a terrifying tailspin. While Bridges struggles to maintain his composure against his mounting fears (or descent into madness?), the gradual revelations of evil beneath their carefully-composed good-neighbor behavior—wolves in sheep's clothing, indeed—anchors Robbins and Cusack's increasingly eerie performances. Bridges and Robbins are excellent, but Cusack is extraordinary. She's delivered many sparkling comedic roles in the past (*Runaway Bride, In and Out, Addams Family Values*, etc.), but her razored use of every expressive tool in her belt to evoke chills instead of chuckles is a real treat. One of the most unnerving shivers here hinges on one of her blissful smiles to Bridges' girlfriend (Hope Davis), a fleeting moment I may never shake. Unlike this year's bigger, sillier conspiracy thriller *Enemy of the State* (which even accommodated a happy ending!), *Arlington Road* bares and plucks the nerve of true paranoia, finding no comfort in the belief—

and the fact—that "they" *are* out to get you. *(Rated 'R' for strong language, gunplay, and violence.)*

In the hideously-titled **HIDEOUS KINKY**—no, it's not a sex-and-bondage or horror flick—the always-radiant Kate Winslet (of *Titanic, Hamlet, Sense and Sensibility,* and *Heavenly Creatures*) plays Julia, a young British single mother who's fed up with London and lets her free-spirit soar, carrying her two daughters along with her to find a new life in Morocco. No doubt the unfortunate title compromised any boxoffice this compelling film may have captured; it's taken from a random word-association game the two young girls play, and has meaning only within the context of the film itself. Set in the early 1970s, *Hideous Kinky* is a fascinating companion piece to the recent *A Walk on the Moon,* which, you may recall, starred Diane Lane as a restless young mother who upsets her daughter by dashing off to the 1969 Woodstock music fest with a dashing young hippie. Winslet's character here goes much further, eagerly cutting all ties with home (save for the occasional check from her estranged husband) and aggressively building a new life, creating a new self, and finding a new partner (a somewhat sketchy juggler) in a new culture. The evocative portrait of the exotic country, community, and craving for new ways of living (Julia embraces the Sufi religion, much to her older daughter's distress) is often exhilarating, the love and tension between mother and daughters is engaging, and the scenery, cinematography, and musical score are ravishing. *(Rate 'R' for language, nudity, and sexual situations.)*

In the first film from her own production company, **NEVER BEEN KISSED** (1999), Drew Barrymore seeks similar solace from the confines of her adult persona by creating a new self. Unlike Kate Winslet's Julia,

Drew's character Josie plunges into the somewhat less exotic (but no less intimidating) culture of the contemporary American high school system, hoping to find a potent enough newspaper story to launch her out of her no-future copy-edit job into "big time" journalism (essentially a gender-reversal of Cameron Crowe's real-life feat that yielded his best-seller *Fast Times at Ridgemont High*; would any of the *Brattleboro Reformer* staff return to high school to score such a promotion?). It's a stretch, but Barrymore toughs it out with the help of her big brother (David Arquette) and co-workers, and on the way finds true love (and aches for her first-ever kiss) with the school's sweetest teacher (Michael Vartan). Once you accept the initial premise, this twist of two very familiar genres—romantic comedy and teen melodrama—does have its charms, including its young cast's fine performances, particularly from Leelee Sobieski (*Joan of Arc* herself!) as the brainy nerd who is the first to befriend Josie. As usual, the clash of cliques and class are the central concern, arriving at a none-too-profound but at least somewhat adult look back at the trials and tribulations of high school life. *Never Been Kissed* is a refreshing female inversion of the recent run of student-teacher seduction narratives presented almost exclusively from the male perspective (*Election, American Beauty*), mature enough to confront the issue with some clarity, and naively romantic enough to contrive a way for Josie to—ah, but that would be telling, wouldn't it? *(Rated 'PG-13' for language and mild sexual situations.)*

With all these attractive young adults aching to find their "real" selves via transformation, it's heartening to find at least one character engaged with the more down-to-earth concerns of finding one's true self in one's roots. Well, okay—so it happens to be Gonzo, the crook-nosed blue Muppet, seeking his roots in the giddy new comedy **MUPPETS FROM SPACE** (1999), a lively family-friendly spin on the the Ben Stiller comedy *Flirting With Disaster* (1995). Though Gonzo has yet to earn the cultural cache of the old Goofy joke ("If Mickey is a mouse, Donald is a duck, and Pluto is a dog, what the hell is Goofy?"), the beloved Muppets crew and creators (the late Jim Henson and his long-time partner Frank Oz) never have been clear about just *what* Gonzo is, or where he came from. Wonder no more! This new Muppet caper lives up to the tradition established by Henson's inventive puppet troupe. Rest assured that the current blend of old and new Muppet performers—Dave Goelz (starring as Gonzo, and others), Steve Whitmore (Kermit), Bill Barretta (great as Pope the Prawn), Jerry Nelson, Brian Henson (son of Jim, and also co-producer), Kevin Clash, and others—still honor and embody the spirit of the original Muppets. The continuing participation of Frank Oz is crucial to this chemistry; Oz has established himself as a fine director (*Bowfinger, In and Out, What About Bob?*, etc.), but he is still cheerfully cutting up the carpet as Miss Piggy, Fozzie Bear, Animal, and Sean Eagle, and anchoring the legacy. The usual procession of Hollywood guest stars (including F. Murray Abraham, David Arquette, Pat Hingle, Ray Liotta, and a surprise cameo from a certain *Dawson's Creek* duo) adds the icing to the cake. Jeffrey Tambor is great as the sinister government investigator who makes life difficult for Gonzo. Don't deprive yourself of an evening of fun by assuming this is just kid's stuff! *(Rated 'G', suitable for all ages.)*

Another fun flick this week is the offbeat **FREE MONEY** (1999), which I got a kick out of. Charlie

Sheen and Thomas Haden Church play a pair of boneheads who fall for prison warden Marlon Brando's twin daughters—all he loves in the world, other than his truck. When the girls claim to be pregnant, the boys have no choice but to marry and (choke) move in with dad, who promptly consigns Sheen to care taking the precious pickup and Church to a hellish job in the prison kitchen. Dad, of course, hasn't much respect for the boys, forbidding any fornication under his roof and savoring the occasional cattle-prod punishments necessary to keeping them in line. Eager to break away from their dead-end obligations to Brando's monstrous patriarch, they scheme a payroll train robbery, but things don't go exactly as planned. It's hard to believe the stellar cast—which also includes Mira Sorvino as an FBI investigator and Donald Sutherland as a corrupt judge crony—slumming in this oddball black comedy, but count your blessings. Mind you, a couple of my best friends *hated* this movie; it isn't for all tastes. Ah, what do they know, anyhoot? I loved every minute of it. *(Rated 'R' for strong language, sexual situations and activity, nudity, gunplay, and violence.)*

Also on the shelves this week is the equally offbeat and endearing ***Me & Will***, starring Sherrie Rose and Melissa Behr (who also co-produced, co-wrote, and co-directed) as a pair of L.A. bikers who take to the highway in search of the chopper Peter Fonda straddled in Easy Rider; Barbara Hershey as the unlucky-in-love actress caught up in a world of hurt with her mob-boss ex (Robbie Coltrane) and cut-throat theater-and-thievery partners in ***Frogs for Snakes***; the equally gritty teen-crime caper ***Born Bad***, and Angie Everhart, James Russo, and Eric Roberts college crime thriller ***Bittersweet***; leaner and meaner still are ***Boiling Point*** and

Violent Cop, the bracing double-bill of Japanese crime thrillers from "Beat" Takeshi Kitano (star and director of Sonatine and Fireworks).

October 28:

CREEPER SLEEPERS: Low-Budget Horrors That Shook the World!

Since the silent era, every generation has had its own equivalent to *The Blair Witch Project*. Sure, *The Phantom of the Opera, The Bride of Frankenstein, The Exorcist*, and *Jaws* are terrific, but often it's the impoverished B-movies and cheapies that crawl out of the woodwork that really raise our collective goosebumps. In hopes of inspiring a few private dusk-to-dawn gatherings in the Valley this Halloween weekend, allow me to introduce you to these "creeper sleepers" that forever changed what a horror film could be, should be, and would be. Major Hollywood studios made a couple of these films, but most of them emerged from regional independents, eager to make their mark. These low-budget horror films captured the public's imagination of their time and made millions, changing horror films forever. I've arranged the titles chronologically, to emphasize the impact these films had on each other, and marked the most significant titles with an asterisk, though please remember that all these films proved influential.

*THE CABINET OF DR. CALIGARI (1919) This startling German silent classic was an international hit, the first cult horror movie. Eager to put the audience in the mind set of the madman telling the tale, the backdrops were constructed and painted in the manner of the expressionistic art movement, with costumes, makeup, and performance stylized to match. Arguably, this is also the first 'zombie' film, though the word didn't yet exist in Western culture.

*NOSFERATU (1921) Another German silent, a dreamy chiller that unveiled the cinema's first and most nightmarish Dracula (Max Schreck), and its first resonant vampire. A truly entrancing, uncanny experience.

*DRACULA (1931) Though produced by an established studio (Universal), this was a major gamble that paid off, ringing in the Golden Age of horror movies. Bela Lugosi remains the archetypal European vampire: "Children of the night, what music they make..." Check out the remastered edition, featuring a new score by Philip Glass; the Spanish language version, shot back-to-back on the same sets with a different cast, is even better, sans the mythic resonance of Lugosi's presence.

FREAKS (1932) Tod Browning's unflinching parable of life, love, and revenge among sideshow freaks prompted patrons to faint or flee. Though MGM produced this, they disowned it, and many countries banned it outright, damning it to obscurity for decades. It was rescued and revived in the late 1960s, earning its place in horror history.

*THE CAT PEOPLE (1942) Note this is the black and white original, not the sexy color remake. The surprising success of this subtle low-budget Val Lewton production introduced an intelligent new approach to horror films: urban, contemporary, driven by psychological nuances, relying on the suggestive power of the unseen and teasing the audience's collective imagination.

*THE THING (1951) Again, see the black and white original, not the John Carpenter color remake (though it's a great film, too, and much closer to the short story that inspired both versions). This tightly crafted, claustrophobic tale of an alien visitor terrorizing a remote arctic base kicked off the entire 1950s monster cycle, introduced the first jump-out-of-your-seat moment (the Thing at the door) to modern horror films, and urged audiences to "Keep Watching the Skies!" They did, and still do.

*LES DIABOLIQUES (1955) Here we go again: see the original French version, not the dreadful Sharon Stone remake. This psychological shocker had audiences lining up around the block in every major city in the US, provoking shrieks during its horrific final act and inspiring a jealous Alfred Hitchcock to make *Psycho*.

*INVASION OF THE BODY SNATCHERS (1956) Don Siegel's paranoid sf classic about a small community supplanted by dispassionate "pod people" crept into the consciousness of a generation, tapping our xenophobia, the ongoing "red scare," and the unspoken "soullessness" of the post-World War suburban lifestyle. Both of the color remakes are very good, but see the original first; together, they actually work as a coherent trilogy.

*THE CURSE OF FRANKENSTEIN (1957) This was the first color Hammer Film, introducing Peter Cushing and Christopher Lee—and an aggressive, graphic new approach to Gothic horror—to the world. The whirlwind international success of this film and Hammer's followup, *The Horror of Dracula*, sparked the horror revival of the late '50s and 1960s.

*I WAS A TEENAGE WEREWOLF (1957) starred Michael Landon as the toothy juvenile delinquent terror of the first-ever teen horror film. Despite the title, this was a great little thriller, and its record-breaking boxoffice success was a major kick-in-the-ass wake-up call to the Hollywood studios.

*PSYCHO (1960) Please, forget the color remake—you owe it to yourself to see the Alfred Hitchcock original, which dared to assault its audience with unprecedented intensity and forever expose the potential for madness lurking in the meekest of souls. Though directed by Hitchcock, this was made without studio support in black and white for very low budget, working with the production team behind Hitchcock's popular TV series, hence its place on this list.

FALL OF THE HOUSE OF USHER (1960) This color Vincent Price vehicle ushered in the popular Poe series which lasted through the 1960s, and legitimized the king of the drive-in quickies Roger Corman as one of America's premiere directors.

CARNIVAL OF SOULS (1962) See the black and white original, not the color remake. This sleeper was rarely screened until its 1989 re-release, but it became a cult favorite for its genuinely spooky evocation of the dream realm, notable for its stylized photography, eerie score, and as a *Night of the Living Dead* precursor.

*BLOOD FEAST (1963) Notorious Herschell Gordon Lewis shocker dared to go where no major studio would, crudely carving out brains, tongues, limbs, and a unique niche as the first true "gore" film. This widely imitated breakthrough hit of the 1960s drive-in circuit was filmed in and around the beaches of Sarasota, Florida.

*NIGHT OF THE LIVING DEAD (1968) George Romero's made-in-Pittsburgh independent bent all the rules of the genre, provoking genuine terror and forever changing horror films. It's impossible to convey how shocking this film was in its day. See the black and white 1968 original, not the colorized version, the color remake, or the dreadful 30th Anniversary Special Edition (sporting a hideous new soundtrack and idiotic new footage). Also beware of bad bootleg editions—the best prints on video are from Hal Roach Studio, Spotlight Video, and especially the restored Anchor Bay edition (or the definitive Elite release, on laserdisc and DVD).

*LAST HOUSE ON THE LEFT (1972) Wes Craven's first film was a drive-in and grindhouse hit, eschewing supernatural horrors for its grim depiction of the cruel murder of two teenagers en route to a rock concert and their upscale family's brutal revenge on their killers. It's almost impossible to see uncut, but even in truncated form, it's a jarring downer. Craven followed this with *The Hills Have Eyes* (1977), which was even better, though it had nowhere near the impact of *Last House*. "Just Keep Repeating: It's Only a Movie, Only a Movie, Only a Movie..."

*THE TEXAS CHAINSAW MASSACRE (1974) Despite the title, this wasn't a "gore" film; there's a reason director Ridley Scott screened this for the cast and crew of *Alien*, and the Museum of Modern Art was quick to secure a print for their permanent collection. Texas student filmmakers Tobe Hooper (who went on to direct Poltergeist) and Kim Henkel's primal grasp of cinema transformed this thin tale of young folk waylaid by a nasty hitchhiker, suspect Texas BBQ, and the most deranged family in film history into the closest approximation of a nightmare ever to kiss the screen.

SHIVERS (1975) David Cronenberg's debut film (also on video as *They Came From Within*, its US theatrical release title) is still a humdinger, detailing the infestation of a Montreal highrise by infectious sexual parasites. Financed in part by the Canadian government, this had members of Parliament screaming until it became the most profitable Canadian film of all time.

*ERASERHEAD (1977) David Lynch's first film remains one of the strangest ever made, and it became a fixture of the midnight movie circuit—though *The Rocky Horror Picture Show* remains *the* Midnight Movie sensation! An estranged father is abandoned in his sordid apartment with his loneliness, fears, sexual longings, and his illegitimate, inhuman baby; there is no way to coherently summarize this uncanny experience, the most tangibly dreamlike of all horror films.

*DAWN OF THE DEAD (1978) George Romero's ultraviolent color sequel to *Night of the Living Dead* was a huge hit, inspiring a new era of zombie and gore films around the world, none of which held a candle to this witty, character-driven, action-packed classic. Romero's sadly underrated final entry in the trilogy, *Day of the Dead* (1986), is also a masterpiece.

*HALLOWEEN (1978) Forget the sequels: John Carpenter's original is the best bogeyman movie ever made, streamlined only to scare you. Even if you have an aversion to "letterboxed" videos, I highly recommend you see the Widescreen edition, as Carpenter uses the entire stretch of the screen to say *"Boo!"*

PHANTASM (1979) An odd, intoxicating curio about inexplicable events in a mortuary, told with the beguiling inventiveness, vigor, and nonsensical lunacy of a preteen boy's campfire tale. It's *Invaders From Mars* (1953) for a new generation: "Boooooooooooy!"

*FRIDAY THE 13TH (1980) The archetypal summer-camp-killer classic may be crude, lewd, and derivative, but this is filmed-in-New Jersey pick-up struck a real nerve in its target audience, earning a fortune and an endless franchise for Paramount.

*THE EVIL DEAD (1983) Sam Raimi's rock 'em, sock 'em, knockabout nightmare debut film energized the old zombie stereotype and grossed—and grossed out—millions. Raimi's sequels, *Evil Dead II* and *Army of Darkness* (now available in a new video/DVD edition featuring the original ending), are highly entertaining, too, but lack the original's horrific go-for-break edge.

*A NIGHTMARE ON ELM STREET (1984) The original Wes Craven classic was and remains an original, genuinely subversive low-budget exercise in fear, introducing the now-cliche, dream-like element of "rubber reality" to the genre.

HENRY: PORTRAIT OF A SERIAL KILLER (1986; unreleased until 1989) This unblinking, raw, and dead-sober Chicago indy distilled the true-life Henry Lee Lucas case history into an indelible meditation on non-supernatural evil, deromanticized and all the more terrifying for its banality and recognizable humanity. Approach with caution.

SCREAM (1996) Wes Craven strikes again, plucking a fresh nerve for a new generation and prompting a new genre revival with this sassy, self-aware revamp of the teen horror formulas.

*THE BLAIR WITCH PROJECT (1999) After over three decades of increasingly explicit mayhem, this inexpensive student venture embraced the Lewton aesthetic of "less is more," reawakening a new generation to the terrors of the unseen—and their own imaginations. If nothing else, though many digital features preceded *Blair Witch* (including *The Last Broadcast*, which provided more than mere inspiration), this surprise hit also confirmed the digital era of filmmaking had arrived and achieved mainstream visibility.

THE TOP HORROR FILMS: S.R. Bissette's Baker's Dozen [11]

With almost forty years of obsessive affection for, viewing of, and studying horror movies, it's damned near impossible to narrow my fave down to just five titles. In fact, I couldn't do it! So, here's my current baker's dozen list. Mind you, I'd name thirteen others on a whim and depending on what day of the week it was.

1., **2.**, and **3.**: George Romero's **NIGHT OF THE LIVING DEAD** (1968), **DAWN OF THE DEAD** (1977), **and DAY OF THE DEAD** (1985): The ultimate apocalyptic American horror movies, one for each decade since the '60s. Romero is one of our finest storytellers; it's a crime the current commercial cinema refuses to accommodate him.[12]

4. James Whale's **THE BRIDE OF FRANKENSTEIN** (1935): I love the classic 1930s horrors, but this and *King Kong* (1933; more a monster movie than a horror movie and hence not on this list) were the jewels of the

---

[11] This piece was originally published in *VMag* #1, November 1997, "The Halloween Issue," pp. 32-33, as part of a collective article entitled "The Top 5 Horror Movies: A Highly Subjective Tour of the Genre," offering 'top horror film' lists from Punco Godyn, G. Michael Dobbs, 'Bill and Dana,' Stanley Wiater, Joseph A. Citro, and yours truly (pp. 27-33). My list is included here as a companion to the Halloween *Video Views* column.

[12] I would certainly add Romero's *Land of the Dead* (2005) to this list today.

crown. Frightening, funny, fierce, heartfelt, and one of the best movies ever made, period.

5. Georges Franju's **EYES WITHOUT A FACE** (1958, aka *Horror Chamber of Dr. Faustus*): The French Grand Guignol tradition brought to the screen with breathtaking beauty, poetry, and horror.

6. Mario Bava's **BLACK SUNDAY** (1960): A baroque black-and-white Gothic arabesque atmospherically photographed around the porcelain (and punctured) features of Barbara Steele. The first horror movie to really scare me—I love it like no other.

7. Ken Russell's **THE DEVILS** (1971): A lethal merger of Church and State conspires to knock the walls of the fortified French village of Loudon to the ground with a sanctioned witch hunt against Father Grandier (Oliver Reed). A delirious adaptation of the Aldous Huxley tract, still impossible to see in this country in its original uncut form.

8. Mario Bava's **BAY OF BLOOD** (1972, aka *Carnage, Twitch of the Death Nerve, Last House Part 2*): I can't possibly justify this title's presence here: simply put, it's the greatest "body count" horror movie of them all. I rushed to see it every time it played theatrically (under a variety of titles). Ravishing Bava cinematography, an ever-escalating string of truly horrific murders (much imitated in the Friday the 13th series) to gain an inheritance, and a hilarious final shot. An unsung classic!

9. Nicolas Roeg's **DON'T LOOK NOW** (1973): Roeg's best films do not pass before our eyes, they explode and implode within the mind. Drawn from one of Daphne du Maurier's short stories, this elliptical psychic thriller never fails to profoundly engage, mesmerize, terrify, and move me.

10. Tobe Hooper's **THE TEXAS CHAINSAW MASSACRE** (1974): On first viewing, one of the most relentless of contemporary horror films; on subsequent viewings, a brilliantly crafted pitch-black comedy, too ("Look what your brother did to the door!").

11. David Lynch's **ERASERHEAD** (1976): Evocative of Bunuel, Polanski, and Samuel Beckett, this one-of-a-kind feature edges from an oppressive urban dreamscape into one of the most tactile domestic nightmares ever committed to film. The Lady in the Radiator is disturbing, but, oh, that baby!

12. David Cronenberg's **THE BROOD** (1980): Cronenberg crawls under my skin like no other filmmaker. In a perverse twist on (and indictment of) recovered memory and "inner child" therapy, "Psychoplasmics" urges its survivor patients to externalize their internal rage, culminating in tragedy and a genuinely startling climactic revelation. The monstrous titular metaphor galvanizes this harrowing portrait of a family ravaged by the cruel legacy of child abuse.

13. Lars Von Triers' **THE KINGDOM** (1996): *The Haunting* (1962), *Carnival of Souls* (1963), and *The Lady in White* (1987) top my list of best ghost movies. Still, Lars Von Triers one-ups them all with this lengthy mini-series set in a haunted hospital that literally sent shivers up my spine. It's also wickedly funny, which doesn't mitigate the chills.

Those are my current favorites, but here are the five most genuinely horrifying films that come to mind. These are not entertainments: these are repulsive, straight-from-the-gut horror movies, dead serious and absolutely no fun; recommended for diehards only.

1. CANNIBAL HOLOCAUST (1979): Ruggero Deodato's parable of soured Third World relations—primitives are butchered by documentary filmmakers, the filmmakers are then in turn butchered by the outraged tribe—is at once the summit and nadir of the notorious Italian cannibal movie cycle. The film-within-a-film structure is cleverly conceived and executed, but the mayhem is, at times, nigh on unbearable.

2. COME AND SEE (1985): An orphaned Russian child's terrifying passage through the hellish WW2 landscape. The most horrifying war film I've ever seen; once seen, never forgotten, comparable to Jerzy Kosinski's novel *The Painted Bird*.

3. HENRY: PORTRAIT OF A SERIAL KILLER (1986): Unflinching amoral snapshot of a contemporary American monster who is excruciatingly familiar and human, a condemnation of the society that created him by failing to in any way connect with or contain him. As such, one of the most moral films of our time.

4. IN A GLASS CAGE (1989): A vicious cycle of sexual abuse entraps an iron-lung bound pedophile (who also conducted experiments on children in the Nazi concentration camps, which he continued in his South American home) when one of his victims, now a teenage boy, becomes his caretaker. Exquisitely mounted, performed, and photographed: you are afraid to watch, but cannot look away, as the debasing spiral between tortured and torturer closes its coils.

5. THE BEGOTTEN (1991): Sans any comprehensible narrative or characters, this is the ultimate nightmare movie to date. A frightful tableau of birth, death, and abandonment dissolves into a dense, dark mire of cloaked figures, writhing forms, vile textures, and unspeakable emotions. Cinema as Dionysian ritual: primal, impenetrable, unshakeable.

November 4:

Family values, indeed. This week's new releases are topped by a trio of 1999 features focusing on broken homes and families in crisis. None of the three weighs the matter with any real gravity, unless you consider Adam Sandler's unstable surrogate father, Vincent Gallo's transvestite witch, or absentee dad Michael Keaton's resurrection as an ambulatory snowman viable role models. What's a poor child to do? Heck, what's a poor father to do, with this week's sorry crop of unwanted, deadbeat, deranged, and downright dead-and-frigid dads on parade?

If you're a fan of Adam Sandler, there's nothing I can possibly write to sway you from **BIG DADDY** (1999), Sandler's furthest step toward the sort of nauseating sentimentality comedians foist on audiences when their careers reach critical mass, recalling the sticky romanticism and paternalism that deep-sixed Jerry Lewis in the 1960s (anyone remember *The Family Jewels*? No? I thought not). It's particularly ill-suited to Sandler's bad-boy, wise-ass, foul-mouthed persona, and the central narrative conceit here is infinitely more insulting and disturbing than fellow *SNL*-alumni David Spade's recent bid for romantic lead in the grating *Lost and Found*. *Big Daddy* asks us to laugh its troubles away for its first two-thirds, then switches gears to tug at our heartstrings during its final act.

The premise here is that star Adam Sandler's archetypal arrested adolescent man-child character takes in l'il abandoned tyke Julian (played by twins Cole and Dylan Sprouse[13]), initially to cover for his slippery brother (who sired the boy during a weekend fling, and doesn't know he has a son), then as a ploy to win the heart of Joey Lauren Adams (the sassy star of Chasing Amy). Sandler's feeble father techniques indulge Julian's crassest childhood instincts, providing a wellspring for either hilarity or anger depending on your age, disposition, and tastes (or lack thereof). Audiences lapped it up over the summer, rocketing *Big Daddy* to the top of the boxoffice charts and further elevating Sandler's rising star. If you're a Sandler fan, he's critic-proof.

Lest you think I'm biased, let me fess up to enjoying many of Sandler's routines and songs and particularly *The Waterboy* (1998), his best vehicle to date. *The Waterboy* (which was an amusing update of silent come-

---

[13] The same Dylan and Cole Sprouse in *The Astronaut's Wife* (see pp. 196-197), Disney Channel's *The Suite Life of Zach and Cody* and currently enjoying 21st century pre-teen superstardom. They also tag-team played the gender-confused child lead in Asia Argento's *The Heart is Deceitful Above All Things* (2003), based on J.T. Leroy's faux memoir.

dian Harold Lloyd's 1925 *The Freshman*) situated Sandler's idiot savant within its own football fantasy world, staying true to its internal illogic. There were no real-world concerns to intrude on the fun—unlike *Big Daddy*, which falls just short of sanctioning child abuse. Aside from issues of taste (bad taste is the basis of Sandler's often-scatological humor, and why should his nothing-is-sacred attitude apply to orphans or child care issues?), *Big Daddy*'s biggest problem is its overt and (in the context of the film) patently phony sentimentality. Charlie Chaplin pulled it off in *The Kid* (1921, starring Jackie Coogan as the little orphan Chaplin takes under his wing), but Chaplin was an artist, a consummate filmmaker and a clown; Sandler will never fill the Little Tramp's shoes—he's a scatological Harry Langdon, really—but make no mistake, this is his first maladroit bid to do just that.[14]

Sandler flirted with similar bathos in *The Wedding Singer* (1997) sans the twisted, manipulative little-boy-lost ploy, a stretch that's particularly ill-suited to Sandler's wise-ass, foul-mouthed persona. *The Wedding Singer* and *The Waterboy* parodied the romantic cliches they reveled in, but *Big Daddy* proposes that Joey Lauren Adam's shrewd legal professional would fall for Sandler; that she does so in part because he's such a sensitive lug once he falls for Julian further strains credibility. Sandler wants it both ways: he's a man-child women lover, a delinquent parent who's the greatest dad in the

---

[14] My editor cut the reference to Harry Langdon, saying no one would know who Langdon was. Sadly, I couldn't argue with her about that. However, Sandler later starred in Paul Thomas Anderson's *Punch-Drunk Love* (2002), which was essentially a revamped Harry Langdon vehicle!

world. He wants us to swallow the transmutation he's orchestrated here (as star, executive producer, and co-screenwriter), though his crude humor is unsettling in the context of parenting an orphan, the romantic claptrap is increasingly ludicrous, and the courtroom finale horrific in its earnestness. I won't give up on Sandler until he's substitute-hosting the Jerry Lewis Telethons, but *Big Daddy* is sliding awfully close to that turf. *(Rated 'R' for strong language, scatological humor, and sexual situations and innuendoes.)*

If you're going to embrace bad taste, go all the way, baby! The most demonic dad of the week pops up my perverse pick of the litter, **FREEWAY 2: CONFESSIONS OF A TRICK BABY** (1999), writer-director Matthew Bright's sequel to his memorably caustic "Little Red Riding Hood" revamp *Freeway* (1995). Bright is one of America's most underrated young filmmakers, upping the ante here with a razor-edged punk retelling of "Hansel and Gretel" as a down & dirty "bad girl" road movie, sending the bulemic Crystal (*Slums of Beverly Hills* star Natasha Lyonne, also associate producer here) and psycho-killer lesbian Cyclona (Maria Celedonio) south of the border to confront the nominal "witch" of the story, the androgynous Sister Gomez (Vincent Gallo of *Buffalo 66* and *The Funeral*). Like its precursor, *Freeway 2* is an absolutely ruthless (but not heartless) black comedy, and it's definitely not for the squeamish, ripe with women's prison and juvenile delinquent exploitation crime movie excesses, sleazeball public defenders and nasty cops, prostitution, drug and child abuse, an over-abundance of binge & purge horrors, foul language, and an apocalyptic finale. Lest you forget, all of this nastiness is surprisingly true to the spirit of the grim Grimm original, and earned the film a *very* strong 'R' rating. You've been warned!

Let me also warn you about our last, and definitely least, major new release, the sorry Michael Keaton vehicle **JACK FROST** (1999). This is the only real family film of the week; too bad it's such a let-down (don't fret, there's a couple of great ones coming in later this month, including *The Iron Giant*). Chronically-absent father Keaton lets his son down big time by getting killed (!), only to magically return as an animated snowman (!!!) to make up for all that lost time and shower his son with the attention and affection he so richly deserved all along. If movies are going to engage with such tragic family losses, even in the framework of a whimsical fantasy, the least one can expect is the sensitivity Disney brought to the subject in *Bambi* and *Dumbo*, which *Jack Frost* is utterly incapable of. This is unimaginative filmmaking-by-committee which squanders whatever promise its premise may have held with its shallow characterizations, surprisingly shoddy special effects (even the design of Keaton's soulful snowman is unappealing), insulting caricatures of parent-child relations, and simple-minded balms for the volatile matters of the heart it pretends to deal with. This early holiday hokum may make a passable afternoon entertainment (though its first third may understandably upset young children, particularly if they're dealing with similar family issues themselves) or a tasty Thanksgiving turkey (if you know what I mean, and I think you do), but don't say I didn't warn you. Twice. Here's hoping that Keaton's next role offers a better showcase for his talents. *(Rated 'PG' for mild language, suitable for all ages.)*

Recent & Recommended:

Drop the crosses and garlic, grab the sticky rice and prayer papers to check out the classic Hong Kong hopping-vampire martial arts action-comedy ***Mr. Vampire***, a delightful blend of exotic comedy, martial-arts action, and horror; sparks fly between a trio of women amid the club and coffee-shop Bohemia of Kristine Peterson's independent gem ***Slaves to the Underground***; and Djimon Hounsou (*Amistad, E.R.*), Akosua Busia (*The Color Purple, Rosewood*), and Eartha Kitt (providing the voice of the inventively-animated spirit of the Wood) star in the riveting black-and-white portrait of the infamous slave-ship revolt of 1869 in ***Ill-Gotten Gains***, African-American director Joel Ben Marsden's independent answer to Spielberg's *Amistad*.

November 11:

Roberto Benigni's long-awaited **LIFE IS BEAUTIFUL** (1998, and postponed from a previously-announced July 1999 video release) is without a doubt the most remarkable new release this week, if only for the audacity of its premise. Daring to find humor in the appalling legacy of the Holocaust concentration camp atrocities is nothing new: *Hogan's Heroes* milked the setting for primetime sitcom laughs for four seasons (1965-1971), while Jerry Lewis deep-sixed his career in the late 1960s fumbling with *The Day the Clown Cried*, a never-released vanity project in which he played a clown in a concentration camp. *Life is Beautiful* director and star Roberto Benigni treads similar volatile ground with this tale of Guido Orefice (Benigni), who woos and wins the woman he loves (a lovely performance by Benigni's wife and frequent costar Nicoletta Braschi) and then struggles to charm his family through the Holocaust and their imprisonment by convincing his young son it's all just a game the adults are playing. Unlike Lewis, Benigni pulled off his tight-wire act with heart, winning critical adulation, his greatest boxoffice success (the highest-grossing foreign film to date in history), and Academy Award recognition.

Benigni established himself as Italy's reigning screen comedian with *Johnny Stecchino* (1992) and *The Monster* (1996), though most Americans were acquainted with his antics in two Jim Jarmusch gems, *Down By Law* (1986) and his absolutely gut-busting turn as a foul-mouthed cab driver in *Night on Earth* (1991). None of these films prepared audiences for this stunning testimonial to family bonds and the enduring power of love tested by the most horrifying circumstances. Consistent with the elaborate game Benigni plays with his son (and the audience), the film downplays the true horrors of the camps, but this can be forgiven in the context of the film's fragile weave. Simply put, the matters of the heart addressed here would have been utterly crushed by a more explicit depiction of the monstrous realities of the camps. It is enough that they smolder in its terrifying shadow, for we all know too well what forces might consume Guido's family (there are many powerful documents and harrowing testimonials of the Holocaust on video store shelves, from *Night and Fog* and *Shoah* to the recent *The Last Days* and *We Were So Beloved*, should you need a reminder). Benigni's tale is set amid these atrocities, but it is not about the Holocaust; it is about family and survival.

Life is Beautiful is Benigni's crowning achievement, and if you fall under its spell, you will never forget it. Better video shops offer both the subtitled and dubbed versions, and I heartily recommend you choose the subtitled version; though the dubbing job is creditable, many delightful nuances of Benigni's performance are scuttled in the translation. Whichever version you choose to watch, this is highly recommended. *(Rated 'PG-13' for some language and non-explicit evocations of the realities of the concentration camps.)*

If you're yearning for more lightweight entertainment, join Julia Roberts and Hugh Grant for their summer boxoffice hit **NOTTING HILL** (1999). Romantic play-acting takes center stage here, too, though the stakes aren't quite life-and-death: Grant stars as a shy British book shop proprietor who unexpectedly falls for a major Hollywood movie actress (Roberts) and she, surprisingly, falls for him, too. Once the press catches wind of the affair, stalking paparazzi aggravate Grant's discomfort with his sudden unwanted celebrity, and Roberts' dire need to protect her image and privacy steers them into inevitably rocky relations. *Notting Hill* rides on its considerable charms, with Grant and Roberts (essentially playing on her own public image and its attendant vulnerabilities) finding an engaging on-screen chemistry that fits these old-fashioned romantic ups and downs like a silk glove. It's particularly amusing to watch Grant nervously skirt the fictional film sets during Roberts' location filmings, as if he didn't belong, but the most consistently hilarious diversion here is Rhys Ifan's performance as Grant's scruffy roommate Spike, whose mugging and bohemian bon mots steal every scene he graces. *(Rated 'PG-13' for some strong language and the expected sexual innuendoes and situations.)*

TREKKIES (1998) is a great little documentary on the curious extremes of the *Star Trek* fan community and international convention scene, narrated and co-produced by *Star Trek: The Next Generation*'s Denise Crosby. The corporate sanction of Paramount undoubtably curbed some of the filmmakers' instincts, but this compelling dissection of the ongoing phenomenon and almost religious devotion spawned by Gene Roddenberry's sf series is quite an eye-opener for the uninitiated. Though the fanaticism occasionally veers close to lunacy and freakshow status, the film is neither overly reverent nor condescending, and the results are well worth an evening's viewing, whatever your attitude toward the *Star Trek* franchise. *(Unrated; Suitable for all ages.)* [15]

Recent & Recommended:

Rachel Weisz (lights years from the action-fantasy of her role in *The Mummy*) stars in the edgy, unsettling British drama ***I Want You***; Vincent D'Onofrio, Salma Hayek, and Thomas Jane delineate the fast-paced, low-lifestyle of the urban disenfranchised in Dan Ireland's ***The Velocity of Gary***; Christopher Lambert headlines the truly disturbed and disturbing suspenser ***Resurrection***, a perverse melding of *Se7en* and *Millennium* that is also a return to form for Australian director Russell Mulcahy (*Razorback, Highlander, The Shadow*).

---

[15] The *Video Views* reviews (or abridgements) for *Trekkies, Austin Powers: The Spy Who Shagged Me, The Haunting, The Last Broadcast* and *Legend of the Chupacabra* were also published in *VMag* #24, November 1999, pp. 38-40.

November 18:

Top draws this week include the most eagerly-awaited comedy of the year, Anthony Hopkins' most recent addition to his fascinating pantheon of characters, and a trio of new films from three of Italy's premiere filmmakers. Let's rock!

What to say about **AUSTIN POWERS: THE SPY WHO SHAGGED ME** (1999)? "You know you want it, baby!" The film's subtitle presented quite a dilemma in the UK, where the term "shag" is the direct equivalent of a word we can't print in a family newspaper, echoing a venerable tradition in international relations initiated by the Al Jolson musical *Hallelujah, I'm a Bum* (in the UK, "Bum" means "Ass") and continued by the family favorite *Free Willy* (where "willy" has other connotations). No doubt the Scots have their own reservations about Michael Myers' new villain Fat Bastard, who demonstrates an inexplicable craving for baby flesh, and most audiences 'round the world groaned at the currently-fashionable barrage of scatological jokes. And what's with Elvis Costello's cute cameo, his second this year (see *200 Cigarettes*)? But, hey, baby, not to worry! How could anyone really take offense at this *Austin Powers* sequel, though it's not about a damned thing except further exploiting, promoting, and merchandising of Myers' fun initial romp as Britian's favorite spy invented by a Canadian? The original *Austin Powers* was actually about something, shallow as its premise (1960s mod spy and villainy culture-clashing with 1990s corporate world) may have been; *The Spy Who Shagged Me* isn't about anything save squeezing another laugh out of you, and otherwise hasn't a thought in its shaggy head. Myers is in great form in his three roles and Heather

Graham is a lovely ornament, though she's nothing to do as Felicity Shagwell, a pale shadow of the original's Vanessa (Elizabeth Hurley, getting short shrift here in the pre-credits opener). Seth Green earns some quality screen-time early on as Dr. Evil's son during the genuinely funny *Jerry Springer* parody, and Dr. Evil's dwarf clone Mini-Me is an inspired creation (inspired, lest we forget, by Marlon Brando's diminutive 'manimal' sidekick in *The Island of Dr. Moreau* remake). It's all fitfully funny, but before the climax it's as tired as the Bond series it lampoons; it took the Bond series four films to fall into this kind of formulaic rut. Here's hoping Myers and company give the inevitable second sequel a conceptual shot in the arm before they squeeze dry whatever charm is left to Powers. In the meantime, enjoy the silly laughs and easy evening's entertainment this will provide—you *know* you're going to rent it, baby!—and do *not* turn the video off until you've caught the gag after the final credits. *(Rated 'PG-13' for language, sexual innuendoes, gross jokes, and coy near-nudity.)*

Austin Powers 2 had big bucks and advertising mojo behind it every step of the way, but my favorite comedy of the week is a little Australian curio entitled **THE CASTLE** (1998). Michael Caton stars as Darryl Kerrigan, the loving head of a decidedly eccentric family whose self-made homestead is threatened when the bordering airport's expansion plans serves government-sanctioned compulsory eviction papers. Rallying his equally eccentric neighbors, Darryl digs in his heels to defend his "castle" against the considerable forces marshaled against the homeowners. As narrated by Darryl's somewhat dense son Dale (Stephen Curry), the tale unfolds with a deadpan wit that provokes laughs without belittling the Kerrigan family's genuine affection, devotion, and decency. This is a gem, and I heartily recommend you give it a look. *(Rated 'R'— there is some strong language here, but this rating seems harsh.)*

Hollywood has always glibly caricatured psychologists and the psychiatric profession, and **INSTINCT** (1999) is no exception. Cuba Gooding, Jr.'s earnest performance stretches credibility with his first quick-fix remedy of a disturbed female patient (an unlikely miracle observed by approving peers and Gooding's doubting mentor played with sleek assurance by Donald Sutherland), but the film rivets our attention as soon as Anthony Hopkins graces the screen. The narrative is pure pop psychology 101 voodoo, woven around a compelling series of confrontations between Gooding's ambitious youth and Hopkins' scarred vet, a renowned psychologist who retreated behind a wall of silence and apparently animalistic behavior after being traumatized by the murder of the African gorillas he had studied and ultimately lived among. This crazy-quilt combo of *Gorillas in the Mist, Silence of the Lambs*, and *One Flew Over the Cuckoo's Nest* constantly stretches and threatens to burst its seams as it pitches Hopkins nose-to-nose against well-intentioned Gooding and the status quo of the asylum's warden and staff, but Hopkins unflinchingly maintains his focus throughout. He sees to it that despite the pulpish trappings and distractions, the film's true emotional climax—the defining moment during the reunion of estranged father and daughter—rings true. *(Rated 'R' for strong language, violence.)*

Three Italian films new to video this week were all filmed in English with predominantly Anglo stars, and all three find their directors (each of whom are renowned for their own stylish excesses) in surprisingly restrained form. Italian maestro Bernardo Bertolucci (*The Conformist, Last Tango in Paris, 1900, The Last Emperor, Stealing Beauty, Little Buddha*, etc.) is arguably the finest storyteller of the three, and his latest feature **BESIEGED** (1998) once again explores the parameters of love and obsession. Thandie Newton (last seen in *Beloved*) stars as a young Nairobian woman seeking solace in Rome after the arrest and ominous disappearance of her husband, only to find herself entangled in an increasingly passionate relationship with the landlord (David Thewlis of *Naked, Seven Years in Tibet*, and—sigh—the ignoble *The Island of Dr. Moreau* remake) of the villa she lives and works in. Like many relationships, this affair of the heart is defined more by what is not said or expressed than what is, by stolen glances and cautious aversions, and Bertolucci weaves a palpable, suffocating emotional tapestry that is far truer to most human experience than the icy sexual romps Hollywood would have us invest in. As always, Bertolucci steeps our senses in sights, sensations, and sounds worth savoring, including the indelible presence of African musician John C. Ojwang. *(Rated 'PG' for language, adult situations, and brief nudity.)*

Franco Zeffirelli's **TEA WITH MUSSOLINI** (1998) is a somewhat less intimate affair, set as it is against the arc of Mussolini's reign and involvement with World War 2. Nevertheless, this is undoubtably Zeffirelli's most personal work (he is renowned for his cinematic Shakespeare adaptations and flamboyant religious epics like *Brother Sun, Sister Moon*), drawn from his own autobiography and childhood memories of the period. The reverie opens in Florence, Italy, in 1935, introducing us to the *Scorpioni*—the Scorpions ("they bite," we are told)—a matriarchal British community of art aficionados whose lives are forever changed by the devastating rise of Mussolini's fascism, and by their communal mothering of the young orphan Luca (played by Charlie Lucas and, as a teenager, by Baird Wallace). This vivid, very touching look back is immeasurably enhanced by its marvelous cast, including Joan Plowright, Maggie Smith, Judi Dench, Lily Tomlin, and Cher. *Tea with Mussolini* garnered lukewarm reviews upon its theatrical release, and certainly isn't for all tastes, but it's a very pleasant surprise, and I heartily recommend you give it a chance. *(Rated 'PG' for language, adult and sexual situations, and brief nudity.)*

The mongrel of the Italian imports in Dario Argento's **PHANTOM OF THE OPERA** (1998), an erratic and occasionally rude adaptation of Gaston Leroux's venerable novel (which has already been filmed at least four times, with Lon Chaney's silent 1925 original still the best of the lot), which repeatedly plunges off the deep end. Julian Sands stars as the uncharacteristically handsome Phantom who haunts the Paris Opera House, and Argento's daughter Asia (whom her director daddy relentlessly tortured onscreen in *The Stendahl Syndrome*) costars as Christine, the diva who remains the focus of the Phantom's obsessive and very dangerous affections. The romantic flourishes are as baroque as the splashes of grue, further enhanced by Ennio Morricone's lavish score and the ornate costumes and setpieces (filmed in the Budapest Opera House and in the Pertosa Caves of Salerno). The playful script was co-written by Gerard Brach, a veteran of the Theater of the Absurd who frequently collaborates with Roman Polanski; it remains true to the particulars of Leroux's tale, from Christine's boat ride through the subterranean canals toward the Phantom's lair to the fatal fall of the grand chandelier, while embellishing the narrative with distinctively European (Edgar Degas has a cameo, sketching the training dancers) and delightfully absurdist touches. Unfaithful to Leroux, though, this Phantom has an amusing origin (washed like Moses into the Paris sewers and raised by rats, like a rodent Tarzan), consummates his affair with Christine, and rescues little girls from pedophile opera house patrons, all while his enemies hunt him with a high-speed slice-'em-dice-'em-vacuum-'em-up ratmobile! Argento's *Phantom of the Opera* has moments of shocking mayhem and vivid beauty, but it's a creaky echo of his most delirious horror films (see *Suspiria, Deep Red, Tenebrae,* and *Phenomena*). Annoying note: though the DVD release claims to be in letterboxed widescreen, it is not, diminishing sorely-needed scope from Argento's patently rich visuals *(Rated a strong 'R' for violence, gore, sexual situations, and nudity.)*

Recent & Recommended:

Ewan McGregor's fine turn as Nick Leeson in ***Rogue Trader*** (1999), chronicling the true story of the rise and plummet of the young stock trader whose wheeling and dealing in the Indonesian markets a few years ago broke the Barings Bank (then the oldest private bank in the world); and ***Inherit the Wind*** (1999), a new and unfortunately still-timely adaptation of Jerome Lawrence and Robert Lee's courtroom drama drawn from the infamous 1925 Scopes "Monkey Trial" which pitched Biblical literalists against the teaching of Darwinian theories of evolution, boasting excellent performances from Jack

Lemmon and the late, great George C. Scott as the dueling attorneys. Not to be missed! [16]

November 25:

GOBBLE! GOBBLE! GOBBLE! The Woodchuck Video Turkey Feast: The Worst Films of All Time

You know, I reckon I like turkey as much as all the rest of you do, but come Thanksgiving weekend, I like other kinds of turkeys, too. I'm talking turkey movies, and I don't mean movies *about* turkeys. I mean turkeys, gobblers, brain dead movies like *Robot Monster* that you might have caught on the late show when you were a kid, and they were so awful you thought you might have dreamt them, only you knew you hadn't. Movies our parents used to dump us off at the matinee to see, back when theaters had matinees like *Santa Claus Conquers the Martians* and *Little Red Riding Hood Versus the Monsters* (being a woodchuck, I saw 'em at the Strong and the Flynn up in Burlington). Once we had our licenses we drove ourselves to 'em by the carload back when drive-ins were real drive-ins (ah, the Twin City drive-in on the Barre-Montpelier road!), showing double features like *I Drink Your Blood* and *I Eat Your Skin* (which reminds me about Marj's favorite part of the table turkey, but never mind). I'm even talking about movies like *Ishtar, Showgirls*, and *Hudson Hawk* that cost more than every one of our whole lifetime's incomes combined would equal, and still gobbled. Movies where you wonder if anyone on the set was awake

---

[16] Portions of the above column appeared in *The Chicopee Herald*, November 24-30, 1999, pg.18.

enough to say, "Hey, this is really bad! Why are we making it?" I'm talking Turkeys with a capital 'T'. Movies so stupid, they'd stand there in the rain with their heads tipped up and fool mouths open till they drowned, if they actually were turkeys.

Here's my list for this year's Woodchuck Turkey Feast, specially cooked up for this weekend. Mind you, these are just my favorites—no doubt, you've got a couple of gobblers near and dear to your own heart you can substitute as you wish. I reckon you could cobble together your own gobbler-fest in no time. Well, clear the table. Here's they are, in no particular order:

*Fave-o-rite Woodchuck Butterball Turkey Classic: Ed Wood's **Plan 9 From Outer Space** (1958) is the King Turkey, so bad it's almost a religious experience. *Plan 9* lives down to its reputation, if you know what I mean, and I think you do. If you're wondering about ol' Ed, check out Tim Burton's bio-pic *Ed Wood* for the behind-the-scenes poop on this cheapjack wonder.

*Fave-o-rite Woodchuck Fast-Food Family Turkey: My neighbors used to go to McDonald's for Thanksgiving, and this movie was made for them. Ronald McDonald liked Steven Spielberg's *E.T.* so much, he ran out and made his own version, **Mac and Me** (1988). Only instead of one E.T., or just one product placement for Reesee's Pieces, McDonald's added a whole ding-dang *family* of cute li'l E.T. knock-offs, named the main one after a burger, and sent the li'l yippers zipping around about 90 minutes worth of product placements, including (of course) McDonald's. It's the definitive family product-placement movie, and it even leaves you choking on

that little clump of snot you get in the back of your throat every time you eat a real Big Mac.

Fave-o-rite Woodchuck Turkey All-Animal Epic: There's only one true contender for this category, America's first all-avian feature-length film, **Bill and Coo** (1947). The entire movie starred only birds—parakeets, parrots, lovebirds, canaries, and their feathered friends, hopping and chirping around a whole teeny-tiny little bird town. Striking a blow for racial harmony everywhere, the villains were crows, which they referred to as "the Black Menace" throughout. This little slice of heaven won a special Academy Award for, um, being special, and it was written and directed by Dean Riesner, who went on to script *Dirty Harry* for Clint Eastwood, which proves, uh, I dunno, it's a good thing they didn't carry Magnums in the 1940s. The second all-avian feature-length film was, of course, *Jonathan Livingston Seagull* (1973), which you might think a possible contender to this perch, but truth be told, it's nary a pinfeather compared to *Bill and Coo*.

Fave-o-rite Woodchuck Western Turkey: An all-bird cast is something to see, you betcha, but you haven't lived until you've experienced the world's one and only all-midget western, **The Terror of Tiny Town** (1938). It's pretty standard oater fare, 'cept all the cowboys and cowgirls and saddle-bums are midgets and dwarves who strut under saloon doors and ride the range on Shetland ponies, and they all sing songs, kinda like Gene Autry and Roy Rogers used to. Except, you know, with higher voices. And not as good. Gosh, I get misty-eyed just thinkin' about it, and wish I could go to Texas—until I think of the next film on the list:

Fave-o-rite Woodchuck Vacation Turkey: Seeing as "manos" is Spanish for "hands," ***Manos, the Hands of Fate*** (1966) actually means *Hands, the Hands of Fate*, which kinda makes you think, don't it? A Texan manure-mogul made this movie about a couple and their daughter waylaid by a satanic backyard barbecue cult and Torgo, a stuttering idiot with big floppy knees. It's just like a real vacation. First, they drive around for a long, long time, and then they drive around some more, and then they drive more, and they drive around again for a while, and not a damned thing happens. Then they find a claptrap fleapit in the middle of nowhere, and a weird little guy (Torgo) checks 'em in. Then they lose their daughter while standing around in their hotel room arguing and she just up and steps out the door and damn, what d'ya know, she's gone, they can't find her. It's real scary, like Torgo's knees or a bad plate of pulled pork.

Fave-o-rite Woodchuck Flatlander Vacation Turkey: Alan Alda starred in, wrote, and directed ***The Four Seasons*** (1981), which everybody chuckled over back when it came out, though I didn't care for it then, and like a crappy bottle of Boone's Farm wine left in the cupboard, my attitude toward it has just turned to vinegar over the years. I hate it when Alan and his muckamuck friends from New Yawk show up in Stowe and proceed to do all kinds of bone-headed flatlander things, like wear embarrassing winter clothing and offend the waiters at restaurants and drive their four-wheeler out onto the ice, which of course breaks through and sucks the fool vehicle down. I was going to Johnson State College at the time, and the best jazz musicians in the school scored a cameo as bad jazz musicians playing at a Stowe club, which I thought demonstrated Alda's contempt for all things Vermontian, save our skiing and scenery. Like I said, flatlander. It's almost as bad as the time the makers of that Chevy Chase movie *Funny Farm* up and killed all the trees in the Townshend Green when they painted the summer leaves fall foliage colors.

Fave-o-rite Woodchuck Turkey Musical Mashed-Potato Extravaganza: There's lots of contenders for the top spud (*Lost Horizon*? *Sgt. Pepper's Lonely Hearts Club Band*? *The Apple*?? *Xanadu*???), but I save my sour cream and butter for that disco-era 'tater tot **Can't Stop the Music** (1980). I was always afraid of New York City until I saw this movie, and realized that, well, people are people everywhere, even if they sing and dance like spring peepers frying on an electric fence. The Village People were the big musical act here, Olympic Decathlon champ Bruce Jenner was the big star, and it was directed by visionary feminist filmmaker Nancy Walker— y'know, Rosie, the lady who used to hustle Bounty paper towels on TV ("it's the quicker picker-upper"). She musta been on some of them thar "picker-uppers" when she made this, and I ain't talkin' paper towels. NASA should fire this into space for other intelligent beings to observe and pass judgment on all mankind.

Fave-o-rite Woodchuck 200-Ton Turkey Monster Movie: Speaking of firing things into space and intelligent beings, the Japanese bred a few contenders for this category, like the two-legged TV-antennaed sorta-poultry monster *The X from Outer Space*, but I'll forever keep a little light on in my soul for **The Giant Claw** (1957). This big turkey buzzard from outer space gobbles up trains, airplanes, and, in one unforgettable shot, little fellers wearing parachutes. Come Thanksgiving, I like a big bird, but this one makes you think twice. It's supposed to be scary, but it looks like a refugee from a Dr. Seuss book and it's a puppet—you can see the strings and everything! In one stirring flash of political insight, the turkey monster pecks away a hunk of the United Nations building, which, come to think of it, may be why our country still hasn't paid its U.N. dues. The movie itself is vintage Grade-A USA turkey, but the giant muppet turkey was actually made in Mexico, anticipating the great benefits the NAFTA treaty brought our way and the blessedly cheap slave labor corporate America has come to depend on.

Fave-o-rite Woodchuck 200-Pound Turkey Monster Movie: None of you have ever heard of it, I'm sure, which proves that God does exist, but **Blood Freak** (1972) was filmed in Florida, which is the strongest argument I can possibly offer for my decision to never, ever move to Florida, even though my parents and sister did. I'll take the snow, thank ye. Anyhoot, *Blood Freak* really *is* a turkey monster movie, in that the monster *is* a turkey, or a turkey-man. You see, he's a screwed-up biker who wants to do right and quit dope and he falls for a born-again Jesus-preachin' woman. But then, a Food-and-Drug researcher slips him a dose of something that, well, turns him into a big turkey, or rather a guy with a big fake turkey head over his own, which makes him kill, though I don't know why. My friend Muskie raises turkeys up around Chester, and his turkeys never do anything but eat and crap and gobble and peck at each other, but this turkey is just plain mean. He needs junkie's blood, which they just don't sell at the feed store. The film's narrator chain-smokes throughout and coughs his fool brains out. This is an important film, really, being the *only* anti-FDA-anti-drug-anti-smoking-pro-Christian-biker-splatter-turkey-monster movie ever made. *Ever*. And that surely counts for something.

*Woodchuck-Pick-of-the-Litter Holiday-Musical Turkey:
Santa Claus Conquers the Martians (1964). The title really says it all—I mean, Santa really *does* conquer the Martians, who, being Grinch-colored, try to steal Xmas—though I should also warn you that li'l Pia Zadora made her debut in green-face as one of the Martian rugrats here, and the lame-o song "Hooray for Santa Claus!" will forever blight your Xmas memories. Why do we know or care about Pia, anyway? She never could act or sing—I mean, how did she ever become a pseudo-celebrity?

Pardon me, I gotta go take a Pia.
See ya around Christmas time.

November 25:

Give thanks, one and all, for one of the best family films in years, **THE IRON GIANT** (1999). Earlier this year, we were graced with the exceptional true-life coming-of-age tale *October Sky* (1999), a moving portrait of a teenage boy awakening to his passion for rocketry, inspired by his first glimpse of the Russian Sputnik satellite in the night skies. *The Iron Giant* is likewise set during that same fateful October of 1957, chronicling the coming-of-age of another boy whose life is forever changed by another airborne object—an extraterrestrial visitor which plunges into the raging sea near his remote Maine seaport village, far from the coal mines of *October Sky*. When young Hogarth (voiced by Eli Marienthal) rescues this visitor, the titular Iron Giant (voiced by Vin Diesel), from electrocution, a unique bond forms between them. Much of the fun lies in the growth and surprisingly heartfelt depth of that bond, while considerable dramatic power emerges from Hogarth's difficulty hiding his newfound friend from, and carefully unveiling him to, the adults around him: his loving single mother (Jennifer Aniston), the local beatnik scrap dealer (Harry Connick, Jr.), and the unwelcome xenophobic government investigator (Christopher MacDonald). Before its rousing conclusion, *The Iron Giant* gracefully touches on many profound issues—matters of the heart, the soul, and the very timely issue of weapons and the moral repercussions when one chooses to embrace violence—without ever losing its endearing sense of warmth for its characters, its rich humor, genuine sense of wonder, impeccable comedic and dramatic timing, or slowing its brisk pace.

Much as I enjoy the Disney animated classics, *The Iron Giant* is hands-down the best American animated feature of the decade; indeed, director Brad Bird's canny direction outstrips almost every live-action film I've seen this year. Bird cut his teeth years ago on the hilarious "Family Dog" episode of the short-lived TV anthology series *Amazing Stories* (1985-87), maturing into one of our finest filmmakers. His adaptation (co-scripted with Tim McCanlies) of Ted Hughes' fine novel *The Iron Man* deserved a fair shot at the audience it was intended to reach—hopefully, home video will provide the vehicle. Regrettably, the powers that be at Warner Brothers buried the film during its truncated theatrical release this past summer. Thanks to the Latchis Theater, a few Brattleboro residents were able to catch this gem on the big screen, which is where I first saw it; after the lights came up, the few adults scattered through the theater were in a daze, genuinely surprised at how excellent the film was, eager to talk to any other adults who'd happened to see it. They won't be alone any longer—there is *plenty* here worth sharing and talking about.

The Iron Giant is my pick of the week, and one I urge every one of you to check out; this was, without a doubt, one of the best films of the year, period. If you're looking for an ideal Holiday home video double feature for the family this weekend, pair up *October Sky* with *The Iron Giant*; it's rare that two family films this good arrive in the same year, and you really owe it to yourself to bring them both home. *(Rated 'G'. suitable—and recommended—for all ages.)*

The best musical-comedy of the year also happened to be an animated feature, though it's definitely not suitable for all ages. Trey Parker and Matt Stone's hilarious **SOUTH PARK: BIGGER, LONGER, & UNCUT** (1999) lives up to, and transcends, its small-screen source series from Comedy Central. This scatological, scathing satire only sharpened its bite on its way to the big screen, daring to sink its teeth into the hands that fed (parent studio Paramount) and tried to restrain it (the MPAA, whose ludicrous attempts to pin an NC-17 on the film further exposed the inherent hypocrisies and worthlessness of the Ratings Board). While the rest of Hollywood fled the long, dark shadow of the Columbine massacre and subsequent political rhetoric, Parker and Stone confront the issues head-on with their absurdist parable in which South Park third-graders Stan, Kyle, Kenny, and Cartman struggle to defuse a nationwide campaign to scapegoat Canada for the cultural pollution of their impressionable young minds—and, while doing so, save mankind from Armageddon. As Parker had already demonstrated in his debut feature *Cannibal! The Musical* (1996), he has always had an unerring ear for parodying Broadway and Hollywood musical conventions, enlivening *South Park: Bigger, Longer & Uncut* with the best and brightest score of the year, sending a barbed harpoon into the carcass of the Disney animated musical archetype. Highly recommended! *(Rated 'R' for incredibly foul language, rude humor, sexual imagery and situations, and adult satire.)*

I'll take Kenny's ghost or the Ghost of Christmas Past of any given year over the DreamWorks remake of **THE HAUNTING** (1999), a hideously over-blown betrayal of the brilliant Shirley Jackson source novel *The Haunting of Hill House* (note that Jackson crafted her most popular novel while living in Bennington, Vermont, lending a certain local color to her classic ghost story). Anything of value in Jackson's novel is jettisoned a mere half-hour into this new version, which unravels the seductive characterizations, subtle unease, and impeccable nightmare-logic of Jackson's novel for its own slavish, misbegotten patchwork dedication to 1990s Hollywood filmmaking-by-committee.

By the time shy shut-in psychic Eleanor (Lili Taylor, giving a fine performance despite the aggressive undermining of her role by the nonsensical script and hack direction by Jan De Bont) finds the house's spectral forces have written her name in blood (instead of the dust of the novel), the film proceeds to lose track of its own story grafts. Is Hill House haunted by the ghosts of long-dead youngsters, victims of its builder's heartless child labor practices? Ya, *that's* it!—well, for ten minutes, anyway. You can almost hear the committee gnashing its teeth as they realized the combined fortunes of Dreamworks Pictures executives Spielberg, Katzenberg, et al were built in part on Third World child labor. Oops! Forget that child-labor tangent! So the reason for the hauntings is changed again and again as the committee changes its mind, phoning in new directions and script concepts to De Bont and the cast, leaving Eleanor shrieking "It's *always* been about family!" (*huh??*) and the film unreeling in an increasingly noisy, senseless plethora of special effects until the narrative vacuum collapses in on itself. One of the novel's (and original film's) most chilling moments—"Who was holding my hand?"—is reduced to a now-meaningless line, tossed off in the wake of another explosion of effects.

On the plus side, the sets are breathtaking and the effects work itself is marvelous, showcasing more fine work from Phil Tippett (*Robocop, Jurassic Park, Starship Troopers*). In the end, this *Haunting* is a hopelessly empty showcase, leaving its technical jewels swimming in Hollywood bile, interesting only as a case study comparing the effectiveness of horrors unseen (as in Jackson's novel, or Robert Wise's original film adaptation *The Haunting*, which is most highly recommend) versus those seen. History has already rendered its verdict: *The Blair Witch Project* and *The Sixth Sense* promptly eclipsed the comparatively feeble earnings of this shameful shambles of a horror movie. *(Rated 'PG-13' for language, violence, and lots of CGI monstrosities.)*

Sorry, I wasted so much space rambling on about *The Haunting* that I haven't the proper space left to discuss **LIMBO** (1999), the genuinely haunting new film by John Sayles (*Lone Star, Matewan, The Secret of Roan Inish*, etc.). Maybe because I'm in my mid-forties and going through some tough life changes (including a change of career after 20+ years invested in an industry I cared deeply for), I identified wholeheartedly with Sayles' cast of characters (led by David Strathairn and Mary Elizabeth Mastrantonio) likewise stranded in a frontier they didn't ask for, harboring regrets over the past, nervous about their future and the legacy left to their children. Sayles' title evokes the barren emotional, physical (Alaska, in all its harsh beauty), and psychological landscape explored here, and should prepare you for its "The Lady or the Tiger" conclusion, which will have some of you ready to toss your remote control through the damned television screen—but it all worked for me. This is challenging, confrontational adult storytelling, and it haunts me still.

Nor is there room to write about ***Entrapment*** (1999), which offers Catherine Zeta Jones much livelier screentime than her role in *The Haunting* affords, herein stalking, capturing, courting, and double-and-triple crossing wits and wile with master thief Sean Connery (who also co-produced the film); Connery and Zeta Jones are the greatest assets on view, lending spark to this high-tech retread of *The Thomas Crown Affair*. Nor can I tell you about ***The Love Letter*** (1999), a pleasant DreamWorks diversion (adapted from Cathleen Schine's novel) in which an anonymous love letter kicks off an amorous comedy-of-errors for Kate Capshaw (who also co-produced) and her circle of friends, turning their seaside small town upside-down. I'd love to write about ***Splendor*** (1999), an erotic romantic comedy from gay bad-boy indy filmmaker Gregg Araki (*The Doom Generation, Nowhere*, etc.) chronicling the ins-and-outs of an unconventional, sustained menage-a-trois between Kathleen Robertson, Jonathan Schaech, and Matt Keeslar, but I can't. There's also Paula Goldberg's very funny short parody ***The Blair Princess Project***, the found-footage fate of three Jewish American Princesses en route to their friend's wedding, but Oy! I can't tell you about that, either. Too bad I can't mention the highly entertaining Spanish apocalyptic horror film ***The Day of the Beast***, or the suspenseful road movie ***Highway Hitcher*** with its taut top-drawer cast (William Forsythe, James LeGros, Elizabeth Pena), or how you have *got* to buy a copy of Rusty Dewess great Vermont one-man-show ***The Logger***, maybe buy a couple more as Xmas gifts for the relatives.

Sorry, no more room. I'm full. Really—I can't eat another thing!

December 3:

This week's hot new releases are a decidedly eclectic bunch, offering the biggest and baddest the big-budget boys can offer, the latest Hollywood flirtation with the Bard, and a grass-roots original that too many might pass over thinking it a *Blair Witch Project* rip.

THE WILD, WILD WEST (1999) is the latest top-dollar remake of a venerable TV series—and one its target youth audience has no familiarity with. Do the kids who have no idea what "mod" means (much less any affinity for—choke—*The Mod Squad*) really have any affinity for James West and Artemis Gordon?

Like all TV series, the original *The Wild, Wild West* (Sept. 1965 - April 1969) was an erratic procession of good and bad episodes, but its premise was inspired, melding the mid-1960s spy craze and television's decade-long passion for primetime westerns with gleefully anachronistic sf concepts, a bevy of Bondian female co-stars, and an often grotesque rogue's gallery worthy of Chester Gould's *Dick Tracy*. Best of the series villains was the evil genius Dr. Miguelito Loveless, played by the brilliant three-foot-ten-inch actor Michael Dunn, who proved popular enough with viewers to become the series' only recurring villain, appearing in ten episodes. Series stars Robert Conrad (as Special Agent James West) and Ross Martin (as master-of-disguise Artemis Gordon) kindled a genuine chemistry that anchored the pendulum-swing of outlandish excesses and impoverished budget constraints.

Eager to repeat their successful collaboration on *Men in Black* (2002, which was streamlined, briskly-paced, and driven by the sparks between live-wire Will Smith and deadpan Tommy Lee Jones), Director Barry Sonnenfeld and star Will Smith can be forgiven for embracing *The Wild, Wild West* as a vehicle, but not for driving it so firmly into the dirt. The conceit of Will Smith as an unlikely black government agent who was raised by Indians and is brash enough to bulldoze his way through the rampant racist elite of the post-War Between the States south is a tough sell; their tactic (supplant good-ol'-boy racism with good-ol'-boy sexism throughout) grows tiresome within minutes. Kevin Kline gives his dual role as Artemus Gordon and President Grant a game go, but there's nary a spark between the co-stars, and Kenneth Branagh's turn as Dr. Arliss Loveless (a nod to Michael Dunn's recurring role who's real-life dwarfism is echoed here by Arliss' lack of the lower half of his body) is sorely underwritten.

There's the string of Bondian women, led by Salma Hayek's thankless role and cameos by super models like Frederique van der Wal, and the expected wielding of gadgetry galore, but nothing works, save the first exchange of words between West and Loveless and one— and I do mean, one—sight gag. The film's central sf conceit—Loveless' eighty-foot mechanical spider war machine—is an apt metaphor for the film itself, which is a wheezing, clanking, ill-conceived, ungainly, oversized, and too-damned expensive entertainment device that absorbed the best efforts of far too many skilled technicians. *(Rated 'PG-13' for language, sexual situations, and violence.)*

Kevin Kline fans will find much more to savor in the latest Hollywood adaptation of William Shakespeare's fantasy **A MIDSUMMER'S NIGHT'S DREAM** (1999), where he shines as the hammy thespian Nick Bottom, a player who becomes a mere plaything for nocturnal netherworld folk amusing themselves tinkering with matters of the heart. Joining Kline in this venerable romantic comedy classic revamp are Rupert Everett (as Oberon, orchestrater of the evening's magic), Stanley Tucci (as Puck, agent of Oberon's magic), Michele Pfeiffer (as the faerie-queen Titania), and the attractive mismatched suitors—Anna Friel and Dominic West, Calista Flockhart and Christian Bale—whose passionate thrashing-about are the sum and substance of the play. Director Michael Hoffman (whose 1988 debut feature *Promised Land* was the first-born of the Sundance Institute) keeps the cast in fine form and the CGI window-dressing to a minimum. The verbal sparring, rich insults, and heartfelt soliloquies are wily Will Shakespeare's work, all right, but the mud-wrestling and anachronistic tinkering with the Bard's text to update the antics to turn-of-the-19th Century Italy (with phonographs and bicycles with unlikely battery-powered lights) is typical of the current wave of Shakespeare adaptations. *(Rated 'PG' for sexual situations.)*

It's tempting to consider the havoc created by Shakespeare's faeries in even more contemporary terms—after all, Bottom and the rematched lovers awaken with a bad case of abduction, missing time, and repressed memories, which would have Mulder and Scully opening a new X-File. Writer-director Jeff Abugov's modest romantic comedy **THE MATING HABITS OF THE EARTHBOUND HUMAN** (1999) chronicles a typical 1990s courtship from first meeting to marriage as an artifact from an extraterrestrial culture: that is, an alien culture's documentary on our mating habits. The conceit is simple, the video box art easily passed over, but this is a charmer. Carmen Electra (*Baywatch*) and MacKenzie Astin (*The Last Days of Disco, Dream for an Insomniac, Iron Will*) are playful and easy on the eyes as the couple under behavioral scrutiny, and *Frasier*'s David Hyde Pierce is the know-it-all analytical alien narrator, whose misperceptions of the rituals on view are as amusing as his dead-on observations. Though occasionally overplaying its hand (in the dinner scenes and flashback memories) and not above borrowing from its betters (the onscreen metaphor for sperm revamps the hilarious climactic sketch in Woody Allen's 1972 satire *Everything You Always Wanted to Know About Sex*), this is a fun, inventive entry in the independent "mockumentary" genre (i.e., *This is Spinal Tap, Waiting for Guffman, The Blair Witch Project*). *(Rated 'R' for sexual situations, nudity, and language.)*

A recent "mockumentary" particularly deserving of attention is **THE LAST BROADCAST** (1998). This is necessary viewing for both fans and detractors of *The Blair Witch Project*, and anyone who is interested in—or part of—the new generation of digital feature filmmakers. This is *not* a fad; this is a new frontier, as revolutionary as the coming of sound in 1927, and just as likely to change *how* we see and think of movies (and devastate and/or change Hollywood) as irrevocably. This new wave has justifiably garnered increasing media attention (via the success of *Blair Witch* and articles in zines like *Wired*), and *The Last Broadcast* is an unsung landmark in this new media landscape—the first feature to enjoy all-digital broadcast theatrical showings (in five concurrent venues in 1998). As your local independent video superstore, First Run Video is proud to bring this overlooked, independently produced and distributed gem to Brattleboro.

The film chronicles the terrible fate of a TV news team that ventures into the New Jersey wilderness to investigate the fabled Jersey Devil. Sound familiar? Don't be so quick to dismiss this as a Johnny-Come-Lately rip-off, which it most definitely is not; if anything, it's the Johnny-Come-Early precursor to *Blair Witch* and one of the key independent films of the 1990s, finally achieving widespread distribution on home video this week after struggling for years to reach its potential audience. *The Last Broadcast* is a nervy, subversive tale, unfolding via a calculated showcase of interviews, investigative TV journalism, and "found footage" of the narrative's central atrocity. Despite ongoing media coverage of their film in at least one major newsstand magazine per month since August 1997, Pennsylvanian independent directors Stefan Avalos (who previously directed *The Game,* aka *The Money Game*, 1994, also on video) and Lance Weiler (currently working on his own solo debut feature) were unable to negotiate a palatable distribution deal for their film, choosing to self-distribute while suffering the frustration of their accomplishments being swept aside in the attendant big-bucks promotion mounted for thunder-stealers *Blair Witch Project* and George Lucas' *Star Wars: The Phantom Menace* (which claimed to be the first digitally-broadcast theatrical feature). Turn off the phone, turn down the lights, and tune in to *The Last Broadcast*. *(Unrated; would most likely be rated 'PG-13' for language, violence.)*

December 9:

There's a mixed bag of new releases this week, along with the ideal Christmas gift for your friends or family—or most of all, those loved ones who moved out of state and could use an undiluted dose of Green Mountain humor right about now. Matter of fact, let me tell you about that one right now:

If you missed Rusty DeWees' live one-man-show **THE LOGGER** (1999) when he was in Brattleboro last month, you owe it to yourself to pick up a copy of Rusty's video version of the show (and if you did see him on stage at Brattleboro Union High School, you don't need me to hustle you to pick up a copy!). *The Logger* captures the first half of Rusty's hilarious meditation on being a Vermonter, with lots of engaging extras, including an interview with neighbors, a peek at the backstage preparations, and more. The tall tales are marvelous (particularly the one about his friend's one-legged dog), the casual insights about life in the boonies are on-the-money, and the comments about the tourist industry are—well, if you're from around here, you'll understand, and if you aren't, you should. DeWees has been one of Vermont's most active performers, popping up on screens little (he was in *The Guiding Light, As the World Turns*, and *Law & Order*) and big (*Black Dog, Mud Season*, and Jay Craven's *Where the Rivers Flow North* and *Stranger in the Kingdom*), but this is his tour de force, and it's not to be missed. He promises the second half of his live show (chronicling his character's misadventures in New York City) will be available next year, but don't drag your feet about getting a copy of the self-contained first volume for your home library. *(Unrated by the MPAA, though Rusty self-rated this 'SC' for "Some cussin'." Like he says.)*

When I was a kid, Walt Disney cranked out one or two formula Americana fantasies a year, usually starring Fred MacMurray, Tommy Kirk, or (later) Dean Jones. I still have a soft spot in my skull for *The Shaggy Dog, The Absent-Minded Professor, Son of Flubber*, and *The Misadventures of Merlin Jones*, and I suspect today's tots have similarly softened their craniums with the new breed of Disney nonsense like *Flubber, My Favorite Martian*, and the new **INSPECTOR GADGET** (1999). These "new" Disney fantasy-comedies are jam-packed with CGI (Computer Generated Imagery) gimmickry and strictly adhere to their own formula, which I have no doubt drives parents up the wall. Unlike the old Disney matinee fodder, the "new" breed are strikingly unoriginal, mining the Disney vaults (*The Absent-Minded Professor* remade as *Flubber*), prime-time TV coffers (*My Favorite Martian*), and now rival cartoon studios for source material.

Inspector Gadget follows the formula to the letter: get a cuddly name star (Matthew Broderick) as the square, innocent hero; tag another name star to play the fey, non-threatening villain, preferably with a touch of a foreign accent (Rupert Everett, having fun slumming) and dimwit lackeys to abuse; give the hetero hero a smart girlfriend (Joely Fisher) and an animated-object sidekick that jabbers incessantly (D.L. Hughley as the Gadgetmobile); spice with product-placement (ABC commercials before the film, a Yahoo plug in the movie), self-referential digs ("Gotta wear seat-belts, baby—it's a Disney movie!"), just a little adolescent naughty humor (Gadget accidentally crunches a guru's groin, then loses his pants during the climactic chase), and a pretty-boy music video (by Backstreet Boys/'N Synch wanna-be's Youngstown). Toss in the not-too-scary evil Doppel-Gadget (Broderick as the destructive RoboGadget) and essential final chase scene (degenerating to shopping carts at one point), and *voila*! Harmless Disney matinee fodder and home video fare.

Inspector Gadget was a short-lived cartoon series with *Get Smart* star Don Adams providing Gadget's voice. It mocked '60s spy fixtures like James Bond (like the Bond villain Blofeld before *You Only Live Twice*, Gadget's nemesis Claw was never shown; only his metal claw-hand was visible, pushing buttons, petting his cat, or clenched as a fist), *Mission Impossible* (in every episode Gadget's note would self-destruct and trash "Chief"), and others, including '60s spy parodies like *Get Smart* (Gadget's boss was "Chief"). The other consistent running joke was that Gadget never solved his cases; that was left up to his abler sidekick Penny (using her marvelous computerized book) and dog Brain (sporting collar and antennae) episode after episode. Penny and Brain are in the film, but get short shrift indeed; maybe if they had written the screenplay, they could have saved the day again.

It's highly unlikely the target audience for Disney's *Inspector Gadget* will pick up on any of the 1960s spy genre references, and they may not appreciate Don Adams' vocal cameo in the coda (as Brain's voice), though *Gadget* fans will. The original cartoon series indeed has its devotees, young and elder, and they may find the film's mere existence gratifying, but I know some pretty die-hard *Gadget* fans and I suspect they'll be vocally critical of the feature film's deviations from the cartoon. At least the catchy *Gadget* theme song (by Haim Saban and Shuki Levy) is left intact. *Gadget* plays more like a family-friendly parody of the vicious, 'R'-rated sf classic *Robocop*, which younger kids probably haven't seen, either (who are these TV remakes intended for, anyway?). But they'll see *Robocop* later in life—when they harbor fond memories of formula Disney fantasies like *Gadget*. *(Rated 'PG' for tame cartoon violence and, I suspect, for the guru-groin gag; special thanks to Daniel Bissette and Ingrid Witherell for their Gadget cartoon series recall and expertise.)*

I've got a confession to make: I love monster movies. Having sat through countless old monster movies just to see a groggy stunt man in a threadbare suit with a zipper up his back, I'm particularly enjoying the new generation of CGI monsters, and the stupider the movie (*Anaconda* or *King Cobra*, anyone?), the more fun I have. I mean, my son and I *loved* the recent American *Godzilla* remake, so you'll have to take anything I say about any monster movie with a grain of salt. Or a zipper up your back.

Having been raised a Catholic boy and made a good confession, I can now tell you about **DEEP BLUE SEA** (1999). If I'm going to watch a wall-to-wall CGI-fest, this is my cup of tea; just put the little ones to bed first. Samuel L. Jackson stars as the big-bucks mogul checking progress at one of his investments, a floating oceanic lab where genetic experiments have yielded a vicious, highly-intelligent breed of sharks (smart move, eh?), all to cure cancer. With impeccable Hollywood disaster/monster flick timing, Sam's arrival jives with the onset of a major tropical storm and revolt of the mutant man-eaters, sending the stellar cast scurrying, scraping, and screaming through the bowels of the crumbling complex until the final frame. Director Renny Harlin (*The Long Kiss Goodnight, Die Hard 2*, etc., though I still prefer his low-budget horror opus *Prison*) effectively tightens the thumbscrews on this diverting retread of two 1970s action-summer-movie archetypes (*Jaws* aboard *The Poseidon Adventure*) upscaled with 1990s CGI effects wizardry. In terms of technical effects, *Jaws* may seem like a puppet show by comparison, but *Deep Blue Sea* doesn't hold a candle to Spielberg's shark-shock classic. If you want to see a good shark movie, rent *Jaws*; if you're in the mood for some lively dumb fun, spiced with some jaw-dropper mayhem, at least one 'Gotcha!' twist that caught me by the short hairs, and an entertaining turn from L.L. Cool as the chef determined not to end up on the menu, c'mon down and chum the video racks.[17] *(Rated 'R' for language, gore, violence, and some spectacular shark-feeding frenzies.)*

There's more mindless fun to be had in **BLACK MASK** (1996), a typically over-the-top Hong Kong thriller that's short on brains but loaded with ass-kicking action. Jet Li (from *Lethal Weapon 4*, for those of you unacquainted with Li's impressive Asian filmography) stars and Danny Lee (who played the cop in John Woo's classic *The Killer*, among others) directed this slight sf tale of a meek librarian who is, in fact, a rogue member of a covert bio-engineered squad of cyborg soldiers. He's also the only survivor to stand against the crime lord who seized control of their ranks, donning a Kato

---

[17] The *Video Views* reviews (or abridgements) for *Deep Blue Sea, Dick, Run Lola Run* and *Teaching Miss Tingle* were also published in *VMag* #25, December 1999, pp. 42-44.

costume (an affectionate nod to Bruce Lee's pre-movie-stardom turn on US television in *The Green Hornet*) and working in uneasy alliance with an obsessed detective. If you've never seen a Hong Kong action film, this is a fine introduction which leaves Western actioners in the dirt, but be warned—the violence is graphic and occasionally fetishized (bondage and heavy bloodshed), and decidedly not for younger viewers. *(Rated 'R' for violence, gore, and some sexual situations.)*

Scott Ziehl's gutsy **BROKEN VESSELS** (1998) beat Martin Scorsese's recent theatrical release *Bringing Out the Dead* to the punch by a year, justifiably scoring numerous independent film festival awards. *Broken Vessels* offers a more satisfyingly linear narrative than Scorsese's calculatingly disjointed take on similar material, chronicling the degeneration of a rogue team of medical-rescue professionals with unflinching clarity. Jason London (*Dazed and Confused*) stars as a young loner who signs on with a rescue service, seeking escape and perhaps redemption from his own past; unfortunately for him, he is paired up with a vet paramedic (Todd Field of *Eyes Wide Shut*, giving a galvanizing performance) whose amoral sociopathic survival skills seize every opportunity for drug use and abuse, casual sex, theft, and manic lunacy. Increasingly jaded and worn to a frazzle by their desperately empty lives and a demanding job where every moment can literally be life-and-death, their lifestyle catches up with them in harrowing fashion. If you're looking for a truly adult drama, check this out, but if you're already timid about dialing "911," approach with caution. This is toxic stuff. *(Rated a strong 'R' for language, violence, sexual situations, drug and alcohol abuse, and things I can't mention here.)*

December 16:

Merry almost-Christmas! It's Kirsten Dunst week at the video store! Yes, the young ingenue stars in two, count 'em, *two* of this week's latest titles, along with John Travolta's latest thriller, and Samuel L. Jackson (all recovered from last week's nasty bout with mutant sharks) hot on the trail of the sexiest violin saga to ever scorch the screen. What's all this got to do with the Christmas season? Ho Ho *Ho! I don't know!!* But those geniuses in Hollywood must know something we don't!

THE GENERAL'S DAUGHTER (1999) is a straightforward, no-nonsense thriller adapted from the 1992 best-selling novel by Nelson DeMille. John Travolta stars as the military investigator whose probe of the most peculiar murder of a female Army Captain (Leslie Stefanson) inevitably uncovers sleazy sex, scandal, and more than one cover-up that upsets her dear old dad (James Cromwell, a long way from the bucolic bliss of *Babe* and too close to *L.A. Confidential* casting mode). Some critics decried the sexual violence, but the film actually downplays its more sordid elements and handles the atrocity at the center of the story with considerable restraint without diminishing its horror. Like Ridley Scott's muddled *G.I. Jane* (1997), though, one comes away a bit dazed at the mixed-messages inherent in this latest exploitation of the women-in-military issue; so, let me understand this correctly—if the chilling cover-up the story revolves around hadn't been indulged, women wouldn't be able to serve, much less excel, in the military? What price glory, indeed! This is slick, sleek, sick Hollywood product at its most polished, efficiently scripted and directed, embellished by fine performances from Madelaine Stowe as Travolta's fellow investigator, Clarence Williams III as the General's toadie, and James Woods as a prime suspect. *(Rated 'R' for language, very strong sexual situations and violence, gunplay, and a horrific rape sequence; for an engaging true-life case history involving civil rights and rape on a military base, also see this week's new release* Dangerous Evidence: The Lori Jackson Story.*)*

In the framing story of **THE RED VIOLIN** (1998), Samuel L. Jackson tracks the 300-year-history of the title instrument, which we experience in intimate detail. Canadian writer/director Francois Girard justifiably scored in his home country's Genie Awards with this expansive, ravishing, sometimes rambling epic, which traces the prophecy and human lives associated with the violin through all their tragic twists and turns; from the hands of its creator (Carlo Checchi) in 17th-Century Italy, where the secret of the instrument's distinctive color lies, through subsequent generations in a monastery in the Austrian alps and the chambers of Vienna, with gypsies and a devilish virtuoso in England, and facing destruction in the cultural revolution in China, until it ends up on the auction block in Montreal. This worthy successor to Girard's marvelous *32 Short Films about Glenn Gould* (1993; note actor Colm Feore, who starred as Gould, here playing the auctioneer) isn't as perceptive or engaging as that classic, casting a wide (and an at times overly familiar) narrative canvas, but the mystique of the instrument and Girard's passion for music and the lives spent dedicated to the art are communicated with heartfelt clarity and power. Its grasp may fall short of its ambitious reach, but this still ranks among the year's best, and is highly recommended. *(Rated 'R' for one vivid sexual encounter, violence, and language.)*

DROP DEAD GORGEOUS (1999) is drop-dead funny if you're in the mood for its in-your-face, mean-spirited brand of satire. Teen beauty contests are easy targets, and this takes plenty of cheap shots. Judging from the talk I hear from my kids and around the video store, Denise Richards (*Starship Troopers, Wild Things, The World is Not Enough*) is the current fave cover-girl everyone loves to hate. Well, you're guaranteed to hate her in this "mockumentary" of a Minnesota teen beauty pageant that pits Denise and her ruthless gargoyle mom (Kirstie Alley) against sweet little goodie-two-shoes Kirsten Dunst and her trailer-park trash mom (Ellen Barkin), tearing open old wounds and resurrecting past rivalries. The humor soars from the heights of Adam West's deadpan cameo as a pageant emcee to the lows of small-town retard-brother slapstick and the most spectacular onscreen barf-fest since 1986 (when David Cronenberg's remake of *The Fly* and *Stand By Me*'s pie-eating contest established a new record for cinematic flash-the-hash excess). If you're looking for less ham-fisted satires of teen beauty pageants and cut-throat stage moms, director Michael Ritchie said it all (with far more merciless wit and intelligence) in two sleepers, *Smile* (1975, with Bruce Dern) and *The Positively True Adventures of the Alleged Texas Cheerleader-Murdering Mom* (1993, starring Holly Hunter in the title role). If you're looking for an easier Denise Richards target, it doesn't get any worse than her debut film, *Tammy and the T-Rex* (1994), in which she has a roll-in-the-hay with a dinosaur (!) sporting her boyfriend's transplanted brain. But if you're just looking for easy laughs this week, *Drop Dead Gorgeous* will fill the bill. Just make sure you're not holding a beer can when the firebomb hits. *(Rated 'R' for language, sexual situations, cartoony* *violence, an overabundance of Technicolor yawns, and irreverence toward all.)*

Nixon, Republicans, and the White House are far more deserving targets, and **DICK** (1999) scores with a pretty amusing "Believe it or not!" rewrite of the Watergate era, in which clueless 1970s teens Kirsten Dunst and Michelle Williams witness the Watergate break-in. They also wander off during a class tour of the White House and meet President Richard Nixon (Dan Hedaya, who was born to play Tricky Dick), and before you know it Williams is tearing down pinups of 1970s teen idol Bobby Sherman to adorn her bedroom walls with snapshots of Nixon. The duo insinuate themselves into the political arena as Nixon's "Youth Advisors," canine caretakers, and they turn on the Oval Office with their "special" brownies; when things go sour, they become the secretive whistle-blower "Deep Throat." If you lived through this era, you'll savor the spin throughout, but the target teen audience might be as clueless as the leads unless they bone up on their Watergate scandal Cliff notes. You can watch (or re-watch) *All the President's Men* first—but who wants to do homework to enjoy a movie this silly? Not as nasty or funny as *Election*, not as brain dead goofy as *Drop Dead Gorgeous*, but ample fun nonetheless, sparked by some clever casting (including Saul Rubinek as Kissinger and *Kids in the Hall*'s Dave Foley and Bruce McCulloch as *The Washington Post*'s Bob Woodward and Carl Bernstein). *(Rated 'R' for language, sexual situations, alcohol and drug references and use.)*

Christopher Walken and Willem Dafoe co-star in (and co-produced) **NEW ROSE HOTEL** (1998), the latest from New York City independent filmmaker Abel Ferrara (*Ms. 45, King of New York, Bad Lieutenant*).

Walken and Dafoe helm a high-stakes futuristic corporate crime caper, kidnapping a Japanese geneticist using sultry Asia Argento as the bait. We see little action or espionage as the film unreels in fits and starts that seem like improvised actor workshop sessions. When Walken, Dafoe, and director Ferrara are in synch, they're dynamite, but the chemistry needs a catalyst which the terminally unfocused script (adapted by Ferrara and Christ Zois from an *Omni* short story by cyberpunker William Gibson) fails to provide. Argento is a limp *femme fatale*, but it's nice to see her reaching outside of the star vehicles crafted by her father Dario (the ultraviolent *The Stendahl Syndrome* and the quirky *Phantom of the Opera*). Fans of Walken, Dafoe, and Ferrara fans can't miss it, but casual viewers will find this murky German/Japanese/US coproduction rough sledding. *(Rated 'R' for language and sexual situations.)*

Back to the teen beat: More teen angst is on display in **TEACHING MISS TINGLE** (1999), the latest from whizkid Kevin Williamson. Lionized (over-praised) for his *Scream* scripts (clever, coy, derivative), his reputation further inflated by the success of his TV series *Dawson's Creek*, Williamson was savaged for *Miss Tingle*, which was his theatrical debut as both writer and director (they should have gone after the boxoffice hit *I Know What You Did Last Summer*, which unreeled like a vapid retread of the same slashers *Scream* satirized). Just like *I Know What You Did Last Summer*, *Teaching Miss Tingle* was adapted from a novel by Lois Duncan, who invented the young adult (aka "Y/A") horror/thriller novel franchise looooong before Christopher Pike or Robert Stine were Y/A brand names. Duncan's source novel *Killing Mr. Griffin* provided the gripping premise (abusive teacher eager to unfairly expel a hard-working student is kidnapped by the student and desperate teenage friends, who see no alternative to murder) and, with a gender change, the film's original title, *Killing Miss Tingle*. Unfortunately, the Hollywood backlash in the wake of the recent spate of high-school shootings neutered more than just the title, with reported refilming and eleventh-hour recuts. Nonetheless, *Teaching Miss Tingle* is pretty engaging fare, an ideal home video rediscovery enlivened by a riveting centerpiece performance from Helen Mirren as Miss Tingle, whose every word, thought, and deed is razored to hamstring anyone in reach. The rest of the young cast tries to hold their own against Mirren's marrow-sucking matriarch, but you know they haven't a snowball's chance in—well, see for yourself. Mirren's career survived *Caligula* (1980), and she'll rise above the stigmatization this film suffered— as will Williamson—though there's nothing here to be ashamed of. I'd give it a B+ or better. *(Rated 'R' for language, sexual situations, and violence.)*

Recent & Recommended:

French auteur Eric Rohmer's latest romance, ***Autumn Tale*** is worth a look, as is the acclaimed portrait of life and love in an Israeli-occupied Arab village, ***The Milky Way***; one of the great cult films of the 1960s, ***Two-Lane Blacktop*** starring James Taylor, Warren Oates, and Dennis Wilson (of The Beach Boys), finally hits video; Armand Assante commands ***The Hunley*** in the true tale of the Civil War's only rebel submarine, the first ever to sink a warship; Christopher Walken and Glenn Close star in the latest chapter of ***Sarah, Plain and Tall: Winter's End***, from Hallmark; and believe it or not, Orson

Welles' final vocal performance graces *Transformers: The Movie*.[18]

December 23:

AMERICAN PIE (1999) was *the* teen gross-out movie of the summer. *American Pie* lives up to its buzz (*The* beer! *The* bible! *The* pie! The Internet Strip-Show! The Laxative Drop in the Girls' Room!), but this is hardly the locker-room raunch parents feared. The set-up is familiar—four horny high school seniors bet they can lose their virginity by prom night—but screenwriter Alan Hertz and director Paul Weitz expose the naivete and basic decency of their clumsy teen heroes, who struggle to bridge the gap between their fantasies and the young women they endlessly, inadvertently alienate and offend. The film catches the male tribal swagger and suffocation, yearning and dread, the constant cuts and tentative support between the boys as they stagger through the opportunistic self-invented rites-of-passage our cultural vacuum abandons them to. With no meaningful barometer, they equate sex with manhood, and all the classroom sex-ed, well-meaning parental talks, porn, and pop cultural baggage provide nary a clue how to connect with their own needs, each other, or potential partners. In its way, this is as touching and insightful as it is laugh-out-loud funny. Jason Biggs (as nominal hero Jim) and Chris Klein (as sensitive jock Oz) are standouts, as are Alyson Hannigan (a great turn from "Willow" of *Buffy the Vampire Slayer*) and Natasha Lyonne (*Slums of Beverly Hills, Freeway 2*) who put up with all the shenani-

---

[18] Portions of the above column appeared in *The Chicopee Herald*, December 22-28, 1999, pg. 17.

gans, waiting for the right moment to provide a wake-up call. Glib critics called *Pie* the *Porky's* of the 1990s, but it's actually closer to *Fast Times in Ridgemont High* (1982), Amy Heckerling's knowing snapshot of sexual awakenings in the suburban mall set—and almost as good a film. *(Available in both 'R'-rated and uncut 'Unrated' versions, though be warned: the restored footage lasts mere seconds, sure to shock parents and utterly disappoint teens.)*

Another raucous coming-of-age comedy, **DETROIT ROCK CITY** (1999), hits the shelves this week—but *only* on DVD, a first for the format (the video won't be available until January 11th, 2000, further evidence that Hollywood wants *you* to have a DVD player in your home). Set in 1978, this follows four Cleveland teen KISS fans (Edward Furlong, Giuseppe Andrews, James De Bello, and Sam Huntington) desperately seeking tickets to a nearby Detroit KISS concert after their's are torched by Huntington's bible-thumping mom (Lin Shaye of *There's Something About Mary* in amusing form). En route, they bust Huntington out of Catholic reform school, encounter vengeful disco fiends, snotty punk kids, horny priests, pick up a female fellow traveler (Natasha Lyonne, once again the street-wise young woman), and Furlong stumbles into a male strip club hoping to earn his ticket money on amateur night. Needless to say, this isn't "role model" material; it hardly rates with *Dazed and Confused* or *American Pie*, but it's a fun road trip with a wall-to-wall 1970s top-40 soundtrack (Cheap Trick, Sweet, Styx, and, of course, KISS). The DVD boasts nifty extras, including audio commentary from director Adam Rifkin and his cast, the original screen test of the teen leads, and two KISS songs exploiting the unique multiple-angle DVD feature, allowing you to choose up to four various camera angles throughout the tunes. Ah, a toy for the big kids! *(Rated 'R' for language, casual drug and alcohol use and abuse, a spectacular vomit scene, sexual situations, and some violence.)*

RUN LOLA RUN (1998) is one of the best films of the decade. Stylish as it is, this isn't just a triumph of style over content; it bursts with substance and heart. Sitting in her Berlin flat, fire-red haired punk Lola (Franka Potente) gets a phone call from her desperate black marketeer beau: if she can't raise the equivalent of $60,000 cash and get it to him in twenty minutes flat, he will be killed. She hits the pavement and doesn't stop running until the harrowing, high-speed odyssey plays itself out—*three* times, and to three very different conclusions, with snapshots of all the infinite alternative realities and destinies in between. Hung on the slight frame of a situation rather than a narrative, this incendiary cinematic device detonates in the eye and mind, leaving the viewer intoxicated and aching for more. It is fast, furious, and more fun than any movie's been in a short-lived dog's age. German director Tom Tykwer doesn't waste a second of celluloid, squeezing more out of just 76 minutes than you thought possible. I've already told you too much; the less you know, the better. Run, rent it, *now! Now!!! (Rated 'R' for language, sexual situations, and violence.)*

SUMMER OF SAM (1999), Spike Lee's latest joint, is a high-energy adult take on the 1970s, light years away from *Detroit Rock City* or *That 70's Show*. It frames its story with the notorious ".44 Calibre Killer"/"Son of Sam" murders that plagued New York City in the summer of 1977. What the film is *really* about, though, is John Leguizamo's twisted attitude toward his wife (Mira Sorvino) and his own sexuality, the fuse for the lethal fireworks on view here. As such, this is a harrowing dissection of misogyny, the justifications and fears that fuel such self-destructive machismo. Meanwhile, in another corner of the movie: The glimpses of David Berkowitz's lifestyle, insanity, and atrocities are calculated to jangle your nerves, derivative of the graphic excesses and kinetics Italian thriller director Dario Argento pioneered in the 1970s. These horrific setpieces are supposed to be catalytic, but they never quite mesh with the breakdown of Leguizamo's marriage and his neighborhood, as he grows increasingly estranged from his best friend (Adrien Brody), whose punk lifestyle and bisexuality make Brody a prime target for the mob-sanctioned vigilante faction seeking a scapegoat for the random murders. Shorn of the shrill "Son of Sam" mayhem and explicit sexual angst, Rod Serling said it all in a half hour with the famous *Twilight Zone* episode "The Monsters Are Due On Maple Street": given the slightest provocation, xenophobic fear of anyone different will prompt people to devour their own family and friends. *(Rated a very strong 'R' for violence, gunplay, nudity, adult and sexual situations, drug and alcohol abuse, and raw language.)*

December 23:

HO! HO! HO! The Woodchuck Guide to Christmas Video Turkeys [19]

---

[19] Due to space restrictions, this column was never published, though it was commissioned and completed ahead of schedule for *The Brattleboro Reformer* A&E section. It appears here for the first time.

'Round my household, we carve up more than one kind of turkey come Christmas. I'm talking turkey, here—real turkeys. Gobblers. *Baaad* movies.

Now, I'm sure some of you have already had your fill of the beloved seasonal favorites like, oh, *Holiday Inn* or *White Christmas* or *It's a Wonderful Life* or any one of about a trillion versions of Dickens' *A Christmas Carol* that come down the chute every so often. Too often for my tastes, really, though I do have a soft spot for the Mickey Mouse and Mr. Magoo versions. When the women folk snuggle into *Bundle of Joy* or some such kleenex-fodder, we woodchuck he-men are indeed fortunate that there is a man's man's man's Christmas movie like *Die Hard* to cotton to. But you know, you can only watch Bruce "Yippee-ki-yi-yay" through the M-80 of Christmas movies just so many times before the little woman finds some more decorating that needs doing. Even wise-ass wonders like *A Christmas Story* or *Gremlins* can get to wearing pretty thin come the arrival of the Yuletide week (though I must confess *A Christmas Story* is a real heart-warmer, 'specially when that little peckerwood's tongue freezes to the flag pole).

But however sick-to-death you may be of those chestnuts, bear in mind it could be worse... I mean, *much* worse. Sick of *Rudolph the Red-Nosed Reindeer* ("Bumbles bounce!")? Can't bear another half-hour with *The Grinch Who Stole Christmas*? (and I *do* mean the half-hour version, not the bloated big-screen movie version directed by li'l Opie and starring that feller who went off and jumped nekkid into Lake Champlain just last year. God, I prit' near snored through all that monkey scat of a movie.) Tired of little nap-haired Linus trotting out on the stage at the end of *A Charlie Brown Christmas* to tell cueball Chuck for the umpteenth time what the true meaning of Christmas is? You better watch out, you better not cry—in fact, you best hunker down and kiss that little rag-toting munchkin's feet for keeping you clear of Pia Zadora in greenface with antennae sprouting out her noggin.

I'm talking Christmas movies *sooooo* bad you want to torch your tree, barf in the stockings, and plug up the chimney to keep Santa out of the house. In fact, a couple of these Christmas Clinkers warn you to steer clear of old St. Nick altogether, lest you be split-and-stacked like a cord of green wood. Now, I could get all highfalutin' here and spout some muck-a-muck academic boo-shwa verbiage about how these chunk-blowers put us in touch with the true roots of St. Nicholas, who was originally sort of a bogeyman kids were a'feared of and all that, but that's neither here nor there. I'm only talking them up here because they're stinkers. Woofers. Technicolor Yawns. *Xmas Arf of the Worst Kind*. Such as:

*BABES IN TOYLAND (1986): No, I'm not talking about the Walt Disney version with Annette Funicello and those dancing trees, nor the Laurel and Hardy version (which is on video as *March of the Wooden Soldiers*, and is a pretty good Xmas chestnut). I'm talking here about the hideous made-for-TV version that starred preteen Drew Barrymore as a little girl from Cincinnati, O-hio who saves Toyland from the evil schemes of nasty ol' Barnaby, played by Richard Mulligan. In the opener, Mulligan also appears as a toy-store proprietor who leches over worker Jill Schoelen, soliciting sexual favors with none-too-much subtlety. That's pretty off-putting in a family movie, but you've yet to suffer through shaggy teen Keanu Reeves (with frosted hair, no less) singing "I

Come from Cin-Cinnati!" while four-wheeling through a blizzard on Christmas Eve. Mercifully, this gut-wrenching number is cut short when Keanu puts his jeep into a spin, sending l'il Drew into a head-on collision with a tree and then she's off to Toyland. Sadly, she doesn't die, though you may want to.

The movie grinds on in a sort of ticky-tack roadside "South of the Border" version of Toyland, with lots of adults in floppy animal costumes. Oh, ya, and Keanu sings some more. Unfortunately, there are no four-wheelers in Toyland to run the brat down. If it were my Toyland, I'd have taken a monster truck to Reeves in short order, you betcha. I hate to give away endings, but Drew saves the day, wakes up back in Cincinnati, survives the concussion with nary a broken neck, and went on to rehab and *Charlie's Angels*.

*There's a really crappy big-budget Dudley Moore movie called *Santa Claus: The Movie* (1985) that's pretty dreadful, but the Mexicans went and made the definitive **SANTA CLAUS** movie back in 1959, and you've gotta see it to believe it. Santa lives in a little fake model castle perched on a cotton ball hovering above the North Pole. The narrator tells us he's "the best friend of boys and girls everywhere," and we see him laughing at a Nativity scene he's just set up, instantly aligning this Mexican Santa with all things good and Christian (though one has to wonder what's so damned funny about his particular Nativity set, until you get a good look at it yerself. Go ahead, *try* not to laugh!).

Then ol' Saint Nick starts playing a magic Hammond organ that tunes into a part of Toyland where "boys and girls of all races and creeds" live, and you just know Walt Disney swiped this whole set-up for the "It's a Small World" ride in Disneyland, which you couldn't pay me to go on again. Santa plays a rocking keyboard for a little ditty from every country's representative rugrats, including some pretty bewildered Chinese kids, a morose pair of Frenchies named Yvette and Pierre, two little Brits singing "London Bridges," and—in the film's most triumphant testimonial to racial equality—a clutch of wee, bare-chested African savages and savagettes beating tom-toms and wearing bones in their hair. The tots from Japan sing painfully off-key, but they're topped by the pathetic American duo butchering "Mary Had a Little Lamb," putting us uppity Yanks in our place. Listen, next time the White House wants to bail out the Mexican banks, you just remember this part of *Santa Claus* and ring up Jim Jeffords in Montpelier and give him a piece of your mind.

Meanwhile, down in Hades, Lucifer dispatches a demon named Pitch topside to stir up some trouble. With his goatee, red jumpsuit, and big phony rubber ears, ol' Pitch just about steals the show as his mission boils down to bedeviling an impoverished little bambino named Lupita, whose craving for "a doll, any doll" invites temptation, desire, and eternal damnation in a sea of hellfire. Santa keeps an eye on Lupita, though, just as he keeps an eye on *all* little boys and girls with his scary "Tele-Talker" machine, a weird computer with a lightbulb nose, severed ear in a radar dish, creepy extendible eye on a stalk, and giant red lips that speak. This is the kind of Santa ol' J. Edgar Hoover approved of. He also has a "Dream Scope" to brain-police slumbering tots, tuning in to Lupita's truly disturbing dream in which giant dolls dance around her. This dream is almost as creepy as that "too many Santas" dream at the beginning of that Frenchie movie *City of Lost Children* (being a Frenchie myself, I'm just the sort to recall that sort of thing). When my daughter saw this video at a tender age and turned to me with her big, wet brown eyes and said, "Daddy, this is the greatest movie ever made!," I knew she spoke the truth for four-year-olds everywhere. 'Scuse me, I gotta go blow my nose.

*There are *two* classic 'killer Santa' movies, but I just can't make up my mind which is worst. Mind you, it's close. **SILENT NIGHT, DEADLY NIGHT** is the one everyone's heard of that kicked up such a stink back in 1984 when the TV commercials scared the bejeezus out of people. It was *banned* in Boston—Really! It's actually a heart-rending tale of a little kid whose parents are raped and murdered by a crazed maniac in a Santa suit. Stuck in an orphanage under the stern vigilance of nuns, including a Mother Superior with a mug like a piece of busted farm-roof slate, the poor little feller grows up to be a pretty scrambled kid who's understandably terrified of Santas and nuns, which a lapsed-Catholic boy like me can relate to. He goes off the deep end when his boss at the department store forces him to dress up as Santa, and there ya go. Heads roll, '80s scream-queen Linnea Quigley gets spiked on a set of antlers, and ya can't help but feel sorry for the poor sap for slipping. I tell ya, it's a real tear-jerker, if you can get past all the slasher stuff, and aren't too scared of nuns. Skip the four sequels. No nuns.

    CHRISTMAS EVIL (1980), on the other hand, is a complete unknown outside of Baltimore, where John Waters declared it the only Christmas movie he'd *force* his kids to watch if he had kids. Maybe he'll adopt one day, y'never know. See, this kid sees Mommy kissing Santa Claus, and then grows up to work in a toy shop.

He *loooooves* Christmas so much, he keeps a list of good and bad kids (including one who wishes for a lifetime subscription to *Penthouse*), and before long goes out and *enforces* Yuletide cheer like a Brattleboro meter maid. *Bad* parents are punished, Scrooges decapitated, party-poopers are snuffed—well, actually, he only kills four people, all in the name of peace on Earth and good will to men. The police try to stop the guy, but the neighborhood kids rally to his defense, and the movie has an absolutely jaw-dropping, heart-fluttering, ring-a-ding-ding transcendental climax. No, I can't tell ya, it's just incredible. *Christmas Evil* is also known as *Terror in Toyland* and *You Better Watch Out*, so's you just better.

*SANTA CLAUS CONQUERS THE MARTIANS (1964): In a perfect world, every blessed school across this great land of our'n would present a live stage show recreation of this corker every December. In fact, I believe that's part-and-parcel of President Select George Dubbaya's educational revamp, in't it? Well, dagnab it, it *should* be. No Child Left Behind, indeed. *Humbug!* Instead of singin' "Rudolph" or "Silver Bells," chorus teachers would mount a full-blown concert composed solely of the songs from this unpolished yule-log of a movie. Believe you me, there is no carol that can hold a candle to "Hooray for Santa Clause!" (or, as they sing it in the movie itself, "Santy Claus"): "He's fat and round, but jumping jiminy / He can climb down any chim-i-ney!" It wouldn't cost nothing to pay for, either: most schools have tons of green greasepaint left over from Halloween (the Martians are green, y'understand, just like the Grinch). The Martian's robot is just a feller in aluminum-foil-covered cardboard boxes with a paint can turned over on his head and his arms and legs sticking out. My son coulda built one of 'em in grade school. Come to think of it, he did.

One of the little Martian tykes is played by the great Pia Zadora, one of those slinky pseudo-celebrities we've all heard of but none of this can remember why or what she mighta done to become famous. In this movie, she's younger than Drew Barrymore was in *Babes in Toyland* and even less lovable. See, the Martian kids don't have Xmas. They want Xmas. So the Martians come down and kidnap Santa, except there's this evil Martian who wants to nip this whole Christmas thing right in the bud. Smart fella. This is the one, the only Christmas movie that works its magic on people of all races, creeds, and such, reducing one and all to tears (I've seen grown men cry when they weren't allowed to fast-forward through this). It's a true melting-pot kinda movie, if you know what I mean. Nor is there a single Xmas movie that comes close to this one's call to arms in the defense of all that's Christmasy—well, the title just about says it all, don't it? Santa *conquers* the Martians. Period. Serves 'em right for messing with Christmas in the first place. If they'd have put Santa in *Independence Day*, it would have been a whole lot shorter of a movie.

*Lest you think I'm just picking on cheapies, let me conclude by declaring the multi-jillion dollar **THE TOY** (1982) and **TOYS** (1992) the worst Xmas turkeys to ever slither out of Hollywood (as for movies made outside of Hollywood, I reckon *Santa and the Ice Cream Bunny* would take the cake, but that's neither here nor there). In *The Toy*, racial harmony is championed by casting Richard Pryor as a down-and-out reporter who's employed to be the "toy" of billionaire oil tycoon Jackie Gleason's son. If that ain't bad enough, the movie ends up lecturing us about the joys of hard-earned friendship after rubbing our noses in 99 minutes of deer droppings. *Toys* is an unfunny, almost endless anti-war movie in which Robin Williams, wishing he was Willie Wonka, turns on the syrup (and I do mean fancy grade: thin and runny, with no flavor) as the heir of a toy factory who has a hard time when his evil uncle changes it into a munitions plant. Unfortunately, uncle cries "uncle" before he gets a chance to blow Williams to kingdom come.

These movies cost more than you, I, and the whole of this blessed state combined earns in a lifetime, and they ain't worth scraping off your boot in the driveway. Come to think of it, the new *Grinch* movie is almost as bad, and cost twice as much as *The Toy* and *Toys* side-by-two. If these Hollywood fellers would donate a fraction of the money they fritter away on such turkeys to a good cause or two, we'd all have a happier New Year.

Now, I'm sure there's more, but that's all I can stomach this year. If I trod on one of your particular favorites, I'm sorry, but it can't be helped. I just call 'em as I see 'em, and I've seen far, far too many. Hey, wait, I got me an idea for a big-budget Christmas movie about these Hollywood muckamucks who come down here in their oversized gas-guzzlers to make a Christmas movie, and we all get together with our snowmobiles and chainsaws, and... heck, it'd be *great!* Wha --? Ah, sorry. Wishful thinking.

Pass me another eggnog—I'll get in the proper spirit yet. Happy Holidays, one and all!

Addendum: The 12th Day of Xmas Viewing: THE GRINCH GORE FEST [20]

I wanted to rhapsodize over *A Christmas Story* or *How the Grinch Stole Christmas* (ah, Boris!), but the editor wouldn't let me. So, Ho Ho Ho, here goes: a crispy Kris Kringle threatened Joan Collins in the original *Tales from the Crypt* (1972) and Larry Drake played the psycho Santa in the remake of this EC Comics classic for the *Tales from the Crypt* TV series premiere (1988). Best of all was the berserk Santa-wannabe in the heartwarming *Christmas Evil* (aka *You Better Watch Out, Terror in Toyland*, 1980), saved from social retribution for his misguided (and murderous) Xmas madness by a ring of singing children. The teens who made *Scream* a theatrical blockbuster last Christmas season should check out *Black Christmas* (1975), first and definitely scariest of all the holiday films, though *Silent Night, Deadly Night* (1984) wins brownie points for being banned in Boston, and *Gremlins* (1984) rates as the only family gorefest we can recommend. For real Xmas perversity there are the fleeting pleasures of Christopher Plummer as the gun-toting St. Nick of *Silent Partner* (1978), but you can't beat Divine crushing Mom under the family Xmas tree 'cuz she didn't get her "cha-cha heels" in John Waters's

---

[20] This piece was originally published in *VMag* #3, January 1998, "Mixed-Up Media Issue," pp. 17, 32, as part of a collective article entitled "12 Days of Xmas Videos." Mine was "Day 12 (and Beyond?)", capping entries from Punco Godyn, G. Michael Dobbs, Bill Dwight, Dana Gentes, Julie Strain, P.A. and J. M. Falla, Chris St. George, Michael Charles Hill, Gene Kane, 'Youngblood,' and 'The Goddess of the Internet' (pp. 16-17). My entry is included here as a companion to the unpublished 1999 Christmas *Video Views* column.

Female Trouble (1974). You don't need to be a fruitcake to revel in festive holiday homo salads: America's favorite man's man action epic *Die Hard* (1988) was a Christmas movie, too. "Oh, the weather outside is frightful…."

December 30, 1999:

This week's Hollywood studio releases are a sorry lot: the romantic comedy **MICKEY BLUE EYES** (1999), the dumb-and-proud-of-it **DUDLEY DO-RIGHT** (1999), and sf actioner **UNIVERSAL SOLDIER: THE RETURN** (1999). More than likely, you've already made up your mind to rent 'em based on your attitude toward their respective stars, Hugh Grant, Brendan Fraser, and Jean-Claude Van Damme. All three are on DVD, too, for those of you so blessed.

Grant mugs shamelessly through ***Mickey Blue Eyes*** as Manhattan art auctioneer Michael, plagued by trucking delays and his misfired marriage proposal to Gina (Jeanne Tripplehorn), daughter of local mob Don James Caan. Despite Gina's warning that everything her family touches "ends up spoiled and corrupted," Mike is game. His trucking delays stop, but other calamities ensue as the mob muscle flexes in the Metropolitan art market. This can't hold a candle to Jonathan Demme's *Married to the Mob* (1988), which was a much sharper piece of work, but I did enjoy Caan and Burt Young (as Uncle Vito, natch) going through their paces—and wait until you see Uncle Vito's son's paintings! *(Rated 'PG-13' for language and sexual situations.)*

It's a sparkler compared to ***Dudley Do-Right***, the latest willfully-stupid TV-remake exercise that boasts none of the snappy satire of Jay Ward's celebrated cartoon series; this movie is more like *F-Troop*. The cast is fun, but Fraser's endearing dolt, Sarah Jessica Parker's Little Nell, Alfred Molina's Snidely Whiplash, and *Monty Python*'s Eric Idle are undone by the lame gags, overblown musical numbers, and absolute paucity of wit. By the time Dudley's dirt-biking with a machine gun and Snidley is manning a tank, you'll want to throw in the towel, but the kids may enjoy it. Just be sure to rent the original cartoons, *please*! *(Rated 'PG' for cartoon violence, sexual innuendoes, and toilet humor.)*

Van Damme and the cyborgs kick ass in the equally brain-dead ***Universal Soldier: The Return***, which ignores the dire cable-TV sequels only to undo the premise of the original in mere moments: Van Damme says, "been there, done that," and we're expected to just roll with the rest. Wrestling fans will enjoy Bill Goldberg's turn as one of the sf super-warriors, but this is a letdown. Re-rent the original, which cooked thanks to the writer/director team of Roland Emmerich and Dean Devlin, who went on to score with *Stargate* and *Independence Day*. *(Rated 'R' for violence, gunplay, gore, language, and sexual situations.)*

But why subject yourself to those? You can savor the off-Hollywood pleasures of Morgan J. Freeman's **DESERT BLUE** (1998) and the latest Sam Elliott western, **YOU KNOW MY NAME** (1999), both steeped in strong characters and assured story-telling.

Don't be put off by the poor box-art for ***Desert Blue***, a leisurely independent gem with a who's-who of young indy performers. If you think teenage life in small town New England can be dismal, check out the ex-Gold Rush town of Baxter, California, population 87, home of the world's largest ice-cream cone—which brings a pop-culture college professor (John Heard) and his self-centered TV-star daughter Skye (Kate Hudson) into town just in time to witness a cola-truck accident that prompts the FBI and EPA to quarantine the town. Chafing at confinement along with Skye are the townies: sheriff's demolition-expert daughter Ely (Christina Ricci), her boyfriend and local motocross-champ Pete (Casey Affleck), beefy Cale (Ethan Suplee of *American History X*), and Blue (Brendan Sexton III of *Welcome to the Dollhouse, Pecker*, and *Hurricane Streets*), who's quietly obsessed with the tragic death of his father and the hope of seeing through his father's failed dreams... and who just might be the one for Skye. The cast is excellent, the pace casual, the characters and chemistry warm and true; pay it a visit, you'll be glad you did. *(Rated 'R' for language, juvenile use of explosives, and casual drug and alcohol use and abuse.)*

Laconic, gravel-voiced Sam Elliott delivers another strong performance in **You Know My Name** as Marshal William Matthew Tilghman. Writer/director John Kent Harrison tells the true story of Tilghman's last tour of duty in Seminole County, Oklahoma circa 1924, portraying Tilghman as a man aware of the transition between the Old West and the new, and his role in each. The encroaching corruption of the new age embodied by a mad-dog Federal Prohibition agent (Arliss Howard) and his cronies sanction the growing "whizbang" (a potent cocaine-morphine mix) black market, relying on tried-and-true tactics (air-drops, body disposal, abuse of federal power, etc.). This solid, moving effort is a fine companion piece to John Cusack's *The Jack Bull*, which was one of the best films of the year. *(This made-for-cable film is unrated; the gunplay, sexual situations, drug abuse, and depictions of corrupt authorities may not be suitable for young children.)*

DANCE WITH THE DEVIL (1998) stars Rosie Perez (*Do the Right Thing, Fearless, The 24 Hour Woman*) as saucy sociopath Perdita Durango in this hellish mutant road movie (*not* to be confused with Ang Lee's current theatrical Civil War drama *Ride with the Devil*). Scorching from Mexico to Las Vegas, she meets soul-mate Romeo Dolorosa (Javier Bardem), an imposing santero *brujo* (warlock), and together they spice a border-run of stolen human fetuses (!) with the sacrifice of two blonde teenage gringos, Estelle (Aimee Graham) and Duane (Harley Cross, fine former child actor who survived *The Believers*, *Cohen and Tate*, and *The Fly 2*). Perez and Bardem are a steaming team you won't soon forget, joined by James Gandolfini and Alex Cox as the DEA agents on their tail, Screamin' Jay Hawkins as a voodoo priest, and vet character actor Don Stroud as the patriarch Romeo inadvertently crosses in this heady, intoxicating brew.

Doesn't sound like a holiday movie, does it? The timid, squeamish, or prudish better back off—this cinematic scorpion expects no favors, takes no prisoners (well, okay, two teenagers), and grants no mercy. If you enjoyed similar fare from independents like Eric Red (*The Hitcher, Cohen and Tate*) and Matthew Bright (*Freeway* and *Freeway 2*, which would make a great second feature), you owe it to yourself to rent this one. Emerging from the volatile new strain of Spanish/Mexican horror, director Alex de la Iglesia (whose Apocalyptic horror-comedy *Day of the Beast* arrived last month) helmed this US/Mexican/Spanish co-production, indulging the passionate excess and dark poetry he shares with peer Guillermo del Toro (*Cronos, Mimic*) and their precursor Alejandro Jodorowsky (*El Topo, The Holy Mountain, Santa Sangre*). De la Iglesia evokes many cultural touchstones throughout (including the wrestler hero Santo, Herb Alpert and the Tijuana Brass, *Vera Cruz*, and beloved Mexican comedian Cantinflas) and revels in a ruthless blend of mysticism and willful cruelty that will put off some viewers, while reminding others of the notorious Matamoros border cannibal-cult murders of 1989. Iglesia co-authored the screenplay in collaboration with novelist Barry Gifford (who reshaped the road movie with David Lynch for *Wild at Heart*— which featured the character of Perdito Durango among its cameo horrors—and *Lost Highway*) working from his novel *50 Degrees and Raining: The Story of Perdita Durango*. It's typical Gifford, populated with human monsters and hapless innocents. Nasty as this puppy is, it's been cut for US release; its original undiluted Spanish incarnation (entitled *Perdita Durango*, natch) is reportedly even sterner stuff. Bring it on, please! *(Rated a very strong 'R' for savage sex, a brutal double-rape, violence, gore, nudity, drug abuse, sorcery, blasphemy, and language.)* [21]

---

[21] Portions of the above column appeared in *The Chicopee Herald*, January 5-11, 2000, pg. 12. The *Video Views* reviews (or abridgements) of *Dance With the Devil, The 13th Warrior, From Dusk to Dawn 3: The Hangman's Daughter, Twin Falls Idaho* and *A Zed and Two Noughts* were also published in *VMag* #26, January 2000, pp. 34-35; those for *The Astronaut's Wife, The Buena Vista Social Club, Grey Owl, The Harmonists* and *Stigmata* in *VMag* #27, February 2000, pp. 36-37.

2000

January 6:

THE THOMAS CROWN AFFAIR (1999) stars Pierce Brosnan and Rene Russo in a polished remake of the sleek, stylish 1968 Steve McQueen - Faye Dunaway vehicle, which I'll refresh your memory on a bit before discussing the remake. With McQueen and Dunaway starring, *The Thomas Crown Affair* was cutting edge Hollywood chic in its day (as was its Oscar-winning theme song "The Windmills of Your Mind," which runs through it with teeth-grinding frequency). Having been dazzled by the 1967 Montreal Expo multi-movie screen displays, director Norman Jewison (like a number of his contemporaries) couldn't resist incorporating the multiple-screen device into the film. Seen today, the gimmick enhances the storytelling only during the opening sequence chronicling McQueen's ambitious jewel-heist, utilizing the screens-within-a-screen technique to visualize the many players McQueen runs through their paces with ingenious clockwork precision. Thereafter, the multiple-screen trickery only gets in the way of the slow-smoldering sparks between cool, efficient insurance investigator Faye Dunaway (in a fashionable array of costume changes and '60s headgear) and McQueen's multimillionaire businessman, whom Dunaway suspects is the mastermind behind the heist. Part of the fascination in '68 was waiting to see which star's cool-as-ice facade was going to crumble (and who would tumble) first, and *The Thomas Crown Affair* remains a compelling entertainment. Unlike so many of the apparently endless 1990s Hollywood remakes of 1960s movies and TV shows, one can understand the desire to revamp this particular title for a new generation.

Enter director John McTiernan, one of contemporary Hollywood's most unpretentious storytellers. After turning a sow's ear into a grisly silk purse with the Schwarzenegger vehicle *Predator* (1987), McTiernan invented the 1990s action movie archetype with *Die Hard* (1988), which remains the best of its breed. He subsequently directed Sean Connery in the Cold War coda *The Hunt for Red October* (1990) and the ecological fable *Medicine Man* (1992) before losing his pace amid studio-tampering (the misbegotten *Last Action Hero*, 1993) and the O.K. sequel *Die Hard: With a Vengeance* (1995). *The Thomas Crown Affair* and *The 13th Warrior* (hitting video stores in two weeks [see review, pg. 185]) find McTiernan back in stride in two very different genres, and both films are models of their kind.

The 1999 *Thomas Crown Affair* seizes on the elements that made the original percolate, and chucks the window-dressing. Gone are the flashy multiple-screens, the pretentious theme song, McQueen's annoying tic of arrogantly laughing to himself, and Dunaway's unconvincing interaction with the peers in her profession. Pierce Brosnan (never in a suit, per his contract with the James Bond producers) eschews the affectations of McQueen, using his unwitting partners-in-crime in the opening heist with even cooler amoral efficiency to manage the actual theft by himself. When this self-made multimillionaire sticks it to the insurance company, or tells the buyers of one of his properties they paid too much, he does so with a quiet conviction that speaks volumes; and as he woos Russo, the same holds true. As in the original, Russo can't resist her target's temptations, but their evolving relationship generates more heat than the austere chess-game one-upsmanship between McQueen and Dunaway did, though Brosnan and Russo haven't the iconic presence of their precursors (does anyone?). Faye blesses the remake with her presence, as an insurance investigator speaking from experience in a sly wink to fans of the original. This is the video pick of the week, warming the winter nights with intrigue, romance, and a good story well told. *(Rated 'R' for sexual situations, nudity, language, and a little violence.)*

Two excellent odes to musicians from other countries are also worthy of your attention. Joseph Vilsmaier's moving **THE HARMONISTS** (1999) lovingly tells the true story of one of the greatest vocal groups in history, Germany's Comedian Harmonists. Charting their formation in 1928 and rise in popularity under the guidance of co-founders Robert Biberti (Ben Becker) and Harry Frommerman (Ulrich Noethen), the film also details the internal and external pressures that unraveled the bond between them, leading to their breakup in 1939. I've no idea if the romantic triangle between Robert, Harry, and the ingenue Erna Eggstein (Meret Becker) was an actuality, but the Third Reich Music Association's targeting of "the non-Aryans in the group" is a matter of historical record, as is the group's triumphant performance in New York City. Resisting the temptation to stay in the US, the Harmonists subsequently endure a harrowing personal encore in the home of a prominent Nazi officer in Nuremberg, which paints a profound, powerful portrait of their predicament. *(Rated "R" for language, violence, and sexual situations.)*

Equally excellent and inspiring is German director Wim Wenders' snapshot of Ry Cooder and son's reunion of the Cuban musicians renowned as **THE BUENA VISTA SOCIAL CLUB** (1999). The gathered musical talents—Ibrahim Ferrer, Ruben Gonzalez, Eliades Ochoa, Omara Portuondo, Compay Segundo, and others—are marvelous throughout, and the spectacle of these performers in their 80s and 90s still burning with music and basking in the opportunity to play before audiences again is truly glorious. Unfortunately, Wenders only savors portions of their performances together, including their historic 1998 live concerts in Amsterdam and NYC's Carnegie Hall, but you can buy the soundtrack CD for that. Wenders wants to steep us in these rare and exceptional people, providing glimpses of their homes and neighborhoods, along with an often amusing glimpse of their visit to NYC as sightseers. Both these films are highly recommended. *(Rated 'G' for all ages.)*

Billy Jack for President! Most political pundits ignored Tom Laughlin's recent bid for the Presidency in the New Hampshire primaries, but old *Billy Jack* fans were paying attention. The **BILLY JACK** film series was an independent film phenomenon in the 1970s, almost as vital to the post-hippie era as *Black Elk Speaks* and Carlos Casteneda's Don Juan novels. Working his way up from roles in obscure Hollywood and fringe-Hollywood movies, actor Tom Laughlin's desire to control his work prompted him to self-produce and direct (under the pseudonym T.C. Frank) the first Billy Jack movie *Born Losers* (1967), which was sold as a biker movie and earned big bucks. Aching for fuller control and higher social causes, the sequel *Billy Jack* (1971) hit a real nerve with audiences, again starring Laughlin as the half-breed martial-arts expert Vietnam war vet who wants to embrace and protect the "give peace a chance" generation but just can't help but kick ass when confronted with racism, corruption, and irrational violence. This inherent contradiction of the character and Laughlin's films—utilizing dramatically cathartic violence to indict violence—is part of their power and naivete, which made Laughlin's politics and piety particularly hard for many to swallow in the idealistic follow-ups, *The Trial of Billy Jack* (1974) and *Billy Jack Goes to Washington* (1976). Laughlin didn't care; he had already bucked Hollywood, legally seizing control of *Billy Jack* from Warner Brothers to self-distribute and make film history with its unprecedented "grass roots" success, but the zeitgeist soon left Laughlin and Billy eating dust. By the time Billy Jack hit Washington, the sequel was practically barred from theaters and remained essentially unavailable until now. Many found Laughlin's politics questionable when he ran for the Presidency, but there's no denying the slice-of-the-70s potency and fascination of his films, which are now available on home video for the first time as a complete series (*Born Losers* and *Billy Jack* had been previously released to home video by their respective distribution studios). If you want to do more than just see the films, check out billyjack.com—and tell Billy we sent ya. *(The* Billy Jack *series is unrated, but its violence, language, and sexual situations—including non-explicit but harrowing rape scenes—makes it unsuitable for very young viewers. The theatrical versions of these films were rated 'R.')*

January 13:

A fine cast and brisk sitcom dialogue brighten **LAKE PLACID** (1999). As I've mentioned before in this column, I love creaky old monster movies, and this by-the-numbers formula 1990s model of the form boasts a lively menace, a 40-foot croc enjoying the good life up in Maine (uh, yes, Maine). Bill Pullman is the no-nonsense Fish & Game hero, Bridget Fonda the perky city-paleontologist-out-of-water, Oliver Platt the rich & eccentric croc-expert, and Brendan Gleeson (who was a revelation as the Irish crime lord in John Boorman's *The General*) is the surly local sheriff, all of whom go through their paces. Only *Golden Girl* Betty White provides any real surprises as the potty-mouthed Mrs. Bickerman, the sole lakeside resident who just doesn't see what all the fuss is about. She's "rooting for the crocodile," and you will be, too. *Friday the 13th* series vet Steve Miner helms with his usual no-nonsense exploitation-movie assurance, but the *auteur* here is TV writer David E. Kelley, creator of *The Practice* and *Ally McBeal*. Kelley is a media darling at the moment and this is a creditable first feature, but John Sayles scripted the classic of the form *Alligator* (1980) with a great deal more wit, sass, and a sharper pencil. *Lake Placid*'s computer-generated croc is an improvement, though. Stan Winston gets the credit for "Creature Effects," but don't be fooled: his crew handled the traditional bigger-the-life rubber animatronics, but Digital Domain deserves the lion's share of the credit for their impressive CGI croc action, which lives up to the promise of those incredibly vicious CGI crocs in the Arnold Schwarzenegger vehicle *Eraser* (1996), the first CGI reptiles (predating *Jurassic Park*'s breakthrough saurians). Despite the rating, this provides monster movie fun for all ages; only the very young should shy away. *(Rated 'R' for foul language from Betty White, violence, and some gore.)*

Having worked in comics for over twenty years, I have a few behind-the-scenes insights to offer you on **MYSTERY MEN** (1999). This amiable shaggy-dog parody of silly super hero movies turns out to be, well, a very silly super hero movie. A little background: When I had dinner a few years ago with Bob Burden, creator of *Flaming Carrot* and the *Mystery Men* comic book this movie was based on, the comic book market had begun its precipitous slide and Bob was outspoken about wanting to enjoy just "one big score" by selling *Mystery Men* to Hollywood. Sonuvagun, Bob did it, and I really, really hope he scored big (here's hoping Bob doesn't blow it all at one big party).

The movie is a mess, but it has its moments. Ben Stiller is Mr. Furious, the ineffectual leader of the unnamed Mystery Men, a ragtag band of impoverished super heroes tired of being scooped by the beloved Captain Amazing (Greg Kinnear). When the arrogant Captain loses his corporate sponsors, he conspires to free archvillain Casanova Frankenstein (Geoffrey Rush, lifting his accent here from Armin Mueller-Stahl, who played his abusive father in *Shine*), and the Mystery Men must rescue Champion City from his clutches. Great casting, with Paul Reubens as the flatulent Spleen, Jeanine Garofalo as the Bowler (bowling her dad's crystal-coated skull), Hank Azaria as the Blue Raja (tossing kitchen utensils and wearing not a stitch of blue), Tom Waits as Dr. Heller the Weapon Maker, and best of all William H. Macy as the rock-solid ordinary-Joe The Shoveler ("I shovel well. I shovel very well."), but the big-budget excess and self-conscious "uncool coolness" is corrosive to the premise.

The inexplicable, subversive charm of Bob Burden's original comic book adventures of the ragtag

Mystery Men (which began as a back-up series in Bob's *Flaming Carrot*) was akin to that of Burden's favorite bohemian beat street-surrealists like Captain Beefheart and Wild Man Fisher, and at times approached the impeccable illogic of Alfred Jarry's *Ubu Roi*. Yes, the *Mystery Men* always satirized super hero cliches, but they were Dadaist creations, by their very nature resistant to the expensive, expansive self-conscious camp inflation of the latter 1990s *Batman* movie franchise. The opulent designs of the movie's Champion City are evocative of *Metropolis* and *Batman*, or comics like Alan Moore's futuristic *Watchmen* and *Promethea*, not Bob's trailer-park, back-alley absurdism. If they had to make the leap to the big screen, something closer to Ray Dennis Steckler's impoverished *Rat Phink A Boo Boo* (1966) would have been truer to the comic—but then, Hollywood didn't want to make that movie, you wouldn't want to see it, and Bob and his publisher Dark Horse Comics wouldn't have pocketed big bucks (Dark Horse mogul Mike Richardson's usual co-producer credit wouldn't have meant as much). Sadly, audiences didn't flock to this high-ticket revamp anyway, and I can see why. I'm also very, very tired of top-40 pop songs strung together into faux musical scores; they should have turned it over to Tom Waites, who might have rekindled the sorely-needed raggedy-ass tone this movie needed. Still, there's some fun to be had if you're in the mood for a very, very, very silly superhero movie. As they say at the frat parties, BYOB. It may help. *(Rated "PG-13" for language and cartoony violence.)*

The premise alone of **OXYGEN** (1999) merits a warning: an arrogant mastermind (Adrien Brody) buries a millionaire's wife (Laila Robins) alive, leaving 24 hours for the ransom to be delivered before she suffocates (hence, the title). Add to this claustrophobic nastiness the female detective lead (Maura Tierney) who has her own problems working out a kinky sadomasochistic sex life (implied, not shown) and poor self-image, cat-and-mouse games with the killer, and occasional glimpses of the poor woman six-feet-under, and you've got a pretty rude evening entertainment. The only meditation on this kind of evil worth the agony is the European classic *The Vanishing* (1988, not the 1993 Hollywood remake), but Brody (who recently scored as the scapegoat punk of *Summer of Sam*) gives this some juice. Here's an actor with chops and great promise, the sole reason to inhale to *Oxygen*. *(Rated 'R' for—well, you know.)*

January 13:

First Run Video Welcomes Last Broadcast *Directors*

Stefan Avalos and Lance Weiler, the directors of the first digitally-produced and theatrically "broadcast" feature length film **THE LAST BROADCAST** (1998), will be visiting Brattleboro at First Run Video (927 Putney Road) on Saturday, January 15th from 4 PM to 6:30 PM. These two young filmmakers from Pennsylvania are being welcomed not only as the second guests in First Run Video's ongoing "Meet the Filmmakers" series (the first, *Stranger in the Kingdom* director Jay Craven, appeared at the store in August 1999), but also as pioneers.

Stefan and Lance's *The Last Broadcast* is significant not only as the precursor and blueprint for 1999's independent boxoffice sensation *The Blair Witch Project*. More importantly, their debut feature stands as *the* first digitally-produced and satellite-broadcast theatrical feature in history—predating the thunder-stealing theatrical presentation via satellite of George Lucas' *Star Wars: The Phantom Menace* by almost a year.

Eventually earning national coverage in *Forbes, Wired, Entertainment Weekly*, and many other magazines and newspapers, *The Last Broadcast* was made in 1997 for about $900 with borrowed digital (and a kid's toy) cameras and edited with available Adobe software and a 166-megahertz personal computer. Through their own distribution firm Wavelength Releasing, Stefan and Lance's film debuted in 1998 in Doylestown, Pennsylvania (long before *Blair Witch*) as a digitally-projected theatrical event. Its successful one-week run was followed by a festival tour and (in conjunction with Cyberstar, Digital Projection, and DLP) momentous satellite-distributed showings in five US cities in October 1998 and five international showings in May 1999 (New York, Cannes, London, Dublin, and Stockholm).

Make no mistake: Stefan and Lance are heralds of a new age in how films are and will be made and shown. They did it essentially on their own, bucking enormous odds—and they would be the first to say *The Last Broadcast* is only the beginning.

Here in our own neighborhood, digital filmmaking has established a beachhead. The technology is being taught in our local high schools and colleges. On December 9th, 1999, director Jay Craven hosted a lively collection of student films at Marlboro College, his second such presentation since taking on the teaching of film studies at Marlboro. These short films demonstrated a remarkable affinity for and skill with the new filmmaking technologies; a few examples were spectacular. The young filmmakers brought an engaging range of abilities, interests, and accomplishments to the screen, proving a significant advance over the previous year's worthy efforts (when Jay hosts his next presentation, I urge all of you to attend!).

As you read this, local filmmakers Joshua Moyse and Nathan Diamond are putting the finishing touches on their own debut horror feature film *Blood Rites*, which enjoyed a successful theatrical "sneak preview" at the Latchis Theater in October 1999. Digital editing and effects are an integral part of Joshua and Nathan's tool kit, providing control over the finished product and fresh opportunities prior generations could only dream about.
In this digital generation, Stefan and Lance stand tall, setting an example for all who follow.

The Last Broadcast is a horror movie, and a mystery film, with much to recommend it. The story is simple, but the telling is tantalizingly convoluted and intricate. In the context of an imagined "documentary" by an obsessed filmmaker David Leigh (David Beard), we are presented with the facts in the case of Jim Suerd (Jim Seward), a young man who was tried and convicted for the murder in the Jersey Pine Barrens of two cable access program creators and their soundman. This amateurish cable "news team" (played by Stefan, Lance, and Rein Clabbers) had wandered deep into the Jersey Barrens in search of the "Jersey Devil," a legendary demon or monster long believed to haunt that wilderness area. Though Suerd was convicted for the crime, Leigh believes someone or something else—perhaps even the Jersey Devil—was the culprit. As the film unfolds its calculating, intriguing tapestry of lies and misperceptions, we discover the horrifying truth of what happened that night.

The often-despised horror genre has provided fertile turf for many debut features: *The Cabinet of Dr. Cali-*

gari broke fresh ground in 1919 for its makers and German cinema as a whole. In recent memory, prominent filmmakers like George Romero (with the "shock felt 'round the world" *Night of the Living Dead*, 1968), Steven Spielberg (TV features *Night Gallery*, 1969, and *Duel*, 1970), Wes Craven (*Last House on the Left*, 1972), David Cronenberg (*Shivers* aka *They Came From Within*, 1975), and David Lynch (*Eraserhead*, 1977) made their debuts with fresh, bracing explorations of the dark side of our human nature. Stefan and Lance's decision to cut their teeth with such a film is an aesthetically and commercially sound one, and it earns them a place in a proud tradition.

Furthermore, *The Last Broadcast* is based in genuine Americana folklore. The event the film "documents" is fiction (the disappearance and murder of the "Fact or Fiction" film team, and conviction of Jim Suerd for their murder never really happened), but Stefan and Lance didn't create the Jersey Devil legend. They grew up with it. Unlike the completely fictional Blair Witch invented for their lucrative successor, the Jersey Devil at the heart of *The Last Broadcast*'s narrative and mystery is—or was—the real McCoy. As mentioned in their own video and DVD extra, the Jersey Devil legend commonly names a woman named Mother Leeds as the wretched mother of the devil, born to an impoverished and overburdened family living in the desolate Pine Barrens during the early 1700s. Her child was either deformed or cursed, depending on which version of this oral legend you subscribe to, prompting Leeds to incarcerate the "devil" in her attic or cellar until it broke loose to haunt the Barrens for the next three centuries. Other versions chalk its origins up to a gypsy curse, Revolutionary War treason, or a documented birth in 1855 in Estellville in Atlantic County, among others.

Whatever its origins, the Devil is described as a bat-winged, serpentine monster with the head of a horse, hoofed feet, and taloned forelimbs. It plagued the area enough to provoke an exorcism in the 1740s; to yield a rash of sightings and barnyard mayhem in 1840, the 1850s, the 1890s, and in 1903. Most astonishing of all remains the cycle of sightings and encounters with the Jersey Devil in January 1909. Between January 16th and the 23th, literally thousands of people in New Jersey and Pennsylvania (including citizens of southern Philadelphia) reported encounters with the Devil or discovery of its footprints that defy rationalization to this day. Among the witnesses were a Burlington, NJ policeman, a priest in Pemberton, two trolley-car conductors, a Trenton City Councilman, numerous search parties, and firefighters in West Collingswood, NJ, who actually turned a hose on the creature and fought with it!

Thereafter, the Jersey Devil receded into memory. More sightings and encounters followed, though none as dramatic or easily mapped or documented as the 1909 week of horrors. Though bounties (from $1,000 to $100,000) were offered and hucksters ballyhooed sideshow Jersey Devil fakery, the Devil was never killed or captured. Reported sightings and encounters periodically hit the newspapers in the 1920s and 1930s, and sporadically in the 1950s and early 1960s, with the last known report filed in 1966. Whatever it was, if ever it lived, the Jersey Devil retired to local lore and folklore circles until

The Last Broadcast disinterred its almost-forgotten legacy for a new millennium.[22]

Like its often-cited successor *The Blair Witch Project*, Stefan and Lance's *The Last Broadcast* is a fake documentary, a genre also referred to as "mockumentary" or (for its more horrific entries) "shockumentary." Furthermore, *The Last Broadcast* uses the form to dissect, critique and condemn the sort of "reality TV" contemporary networks so recklessly exploit. It also cuts much deeper to probe the psychology and pathology behind the making of such fare. The conceit is central to the film itself; indeed, the opening credits do not acknowledge Stefan and Lance as the directors, but rather announces itself as "A Film by David Leigh," placing the fictional filmmaker at its center from the beginning.

The Last Broadcast has many precursors, including Peter Watkins' *The War Game* (BBC, 1967) and Ruggero Deodato's notorious *Cannibal Holocaust* (1981), which also attacked the ethics of filmmakers responsible for once-popular "shockumentaries" like *Mondo Cane* (1963) and *Faces of Death*. Let us not forget Orson Welles hysteria-inducing Halloween, 1938 broadcast of H.G. Wells' *The War of the Worlds* that terrified listeners into believing the Martians had landed! There have been plenty of playful "mockumentaries," too, prominent among them the popular rock parody *This is Spinal Tap* (1984), and *The Last Broadcast* belongs in their ranks. In their engaging DVD commentary, Stefan and

---

[22] Actually, *The X-Files* episode "The Jersey Devil" was broadcast October 8, 1993. Also note Steven Stockage's *13th Child: Legend of the Jersey Devil* (2003), shot in Pennsylvania and Philadelphia's Holmsburg Prison, and Dante Tomaselli's *Satan's Playground* (2006), shot in NJ's Pine Barrens.

Lance also cite the "autobiographical" independent classic *David Holzman's Diary* (1967), in which writer/director Jim McBride and co-author and lead actor L.M. Kit Carson (playing Holzman) targeted the pretensions of student filmmakers with droll precision and wit. The fictional Holzman, a geeky and endearingly earnest youth aching to pierce to the "truth" of his life via his obsessive filming of every aspect of it, brought a new satiric archetype to the cinema that has been imitated ever since. Thus, McBride (who went on to direct *Breathless*, 1983, *The Big Easy*, 1987, etc.) and Carson (who later wrote *Paris, Texas*, 1983, and appeared in *Running on Empty*, 1988) mirrored the narcissism of all who followed in their footsteps, and anticipated the intrusive effects of bombshells like the PBS documentary series *An American Family* (1973). Clearly, "David Leigh" is Stefan and Lance's "David Holzman," with a much darker twist relevant to its generation.

This is a rare opportunity for any and all interesting Brattleboro area residents, filmmakers, and aspiring filmmakers to meet these pioneer entrepreneurs.[23] They will be at First Run Video to meet and talk to you, sign autographs, sell their own collector's edition of *The Last Broadcast* and *Last Broadcast* one-sheet posters.

---

[23] Stefan and Lance recently wrote and directed solo digital features: Stefan Avalos's *The Ghost of Edendale* (2004) and Lance Weiler's *Head Trauma* (which screened for cast and crew on October 8, 2005, released 2006). Stefan also executed the Terry Gilliam-like animation for the documentary on Gilliam's scuttled *Don Quixote* project, *Lost in La Mancha* (2003).

January 20:

BOWFINGER (1999) lies somewhere between Tim Burton's biopic *Ed Wood* (1994) and the new documentary *American Movie* (1998) in its portrait of a maladroit filmmaker intent on making a movie—*any* movie—at any cost. Star Steve Martin's clever, funny script brings him together with Eddie Murphy (in dual roles) and director Frank Oz (*Little Shop of Horrors, What About Bob?, In and Out*, and Muppets co-creator) to chronicle the giddy misadventures of wanna-be Hollywood player Bowfinger (Martin). All are in top form here, but it seems to me that Hollywood thinks we're all far more interested in movies-about-people-making-movies than we really are (Albert Brooks' *The Muse* will be out on video in February [see review, pg. 203]). That said, Martin, Murphy, and their costars squeeze some real laughs out of this material, and you'll never look at a Federal Express truck the same way again. Amusing, filled with engaging characters and lively set pieces, and a step toward a return-to-form for Eddie Murphy, who could maybe use a real-life dose of Bowfinger magic to resurrect his career slide. This is only a slight extrapolation on the sad career of the late, lamented filmmaker Ed Wood, Jr. and the conditions under which Wood crafted such beloved cinematic atrocities as *Glen or Glenda?* (1953), *Bride of the Monster* (1956) and *Plan 9 from Outer Space* (1958). If you enjoy *Bowfinger*, you might want to refresh your memory with *Ed Wood*, which was the obvious blueprint for Martin's screenplay. *(Rated 'PG-13' for language and behavior that should not be imitated by inexperienced aspiring stunt men.)*

Believe it or not, **FROM DUSK TO DAWN 3: THE HANGMAN'S DAUGHTER** (1999) is far, far superior to the prior direct-to-video sequel to Robert Rodriguez and Quentin Tarantino's 1995 theatrical feature, with founders Rodriguez, Tarantino, and co-executive producer Lawrence Bender steering the runaway train back on track. Mexican outlaw Johnny Madrid (Marco Leonardi of *Like Water for Chocolate*) escapes his execution and runs South-of-the-Border toting the hangman's daughter (Ara Celi) with daddy (Temuera Morrison of *Once Were Warriors*, *Island of Dr. Moreau*) in hot pursuit. But all paths lead to the weird brothel-bar, where the hangman's secrets with the whorehouse madam Quintla (Sonia Braga) and a bevy of blood drinkers are revealed. This turn-of-the-century Western-horror (scripted by Robert Rodriguez and his brother Alvaro) provides considerable background for the barroom-vampire mythos of the original, and has a nifty historical hook with sardonic writer Ambrose Bierce as a lead character (played by series regular Michael Parks in his best role since the *Twin Peaks*); "Occurrence at Owl Creek Bridge" author Bierce actually did disappear in Mexico, never to be seen again. The only other series regular, character actor Danny Trejo, returns as the bartender Razor Charlie, and the KNB makeup effects group are back in the saddle delivering the gross-eries again. Though director P.J. Pescoe peppers the film with homages to Sergio Leone and Sam Peckinpah's classic westerns, *The Hangman's Daughter* has a beginning, middle, and end, which is more than the prior two entries offered. It's less kinetic than the no-holds-barred original, but the most entertaining of the lot, narratively the strongest and most cohesive of the series. Give it a chance, you won't be sorry. *(Rated 'R' for violence, gore, nudity, sexual situations, alcohol, and language.)*

Antonio Banderas is Ibn Fadlan, **THE 13TH WARRIOR** (1998), an Arabian outcast who rides with a select band of Vikings against the terrifying Ven, the Eaters of the Dead. Studio timidity left this on the shelf for almost two years, but it's a triumphantly lean, mean, and muscular medieval heroic fantasy despite evident tinkering (trimming the violence) and a clumsy retitling (the original title, *Eaters of the Dead*, was drawn from writer/co-producer Michael Crichton's best-selling 1976 novel). *The 13th Warrior*'s director John McTiernan ushered in the 1990s action film era with his masterful *Die Hard* (1988). He realizes Crichton's tale and its brutal tribal rituals and battles with ferocious clarity and conviction, and the cast is in top form. McTiernan describes his own films as "boy's adventure movies—big boys, little boys, they're still boy's adventure movies" (he considered his adaptation of *The Hunt for Red October*, 1990, a reworking of Robert Louis Stevenson's *Treasure Island*). This is a prime high-octane boy's adventure, a romantic fusion of chain mail and hammered iron, mist and mud, water and fire, blood and fire, beauty and horror. Critics tend to devalue this genre (apart from the classical Japanese samurai medieval epics), but this is the best of its kind since Paul Verhoeven's underrated *Flesh + Blood* (1985) and Nils Gaup's marvelous *Pathfinder* (1987), which I highly recommend, too. Crichton's central fantasy conceit—the exotic blend of Arabian and Nordic elements—recalls the heyday of Hollywood adventure spectacles like *The Long Ships* (1964), though this is closer kin to Richard Fleischer's magnificent *The Vikings* (1958). Great fun! For a very different recent McTiernan effort, also see (if you haven't already) this month's remake of *The Thomas Crown Affair*, which honors its 1967 source material while providing stylish adult entertainment of a very different breed. *(Rated 'R' for violence, gore, sword play, and nudity.)*

Though we've seen plenty of films about twin brothers (Ivan Reitman's *Twins*, David Cronenberg's *Dead Ringers*, etc.), and plenty of films written and directed by brothers (the Coen Brothers, the Wachowsky Brothers, etc.), **TWIN FALLS, IDAHO** (1999) is the first film about twin brothers made *by* twin brothers. This odd slice of American Gothic finds the conjoined "Siamese" twins (Michael and Mark Polish) falling in love with the same beautiful woman (Michelle Hicks). She's a hooker who finds herself in way over her head when her initial concern for the declining health of her unexpected 'trick' blossoms into something more. Hicks is appropriately aloof throughout, bearing a striking resemblance at times to Bridget Fonda, but the Polish brothers are truly haunting as the twins, obsessed with their search for their mother (Lesley Anne Warren), the forever-lost affection they ache for, and a way out of their dire agoraphobic existence. The influence of David Lynch echoes through more than the title—the deadpan humor, the intensive focus on claustrophobic living spaces, the evocative dream life of the twins—and there are obvious debts to Cronenberg's *Dead Ringers* (1988), but this affecting drama establishes and stays true to its own interior rhythm, creating a memorable emotional landscape. Michael Polish is the credited director, but this was most likely an organic collaboration, resonating with strangely moving insights about loneliness, intimacy, and family. Not for all tastes by a long shot, but adventurous viewers will find much to enjoy here. *(Rated 'R' for sexual situations, nudity, and strong language)*

Recent & Recommended:

A Zed and Two Noughts (1985): Ah, more twins! This is a precursor of sorts to *Twin Falls, Idaho*, a sly, visually intoxicating, and infuriatingly schematic early effort from British director Peter Greenaway (*The Draughtsman's Contract, The Cook, The Thief, His Wife and Her Lover*, etc.). The title refers to the word 'zoo' as well as the sexual dynamic at work, and it all opens in the glare of an outsized neon 'zoo' sign where a Fortean event occurs. The event is summarized by one of the husbands of the dearly-departed: "The wives of two zoologists die in a car driven by a women called Bewick (read: "Buick") who's attacked by a swan on Swan's Way!" The bereaved twins work at the zoo in question. They are named Oswald and Oliver Deuce (played by brothers Brian and Eric Deacon), and the accident sends them into an agonizingly slow spiral into madness, obsessed with decay and creation. Together, they sexually fixate on the surviving driver, a one-legged female sophisticate (Andrea Ferreol) who indulges their every whim. Frances Barber and Joss Ackland are the malicious schemers in their orbit, but (as in most Greenaway confections) any empathy or human emotion is lovingly smothered in the freeze-dried black comedy and precision-tooled intellectual gaming. These conceits toy with duality (black and white and mirror motifs; one brother is blonde, the other brunette), amputation, art, architecture, rot, snails, and the juxtaposition of raging crimson costumes and props and unadorned human flesh. Among the cinematic artifacts woven into the dense tapestry are clips from David Attenborough's nature documentaries and a dazzling, disgusting array of time-lapse photography sequences detailing the rot of vegetables and animal carcasses, which provide the *de rigueur* horrific element Greenaway imposes on all his compositions (the scatology and cannibalism of *The Cook, The Thief, His Wife and Her Lover*; Ewan McGregor's body reduced to a human book jacket for *The Pillow Book*). As always, Greenaway's oddity is sumptuously mounted, performed, photographed, costumed, composed, and scored (by steady collaborator Michael Nyman, and persistent use of a vintage recording of "Teddy Bears' Picnic"). David Cronenberg fans should give it a look, as Cronenberg screened this curio for the cast and crew of his masterpiece *Dead Ringers*, and the influence is clear—I don't recommend them as a double-feature, though, unless you absolutely crave suicidal depressions. *A Zed and Two Noughts* is an acquired taste, absurdist and austere, precious and perverse, an exquisite eccentricity that will fascinate many, but frustrate and bore far more viewers than it will win. As a Greenaway fan, I'm thankful for this reissue; the film was previously released uncut to home video by Michael Nesmith's Pacific Arts Video, but the Fox Lorber/Winstar re-release has been handsomely remastered and letterboxed to preserve the visual integrity of Greenaway's widescreen compositions. *(Unrated, but this is definitely adult fare.)*

January 27:

(A Note from the Editor: This week's "Video Views" column ran short, so we decided to publish this letter from Steve that was attached to the manuscript. It's marked "Personal," but we figured, what the heck. Steve needs the word count to pad his check.)

Dear April,

Because we're friends and co-workers at First Run Video, I had to write and let you know why I wouldn't be able to review **RUNAWAY BRIDE** in this week's "Video Views" column. Don't be offended, please. Believe me, you would have been more offended if I had reviewed it. Knowing that you like the film and are going to be getting married soon and everything, I was worried you'd think I was down on marriage or something. I mean, what do I know, anyway? Most people agree with you on this one, so why set myself up for the grief? *Runaway Bride* was one of the top moneymakers last year, it's a feel-good Valentine's Day season release, it's all gushy and everything, and every independent video store in America will be carrying a million copies of this title to satisfy the demand. We'll sure have a ton of them.

Let me tell you, I tried, I really tried to like it, April. I sort of liked Julia Roberts' last outing with Hugh Grant, the one where she was the actress and he owned a bookstore, mainly because Hugh Grant's roommate was pretty funny. I know everyone else on planet Earth thought *Pretty Woman* was great, and couldn't wait to see Julia get back together with Richard Gere in a movie and all. This one's even directed by Garry Marshall, the same guy who made *Pretty Woman*. Well, I loathed *Pretty Woman*. At least this one didn't romanticize prostitution, and Roberts wasn't as psycho as she was in *My Best Friend's Wedding*, which was real horror movie material, if you know what I mean. Friends like that you don't need at your wedding. Of course, friends like Joan Cusack (who plays Julia's best friend in *Runaway Bride*) you don't need either. She's way scarier here than she was in *Arlington Road* as a terrorist killer. Oops—Sorry.

See what I mean? I can't help myself. I really can't review this one. It's just not my cup of tea. In fact, it's the same movie as *Pretty Woman* all over again, which I'm sure was the whole idea. Here's Gere—again—as a debonair, arrogant self-centered professional male who initially exploits Roberts' attractive, vulnerable self-centered woman, until she lashes out, they parry, have a change of heart after too much screen time and top-forty hits on the soundtrack, and fall for each other. Again. Not only did I not melt like I was supposed to, I'm afraid my skin almost sloughed off. I had to watch an Italian zombie movie after to regain my passion for life, love, and movies, though I suppose watching *An Ideal Husband* instead would have been a much healthier choice. After all, that at least involves weddings, too, and it was much funnier and nastier and so Victorian-era smug about the whole marriage thing. That Oscar Wilde. He was a much better writer than the team behind *Runaway Bride*.

So what's not to like, you ask. Look, let's not go there, okay? If I don't write this one up, can I still go to your wedding? I'll get you guys a great gift.

If you don't run away.

See you at work,

Steve

(*We now return to the regularly scheduled column.*)[24]

---

[24] Note that this review was botched in its original publication in *The Brattleboro Reformer*: the nervous editor removed the references to April Stage, making nonsense of the fake "letter-to-April" format! It appears here as originally written.

MY SON THE FANATIC (1998) Harks from the UK (a co-production with BBC Films) and tells the tale of a Pakistan immigrant (pock-faced Om Puri in grand form) who's been driving cab in London for 25 years. His unceasing devotion to his wife (Gopi Desai) and son (Akbar Kurtha) is shaken by the fallout from a dubious relationship with his latest fare from the airport, a foreign businessman named Shitz (Stellan Skarsgard from *Breaking the Waves*). The cabbie ends up essentially pimping for Shitz, and in the process he falls in love himself with a prostitute (Rachel Griffiths). The conflict between his growing love for the woman, qualms with Shitz's affairs, distance from his wife, and friction with his son over the young man's rejection of their adopted country and an arranged marriage lends this engaging drama its edge. Simmering emotions come to a boil when his son's increasing fanatical religious devotion detours into an aggressive hatred and public campaign against the local house of ill repute, which inevitably forces father, son, and mother to confront their fraying family ties. Perceptively scripted by Hanif Kureishi from his own short story and directed by Udayan Prasad with heart and a strong sense of place—the home life, street life, and community—*My Son the Fanatic* is a fine film. It's compelling meditation on the human toll of placing the individual's needs before those of the family, hazarding the risks, rewards, pain, and even the necessity of doing so. *(Rated 'R' for language, adult and sexual situations, and nudity.)*[25]

---

[25] The *Video Views* reviews (or abridgements) of *My Son the Fanatic, The Brandon Teena Story, Breakfast of Champions, The Dead Hate the Living* and *In Too Deep* were also published in *VMag* #28, March 2000, pp. 40-41.

Fathers, mothers, sons, and the tolls and temptations of adultery also color **MY LIFE SO FAR** (1999), a beguiling recreation of a ten-year boy's life on his family's Scottish estate in the mid-war limbo of the 1920s. The narrator and nominal hero Fraser (Robert Norman) is struggling through his adolescent sexual awakening, furtively indulging in his grandfather's forbidden library in the attic and using all the big words he's discovered (like "prostitution") as dinner table *bon mots* while trying to grasp the momentous life changes and perplexing, volatile behavior of the adults around him. Most perplexing is the jealousy fired between Fraser and his father (Colin Firth), his father and mother (Mary Elizabeth Mastrantonio, in stellar form), and Da and Uncle Morris (Malcolm McDowell in the best role he's had since *A Clockwork Orange*) when the latter brings his very young French fiance (Irene Jacob) to their beloved Kiloran castle to visit. This is a marvelous gem, modest in content and intent, brimming with likable characters, the rugged beauty of its Scottish setting, and the bygone era it so fondly evokes. Hugh Hudson (*Chariots of Fire, Greystoke*) directed, working from Simon Donald's spry screen adaptation of Sir Denis Forman's memoirs, and delivers his best work. *(Rated 'PG-13' for adult situations, language—mostly from Fraser testing his growing vocabulary—and the nude portraits Fraser lingers over in grandfather's book collection.)*

February 3:

A STIR OF ECHOES (1999) is a sharp reworking of a minor but very effective novel by Richard Matheson (author of *The Shrinking Man, I Am Legend, Duel, What Dreams May Come*, and many of the best *Twilight Zone* episodes), consolidating the novel's characters and events without betraying Matheson's characteristically subversive agenda and tightly-woven plot. A working class stiff (Kevin Bacon), complacent but profoundly unhappy with his Chicago-suburban family life, is hypnotized as a party entertainment, after which his life is shattered by sudden premonitions and psychic flashes, with the most nightmarish visions increasingly centered on an apparition haunting his own home. Bacon and the supporting cast are excellent throughout, and the terror mounts with impressive, suffocating power. Writer/director David Koepp helms Bacon's descent into waking hell and escalating alienation from friends, family, and community with urgent conviction, suffering only one real misstep (the enigmatic and unnecessary diversion of a black cop who "shines," to use Stephen King's expression). An element imposed on Matheson's narrative frame (the psychic ability of Bacon's son) works well on the film's own terms, but unfortunately suggests a knock-off of *The Sixth Sense*, which this most definitely is not: they were produced simultaneously, and Matheson's novel is over three decades old. Tripping over themselves in the shadows of *The Blair Witch Project* and *The Sixth Sense*, critics belittled this fine effort, though the excellent trailers sparked audience interest. This "sleeper" (as in underrated gem, not cinematic Sominex) didn't get the theatrical play it deserved: it's a prime home video rediscovery. Like Koepp's directorial debut *The Trigger Effect* (1996, which I also liked a great deal), this is a modest thriller, intimate in scale and effect, further proof of Koepp's devotion to the aesthetic pioneered by *Twilight Zone auteur* and TV playwright Rod Serling. He's done Serling and Matheson proud, sharpening his own scalpel to continue their dissection of the underbelly of the deceptive, illusory comforts of the middle-American mind-set and landscape. Recommended, particularly for late-night viewing! *(Rated 'R' for adult and sexual situations, strong language, nudity, violence, and the harrowing 'visions,' which are often gruesome.)*

Walt Disney Studios' **TARZAN** (1999) owes only its set-up—the adoption and raising of an orphan human child by apes—to the venerable Edgar Rice Burroughs classic pulp fantasy. The rest, Phil Collins music and all, is pure Disney, which is good and bad, depending on your disposition to the Disney empire. With three screenplay writers credited, but 23 additional story credits in the final crawl, *Tarzan* is real "storytelling-by-committee" fluff. Forget about Burroughs' evocative ape-language: this *Tarzan* plunders its gorilla lore from *Gorillas in the Mist*, *Mighty Joe Young*, and *Instinct* as well as the marvelous opening half-hour of Hugh Hudson's *Greystoke*, which, you may recall, was the revisionist *Tarzan* for the 1980s (with Caspar Van Dien's turn in *Tarzan and the Lost City* standing as the "Saturday matinee *Tarzan*" of the 1990s). Disney Studios' version of Tarzan (voiced by Tony Goldwyn) boasts dreadlocks and slick skate-boarder moves through the trees, the icing on a nifty animated characterization sparked with the apeman's expressive body language, odd simian posture, and a ferocity and fluidity of movement that embodies this feature's greatest strengths. The celebrated merger of computer-generated animation and traditional line-drawn cartooning works well throughout, though it's hardly seamless: the visually-intoxicating delineation of the sea, waves, and water becomes an intrusively distinctive visual element, belonging to a reality apart from the hand-drawn animation. The rest of this lightweight confection works surprisingly well, thanks primarily to the top-drawer vocal performances from Minnie Driver (Jane), Brian Blessed (Clayton, whose namesake in the novel was hardly the villain he's made out to be here), Glenn Close (the ape-mother Kala), Nigel Hawthorne (Porter), Lance Hendrickson (lending authority to the simian patriarch Kerchak), and Rosie O'Donnell (as the anachronistic Bronx-accented ape Terk). Do your kids a favor, though: read them the real *Tarzan of the Apes*, or leave a copy of the Burroughs original laying around. *(Rated 'G' though some might object to the usual Disney stereotypes and occasional jungle mayhem, which is dramatically staged but never gruesome.)*

Hate crimes—vigilante executions targeting race, religion, and gender—are among the most terrible legacies of contemporary America, and Susan Muska and Gret Olafsdottir's **THE BRANDON TEENA STORY** (1998) chronicles one of the most unusual and heartbreaking of these recent atrocities. Early in this compelling documentary, one of the many teenage girls who dated Brandon describes him as "a woman's man, every woman's dream." The problem for many was the fact that Brandon was actually Teena Brandon, a transgender whose self-transformation into Brandon Teena in the limbo of small-town Nebraska rubbed two redneck youths the wrong way, ending in a horrific Christmas Eve rape and New Year's Eve triple homicide (only 19 days after Brandon/Teena's 21st birthday) in 1993. This deceptively straightforward chronicle negotiates a treacherous maze of emotions, gender issues, police incompetence, and irrevocable loss. The feature "docudramatization" of this story, *Boys Don't Cry*, earned critical acclaim and is currently playing in urban theaters; by all means, see this first, now available at your local independent video store. Recommended. *(No MPAA rating, but recommended for mature viewers due to adult situations, explicit language, and the violent nature of the crimes discussed.)*

Fans of jungle-music's Goldie may want to catch **B.U.S.T.E.D.** (1998) despite the poor word-of-mouth. After crafting hypnotic CDs like *Saturnzreturn* (1998), Goldie extended his range into acting with this low-rent British gangster flick before cranking up the villainy for the James Bond adventure *The World is Not Enough* (1999). Originally exhibited in the UK as *Everyone Loves Sunshine*, this mannered, meandering snapshot of the nastiness lurking beneath the club scene was written and directed by Andrew Goth, whose narcissistic star turn as Goldie's skinhead cousin grows tiresome fast. "You ain't no bad man," a character tells Goth, "You want to create, you want to make music," and sure enough, the raves and the jungle music play their part. But Goldie *loves* playing the sociopathic bad man, flashing his gold teeth like a bandito and torturing Goth's girlfriend (Rachel Shelley). David Bowie's on hand as the veteran crime lord, advising temperance as Goldie teeters off the deep end. Temperance? In a contemporary British gangster movie? Tut, tut, white duke; just keep your own hands clean. *(Rated 'R' for violence, gunplay, strong language, adult and sexual situations, and some particularly misogynist mayhem.)*

February 10:

THE ASTRONAUT'S WIFE (1999) stars Johnny Depp as a NASA astronaut who goes up a sweetheart and comes down with a nasty reproductive agenda.

Charlize Theron is his loving, long-suffering wife who's gradually awakening to the fact that her hubby is acting just a wee bit off of late. The couple is incredibly easy on the eyes (as always) and work with all they're given, which unfortunately is just two notches above *Species* in the alien "take my seed" sweepstakes. Theron was riveting in *The Devil's Advocate* (1997) and lent considerable heart to the remake of *Mighty Joe Young* (1998). Johnny Depp is, well, Johnny Depp; the camera loves the man, even when he's sleepwalking, space-walking, or giving Charlize that furtive "come hither, Earth woman" look. The skeletal plot pirates Nigel Kneale's *The Quatermass Experiment* (1955, US title: *The Creeping Unknown*), which covered similar ground with a great deal more skill and intelligence for less than the catering fees on this picture. The other obvious source here is Ira Levin's chilling novel *Rosemary's Baby* (1967), which Roman Polanski brought to the screen with breathtaking clarity back in 1968. Heck, even a low-budget British shocker entitled *Xtro* (1982) handled the same premise with more ingenuity. The strong residue of those films, coupled with the fine cast, superficially-competent direction from music-video director Rand Ravich, and one nasty wish-fulfillment sex scene between the two leads in a secluded corner of a crowded, posh party almost yields a movie—almost. I hate to give anything else away, but look for the twins who played the orphan in Adam Sandler's *Big Daddy*. It's the film's best moment, *if* you recognize the tykes, which I sincerely doubt the filmmakers intended. *(Rated 'R' for language, nudity, sexual situations, violence, and some gore.)*

Martin Lawrence gets another shot at the big-time in **BLUE STREAK** (1999), a caper action-comedy rigged to put him through his paces without once breaking a sweat. Lawrence stars as jewel thief Miles Logan whose "big score" gets deep-sixed by the treachery of a greedy partner (Peter Greene). Before the police handcuff Miles, he manages to hide the diamond rock inside an air conditioning duct in a skyscraper that's under construction. No problem: he serves his two-year sentence, marches on down to the building, and—*whoa!* It's the Los Angeles Police Department's new digs! In order to gain access to his hiding place, Miles has no choice but to impersonate a detective—no, wait, make that an internal affairs investigator—no, uh—well, you get the idea. With his evil ex-partner sniffing around, and an incompetent ex-partner in custody for armed robbery threatening to spill the beans at any minute, Lawrence should be squirming like a worm on a hot brick. But the man is cool as a cucumber. Luke Wilson plays his oblique rookie partner as *un*cool, providing some amusement, which is all this movie's concerned with anyway.

Lawrence has been busy making movies since the sleeper hit *House Party* a decade ago. For my money, his team-up with Tim Robbins in *Nothing to Lose* (1996) is still his best piece of work, primarily because the script and Robbins gave the man something worth bouncing off of. This'll do for an evening's entertainment, but I hope Lawrence gets a shot at something with a little bit of meat on its bones next time around. *(Rated 'R' for language, gunplay, and—jeez, you know, I'm not at all sure why this got an 'R'!)* And speaking of meat on bones...

Local boy makes good! A good zombie movie, that is. In **THE DEAD HATE THE LIVING** (1999), young filmmakers inadvertently activate a device that resurrects the dead and opens a portal to a deadly netherworld, releasing a murderous pack of undead creatures intent on bringing the living into the fold. This nightmare material was a dream-come-true for Vermont filmmaker David Parker, who shot this under a tight schedule and lean budget in Hollywood. The tale is a familiar one for horror fans, derivative of curios like *Children Shouldn't Play With Dead Things* (1972), *The House of Seven Corpses* (1973), and the late Lucio Fulci's Italian zombie classics *Zombie* (1980) and *The Beyond* (1982), revamped for a new audience who cut their teeth on horrors that would have been unthinkable when I was a kid. As zombie movies go, it's a solid first effort, aimed at fans of the *Resident Evil* video games, which is what makes *The Dead Hate the Living* significant.

Resident Evil (1996) made a plethora of walking dead and mutants the focus of the action, and quickly became the blockbuster success that defined the graphic "shoot 'em up" adventure-horror game format. Horror-adventure games continue to be very popular, with many of them featuring the now-cliche hordes of the walking dead, mutant monsters, and reanimated body parts. The impact of these games on other media is already evident. Vermonter Parker's debut direct-to-video feature affectionately acknowledges its debt to George (*Night of the Living Dead*) Romero and Lucio Fulci's classics (its finale expands upon the eerie climax of *The Beyond*), but Parker and makeup designer Thomas Surprenant patterned the look of its zombies after those in *Resident Evil*. "Like the creatures in that game," Parker says, "our zombies look more like strange experiments gone awry than just hollow-eyed corpses coming back from the dead."[26]

This certainly isn't everyone's cup of grue-brew, but I still haven't recovered from *Runaway Bride*. I *needed* a good zombie movie this week. Every filmmaker has to start somewhere—and I for one can't wait to see what Dave has up his sleeve for his next trick. *(Rated 'R' for language, gore, sexual situations, nudity, and zombie-mayhem.)*

Oh, while I'm wallowing in this vile stuff, I might as well mention Joe Castro's monster mockumentary **LEGEND OF THE CHUPACABRA** (1997). Though it's spent a couple of years on the shelf, this is the latest offering from Troma, the cheapjack NYC-based independent renowned for *The Toxic Avenger* (though much of their video slate is comprised of pickups—that is, films by other independent filmmakers—like this one). This release is timed and ballyhooed to capitalize on the crosscurrents of *The X-Files, The Blair Witch Project*, and ongoing tabloid fascination with the Chupacabra legend, but like *The Last Broadcast*, Castro's opus in fact predated *The Blair Witch Project*. Unlike either of those films, Castro is never content to leave his horrors unseen when he can splash gore on the camera lens or rub our noses in slippery ribbons of innards. Female cryptozoologist and film journalist Maria Esperanza (Katsy Joiner) and her crew, well-armed with cameras and guns, are determined to unravel the mystery of the latest Latino bogeyman, the "goat sucker" of contemporary urban and rural legend. This Troma pick-up amusingly synthesizes all manner of recent pop-horror arti-

---

[26] Note Dave Parker's co-writer credit on the later zombie video-game-to-movie opus *House of the Dead* (2003).

facts, including *The X-Files, Alien Autopsy* footage, and more. Castro also designed and executed the toothy titular monster, which gets plenty of onscreen exposure before the final credits roll. Not to be confused with *Guns of the Chupacabra* starring Kevin Eastman (co-creator of the *Teenage Mutant Ninja Turtles*), which has yet to surface on video in the US. Pass the goat chips, please! *(Rated 'R' for language, gore and violence.)*

MURDER IN NEW HAMPSHIRE (1991) offers another kind of "vile stuff"—true-crime sex and death involving teenagers. This has just been re-released as if it's a brand-new title, but don't be fooled: this made-for-cable softcore account of the notorious Pamela Smart murder-most-foul affair has been on video for almost ten years. They've just gussied it all up in a hot new box to trick you, just like Pamela tricked her students. Helen Hunt delivers a rich performance as the seductress who wrapped her legs around a virginal high school student (Chad Allen) and banged him into a murder plot to take out her husband, but the unimaginative approach to such a volatile, sordid crime leaves Hunt out on a limb by herself. Though this may have some regional interest for readers, but please remember that Gus Van Sant and Buck Henry's inventive black comedy take on the story *To Die For* (1995) offers far, far more as a movie, and most likely will remain the last cinematic word on this tragic crime. *(Unrated, but sexual situations and adult content is recommended for mature viewers.)*

February 17:

BROKEDOWN PALACE (1999) is a revamp of the French film *Force Majeure* (1989), which Hollywood already remade as *Return to Paradise* (1998), in which two friends returned to face a harsh Malaysian penal system for drug charges that had imprisoned a third friend. *Midnight Express* (1978) related a similar true story of the Turkish prison ordeal suffered by Billy Hayes (Brad Davis) after a drug bust. *Brokedown Palace* retreads this tortured turf: Darlene (Kate Beckinsale) and Alice (Claire Danes) are imprisoned in Thailand after being set up for a bust by a seductive stranger (Daniel Lapaine). Benevolent attorney Hank Greene (Bill Pullman) mounts their case against overwhelming odds, including a corrupt DEA agent (Lou Diamond Phillips) and a system that could care less what happens to the girls. The story is competently told, but the film timidly skirts any real confrontation with the very real human evil, violence, corruption, and repression at work here. Once again the current pop cinema's reliance on musical scores comprised of rock tunes dissipates rather than enhances the emotional impact, and the attempt to soften the blow of the climax rings hollow. *(Rated 'R' for language, violence, and some violence.)*

Human evil is in sharp focus with **IN TOO DEEP** (1999), based on a true story. Charting the harrowing tightwire walk undercover cop Jeff Cole (Omar Epps) treads between duty and the depths, this is a taut, potent film with real teeth. Under the cool, experienced watch of his supervisor (Stanley Tucci), Cole become "J. Reid," street-wise insider, confidante, and eventual right-hand man to his target Dwayne Gittens aka "God" (LL Cool J), who we meet casually cutting the tongue out of a squealer. This is strong drama, not an exploitative bloodbath: the most horrific violence—including the atrocity I just mentioned—is kept tastefully offscreen, but the worst of it is so vividly set up and conveyed that it is at times nigh on unbearable (if you're squeamish, when "God" asks for the pool cue, please, look away). Epps and Cool J deliver in their roles, aided by support from Pam Grier (Jackie Brown, Coffy) and tight direction by Michael Rymer. *(Rated 'R' for violence, nudity, adult and sexual situations, and drug abuse.)*

Albert Brooks' dry, deadpan brand of satire is an acquired taste, and **THE MUSE** (1999) is an amusing idea rendered extra-dry; a rarefied flavor indeed, even among Brooks fans. Sharon Stone is the possibly mystical Muse (as in the daughters of Zeus in Greek mythology) living incognito under the name of Sarah, a living, breathing, walking, and all-consuming wellspring of inspiration and success for a select Hollywood few. Screenwriter Steven Phillips (Brooks) finds his career on the skids, so one of his buddies (Jeff Bridges) puts in a good word for him with Sarah, raising the suspicions of Steven's wife Laura (Andie MacDowell) until she ends up on the receiving end of Sarah's magic.

There's meat for satire here—the friction between Steve and Laura as her new career launch soars and his sours—and a few amusing cameos (directors Rob Reiner, James Cameron, and Martin Scorsese, among others), but writer-director-star Brooks seems to be shaving with a dull razor this time out; only Steven Wright scores as "Stan Spielberg." Hollywood seems to think there's a vast audience out there for this kind of industry navel-gazing, but only those concerned with its fringe crazies—*Ed Wood, Bowfinger*—have proven worthwhile. *(Rated 'PG-13' for language, adult situations.)*

If you do enjoy this genre, though, check out this week's **ENTROPY** (1999), starring Stephen Dorff as a young hotshot music video director suffering through his first feature. The tough-talking, chain-smoking kitten (as in "meow") provides a startling highlight; U2 fans should give *Entropy* a look and listen, too, as the band and their music play key roles here. *(Rated 'R' for language, adult and sexual situations.)*

The Muse implies that director Rob Reiner has a real "in" with his Muse; Reiner indeed scored through the 1980s (from his debut feature *This is Spinal Tap* to 1990's *Misery*), but he's in the same position as Brooks this week with **THE STORY OF US** (1999), a coy comedy-of-ill-manners about marriage, separation, and divorce. The film dances around the strained marriage of Ben (Bruce Willis) and Katie (Michelle Pfeiffer); she can't share his "special moments" (like the demolition of their first apartment), and they're both enduring quips from their friends like "marriage is the Jack Kavorkian of romance." Katie describes their situation early on as one in which "fighting becomes the condition rather than the exception, [turning] into the language of the relationship," in which "your only option is a silent retreat to neutral corners." We're given privileged looks at this painful state of affairs, including their lies to their preteen son (Jake Sandvig) and daughter (Colleen Rennison) as they maintain a facade that 'all is well,' carefully timing their separation for the kids' summer camp trips (a seat-squirming subplot in which their daughter mounts a pathetic attempt at parental reconciliation).

Tread carefully, folks: depending on your own personal situation, you'll either like or loathe Reiner's superficial portrait of such volatile emotional issues. A true populist, Reiner avoids the rigorous dissection of Ingmar Bergman's *Scenes from a Marriage* (1973) and Alan Parker's *Shoot the Moon* (1982), or the division-of-property issues that fueled Danny DeVito's savage black comedy *The War of the Roses* (1989). The comparison may seem unfair, but the Pandora's Box of separation and divorce isn't one to be opened lightly, and *The Story of Us* very much wants to maintain its light touch. Eric Clapton and Marc Shaiman's score is appropriate to that effort, and Willis and Pfeiffer (in another onscreen maternal trial like those of *One Fine Day* and *The Deep End of the Ocean*) give it a game try. You might want to, too, but remember what I've said here. *(Rated 'R' for language, adult and sexual situations.)*

The devastation of disintegrating marriages and broken homes is the core of actor Frank Whaley's impressive directorial debut **JOE THE KING** (1999), chronicling the steady slide toward juvenile hall endured by unwashed 14-year-old Joe (Noah Fleiss), who ineffectually assumes the titular moniker in one of his feeble attempts to keep his footing and a shred of dignity in a decidedly unfriendly world. At the bottom of the pecking order in every corner of his existence—at home, at school, at his job as a dish-washer, and definitely in life—Joe survives by staying below the radar as best he can. He indulges in petty crime and theft to stay afloat as he suffers the verbal and physical assaults dished out by his surly alcoholic father (Val Kilmer in rare form) and well-meaning attempts by co-worker John Leguizamo and guidance counselor Ethan Hawke to pay some attention to the lad. Joe's unyielding stoicism, his relationship with his older brother Mike (Max Ligoshi), and attempt to find some kind of redemption and a niche for himself remains the absolute focus of Whaley's screenplay and direction. Highly recommended! *(Rated 'R' for language, domestic violence, and adult situations.)*

February 24:

The 1990s have been dominated by 1940s programmers disguised as big-budget "event" movies, but those low-budget B-movies of yore often boasted tighter scripts, direction, and performances than today's "package" movies. **DOUBLE JEOPARDY** (1999) is such a package—solid cast (Tommy Lee Jones, Ashley Judd), director (Bruce Beresford of *Breaker Morant, Driving Miss Daisy, Black Robe*, etc.), and a sure-fire plot. Libby Parsons (Judd) is arrested, tried, convicted, and imprisoned for the murder of her husband (Bruce Greenwood). While serving her time, she discovers the bastard set her up and he's still alive, free of debt and raising their son under an alias, while she rots in prison. She also learns about "double jeopardy": a person cannot be tried for the same crime twice. Having served her time, Libby goes a-hunting, hindered by tough parole-officer Travis Lehman (Tommy Lee Jones).

With such attractive talent in place, *Double Jeopardy* should have been a no-brainer. Well, it is, but not the way it should have been. The film trades on the "all men are heels" adrenaline rush *Thelma and Louise* and *Sleeping with the Enemy* deftly exploited while capitalizing on Judd and Jones' skills, but they're caught in a vehicle unworthy of their talents. The galvanizing, Academy Award-winning conviction Jones brought to his role in fine revamp of *The Fugitive* (1993) dwindled in the lackluster sequel *U.S. Marshals* (1998) and is completely squandered here. Ashley Judd is an excellent actress who deserves far, far better than contrived potboilers like *Kiss the Girls* and this slippery mishmash. Still, there's some pleasure in these pros at work: Greenwood plays a great slimeball, Jones redeems his gender, and Judd righteously spits bile with style. *(Rated 'R' for violence, language, adult and sexual situations.)*

Far, far more entertaining echoes of the gritty B-movies of the '40s can be savored in this week's **BEST LAID PLANS** (1999) and **LETTERS FROM A KILLER** (1998). These modest, unpretentious direct-to-video pleasures out-perform *Double Jeopardy* with every twist, turn, and double-cross of their narratives. *Letter from a Killer* is the more straightforward of the two: death-row inmate and best-selling author Race Darnell (Patrick Swayze) bides his time courting four women via the post office (male-by-mail jail bait). But when jealous guards switch two of his juicy audiotape love-letters, deliberately sending them to the wrong women, and Darnell becomes a free man, someone frames him for a quick return-trip to death row. "Hell hath no fury like a woman scorned," and director David Carson milks the premise for all it's worth. Swayze delivers the goods as he did in sleepers like *Roadhouse* (1989) and *Black Dog* (1998); Gia Carides, Roger E. Mosley, and Bruce McGill provide rock-steady support.

Best Laid Plans is even better, fueled by the crafty script (by Ted Griffin) and direction (from Mike Barker) coiled like a rattlesnake around its three leads. The less you know, the better. At first, it appears that down-and-out Nick (Alessandro Nivola) has been drawn into a shaky scheme to extract an old college roommate (Josh Brolin) from a date-rape rap threatened by an under-age girl (Reese Witherspoon); but she ain't jailbait, Nick's no pal, and nothing, but nothing, is what it seems. *Best Laid Plans* evokes the reptilian allure of film *noir* gems like Edgar Ulmer's *Detour* (1946) and Irving Pichel's *Quicksand* (1950), milking genuine surprises and suspense out of the plight of its increasingly desperate bottom-feeders. This isn't another imitation *noir*, though: *Best Laid Plans* is absolutely of its time, and the sting in its tail is well worth the rental. Highly recommended! *(Both films are rated 'R' for sex, violence, language, and adult situations.)*

Not all B-movie genetic strains are worth reviving. If you thought *Lake Placid* and *Deep Blue Sea* were silly—that they were, but they were also very entertaining monster movies—watch out for **BATS** (1999), which makes *Lake Placid* seem like sweet Shakespeare. *Bats* had a very cool preview, didn't it? Leave it at that. At first, the giddy speed with which *Bats* skips like a stone over character development, linear plot elements, and the genre's cursory cliches is intoxicating. But just when it seems this thin gruel about a Southwestern border town being pillaged by high-octane vampire bats might somehow maintain its slippery footing, ass-over-tea-kettle it goes. By the time the two leads (Lou Diamond Phillips slumming after some great character roles and *Starship Troopers*' Dina Meyer sorely in need of Caspar Van Dien) are up to their nipples in a lake of bat guano, you'll realize you've been wading in the same for over an hour, and it's getting *mighty* deep.

When I was a kid, the monster movie cliche we laughed at had slow, shuffling monsters catching their victims. I mean, the Lon Chaney Jr. Mummy throttled almost all his targets despite a bum leg, one eye, and an arm in a bandage-sling; we knew you could have been in full traction, fall-down drunk, or an amputee and you could still outrun *that* Mummy. The equivalent 1990s monster movie cliche insistently shows us the opposite, as heroes and heroines impossibly outrun the greased-lightning menace of choice (raptors in *The Lost World*, the flaming monster in *The Relic*, the faster-than-aspeeding-bullet *Anaconda*, etc.). These days, CGI effects can dazzle us with anything the filmmakers' slushy little gray matter can conceive, but *Bats* blows it repeatedly by "showing" us it is sho' nuff possible to outrun a horde of giant bats that are flying 542-miles-per-hour, even while wearing bulky bat-dung-encrusted astronaut gear and climbing up a series of ladders in dark, narrow mine shafts. I do believe the leathery-winged wonders would have been nesting in Lou and Dina's rib cages long before the dagnabbit duo reached daylight. Director Louis Morneau previously directed *Carnosaur 2* for Roger Corman, a tacky little trifle that did more with less than this loser. There have been some other historic bat clunkers (*The Bat People* aka *It Lives By Night*, 1973; *Chosen Survivors*, 1974; *Nightwing*, 1979), and the *World Weekly News* had its risible cover star, the Bat-boy (reportedly heralding from exotic-sounding Rutland, VT!), but *Bats* is even lamer. Can it really be that the silly old Bela Lugosi chestnut *The Devil Bat* (1941) still holds its place as the best (choke!) killer bat movie ever made? Yes, I'm afraid so. *(Rated 'R' for typical, tame Hollywood gore effects and language.)*

Pierce Brosnan is James Bon—no, sorry, he's **GREY OWL** (1999), a white trapper named Archie (really) who goes all Native North American and looks uncomfortably like Pierce Brosnan in a long-haired wig and, well, you know, all Indian-like. Still, he also ends up spearheading the 20th Century ecology movement decades before Rachel Carlson wrote *The Silent Spring*. Director and co-producer Richard Attenborough mounts another lavish production—one of the most expensive direct-to-video titles to date, right up there with Van Damme's *Legionnaire* and Whoopi's *Theodore Rex*, which isn't the kind of company ol' Richard tends to keep. As ever, Attenborough is a completely pedestrian filmmaker, but he's a fine storyteller. His heart is in the right place, the film is tastefully done, and the compelling true tale is well worth the telling. The mewling baby beavers may get on your nerves (they sure got on mine), but the sequence in which Archie visits his childhood home provides the quietly moving core which you will recall long after the beaver-whining fades from memory. It's mighty hard to get past Brosnan so badly miscast in the central role, and Attenborough never did demonstrate the restraint or grace as a director this kind of material deserves (see Bruce Beresford's marvelous *Black Robe*, 1991). It's a kinder, gentler *A Man Called Horse*, and if you were able to swallow Richard Harris in that one, maybe you'll be able to ride with Brosnan in this one. I'll have vanilla. The DVD features some engaging extras, including rare footage of the real Archie Grey Owl; still, it's acceptable family fare. *(Rated 'PG-13' for restrained, non-gratuitous violence—involving self-defense and Archie's animal trapping—brief harsh language, sexual situations, and pierced nipples—no, I meant Pierce's nipples.)*

February 24:

From **POKEMON** *to* **MONONOKE***:*
The **Anime** *Alternative*

There were only a handful of parents and children in the theater. As the lights came up after 195 minutes of breathtaking adventure, we all looked at each other and smiled. Accustomed to the narcotic effect of Disney extravaganzas or the Spielberg-Lucas roller-coaster thrill-machines, we had all been stirred and awakened by a rare American theatrical showing of Hayao Miyazaki's animated feature *Laputa* (1986, aka *Castle in the Sky*). Miyazaki's tale of a little girl named Sheeta, her orphan friend Pazu, crafty Ma Dola and her sky pirates, villainous government agents, and their shared destiny in the ruins of the miraculous aerial city Laputa (a knowing reference to the realm in Swift's *Gulliver's Travels*) unfolded like a series of flowers within flowers, each more eye-popping than the last.

This was truly epic filmmaking, realized with bravado, imagination, and heart. Thankfully, my daughter Maia was with me (alas, my son Daniel was too young at the time). We were both hooked from that day on, and soon introduced Daniel to the wonders of *anime*, the preferred term for Japanese animation. As my children matured, we built our own video library of Miyazaki's masterpieces: *Warriors of the Wind* (the dubbed and cut US version of *Nausicaa*, 1984), *My Neighbor Totoro* (1988), *Kiki's Delivery Service* (1989), and others. We had the distinct pleasure of seeing Miyazaki's latest feature, *Princess Mononoke* (1997; US release 1999) on the big screen in Boston.

To call Miyazaki's features the greatest animated features ever made is an understatement: they are among the finest films ever made, period. And yet, Miyazaki and his masterworks remain largely unknown in the US. Hopefully, all that will change very soon, thanks to the recent infestation of cute little monsters like Jigglypuff, Eevee, Golem, Blastoise, Mew, Gengar, and the lovable Pikachu.

Most American parents are now all-too-familiar with the anime import *Pokemon*, which is currently sweeping our pop culture with the same tsunami force with which it hit Japan in 1996-97. Created by Satoshi

Tajiri for Nintendo's Game Boy system, *Pokemon* quickly spawned a successful anime TV series. When the strobing color effects that used to spice *Pokemon* induced seizures in 700 children all across Japan in December of 1997, American newspapers headlined the story. The seizure-inducing special effects were immediately and forever cut, and *Pokemon* soon made the transition to American pop culture—and how! The series hit the cover of *Time* magazine in November 1999 as *Pokemon* cartoons, toys, video games, and merchandise of all manner became fixtures of most local homes. *Pokemon: The First Movie* broke boxoffice records, with the sequel poised to do the same, and *Pokemon* cards are hot ticket items on playgrounds.

Local kids are on top of the trend: 7-year old Chris Johnson of Brattleboro boasts a huge *Pokemon* card collection, and he has eased his cousin Gregory Johnson of Guilford into the habit. The cards are necessary to the "battle" games (which usually last about an hour), but Chris says trading is his favorite aspect of the card scene. Chris says the card for the *Pokemon* monster Mew is the toughest card to find these days; vet collector Kirby Veitch of Townshend, age 10, has an even larger collection, and he judges card rarity on their respective price guide values, where Charizard and Aerodactyl command top dollar. All agree that the hologram cards are the most desirable.

Kirby bemoans his school's rule against trading cards (due to theft: "It's a big problem," Kirby told me). He's also unhappy about the difficulties finding places to buy cards in southern Vermont, but there are still some local venues. And there are other alternatives: this coming Sunday, February 27, First Run Video hosts one of the area's first *Pokemon* Swap Meets from 1 PM to 4 PM. It won't be the last.

When I asked Chris and Greg if they'd ever outgrow *Pokemon*, they shook their heads; "No—probably when I'm about 96," Chris replied. Older and wiser Kirby circumspectly said, "Sure." But don't hold your breath, mom and dad!

Where do these weird creatures come from? What is—or are—*anime*? *Anime*, like the *manga* (Japanese comics) they are often drawn from, are literally a world apart from American animation. Both *manga* and *anime* have lifted stylistic archetypes from Western animation (i.e., exaggerated large eyes to denote youth or cuteness, etc.), but the differences between Eastern and Western animation are far more pronounced than the similarities. Until recently, Western animation was primarily marketed as a children's entertainment; *anime* targets all ages, with many designed specifically for adult audiences.

With few exceptions, American commercial animation is derived from either the vaudeville tradition of gag and/or musical comedy (Warner Bros.' *Looney Tunes*), the fairy tale, or the Broadway musical format (both standbys of the Disney mold). *Anime* embrace humor, fairy tales, music, and so much more. Nurtured from completely different cultural and artistic roots, *anime* have their own iconography and dramaturgy, embracing a far wider range of issues, graphic styles, stories, genres, and approaches. *Anime* constantly push the envelope: *anime* "cute" puts Western "cute" to shame (see *Pokemon, Hello Kitty*, etc.), *anime* mayhem makes Western violence and horror seem tame, and *anime* often burst with a sensuality and sexuality Western cartoons shun. When atmospheric *mise en scene*, character, or spectacle invites it, *anime* can engage the audience's senses with meditative focus. Intent on tickling funny bones, plucking heartstrings, or rushing to the next plot point or song, Western animation would never indulge the extended tour of a future metropolis *Ghost in the Shell* (1995) gives us, stretch mass destruction to the intoxicating limits *Akira* (1988) revels in, or send us soaring silently amid the clouds in the extended biplane flying sequences of Miyazaki's *Porco Rosso* (*The Red Pig*, 1992; not yet available in the US).

It should come as no surprise, then, that an entire generation of Americans has embraced Eastern *anime* as an alternative to the pervasive Disney and Warner archetypes. *Pinocchio* and Bugs Bunny belong to prior generations: the polar extremes of *Pokemon* and *Princess Mononoke* belong to today. As celebrated Czech surrealist filmmaker and stop-motion animator Jan Svankmajer (director of *Alice* and *Faust*) puts it, "Disney is one of the great liquidators of Western culture... It destroys children's souls."[27] Though they revered Disney, *anime*'s founding father Osamu Tezuka and artistic heirs of Mijazaki's caliber have transcended Disney's legacy with a pantheon of adventures featuring young characters whose moral integrity, courage, and vision can truly be called soul enhancing.

Not all *anime* are so upbeat. Many are darker but equally compelling, ranging from the crime *noir* of *Crying Freeman* (1988-92) and the dystopian cyberpunk of *Akira* and *Ghost in the Shell* to the libido-lashing horrors of *Wicked City* and *Urotsukidoji* (both

---

[27] Svankmajer is quoted from "Kafka's Heir" by Anthony Lane, *The New Yorker*, October 31, 1994.

1987). Many are punctuated with excruciating snapshots of Armageddon: no pop culture on Earth has explored apocalyptic dread with the unflinching clarity of that which emerged from the ashes of Hiroshima and Nagasaki. *Anime* provide the ideal vehicle for such terrifying visions, including the real-life nuclear holocausts detailed in Masaki Mori's *Barefoot Gen* (1983, adapted from Keiji Nakazawa's *manga* classic), or the grim final days of two firebombing orphans in Isao Takahata's profoundly moving *Grave of the Fireflies* (1988).

Admittedly, there is also a good deal of mediocre and poor *anime* product—with over a hundred direct-to-video productions being produced every year, how could it be otherwise? But much of it is very good indeed, and some of it is truly great.

As luck and the vagaries of pop cultural commerce would have it, Americans were introduced to *anime* with its first hero, a robot boy who wanted to be human, a Pinocchio for the 21st Century. Osamu Tezuka, justifiably revered in Japan as "Manga no Kami-Sama" ("The God of Comics"), embraced the comparatively modest resources of black-and-white limited animation for television. Tezuka brought his popular *manga* creation *Tetsuwan Atom* to Fuji TV on New Years Day of 1963. NBC Enterprises bought the syndication rights for America, debuting the series in September 1963 under its new moniker *Astro Boy*.

By October of the following year, *Astro Boy* was one of the most popular cartoon shows on American television, ushering in a succession of *anime* heroes like *Gigantor* (1966) and *Speed Racer* (1967). The vigor of *Speed Racer*'s weekly adventures with the super-charged Mach Five racecar superseded its limited animation and production values, becoming a particular favorite among American children. Tezuka's own successor to *Astro Boy* was *Kimba the White Lion*, which premiered in the US in September of 1966. Almost three decades later, *Kimba* was the unacknowledged inspiration for Disney's feature *The Lion King*.

Television remained *anime*'s international magic carpet well into the 1980s. Hence, *Space Battleship Yamato* (debuted 1974) became *Star Blazers* (debuted 1979) in the US, and multiple Japanese titles were combined to yield *Force Five* (1980-81), *Voltron* (1984-85), and *Robotech* (1985). Go Nagai's *Mazinger-Z* (1972-79) became *Tranzor Z* (1985), spawning the whole transforming giant robot toy and cartoon craze.

In 1983 and '84, original animation videos (OAV) surfaced in the booming videocassette market in Japan. Science fiction and giant robots reigned, but new genres emerged: free of broadcast standards, erotic *anime* constituted almost a quarter of the OAV market by 1985. Horror OAV surfaced with the gothic *Vampire Hunter 'D'* (1985), the monster-filled *Guyver* series (1986-92), and others. The inevitable merger of sex and horror followed, though by 1987 erotic *anime* commanded a far smaller share of a rapidly expanding market as children's *anime* reasserted the appeal of all-ages *anime*.

While TV and video fueled the *anime* explosion, theatrical *anime* continued to be produced. Precious few played US screens. All that changed with the international success of Katsuhiro Otomo's high-octane science-fiction epic *Akira* (1988). The staggering scope and depth of Otomo's *manga* was compromised, but *Akira*'s dense visuals and riveting tale of a teenage biker-gang punk named Tetsuo empowered and ultimately consumed by latent psychic powers which nearly level the future city of Neo-Tokyo thrust *anime* into the spotlight worldwide. The international theatrical release of Mamoru Oshii's *anime* adaptation of Masamune Shirow's complex cyber-punk *manga Ghost in the Shell* (1995) was another landmark. *Akira, Ghost in the Shell*, and the video success of adults-only titles like *Urotsukidoji: Legend of the Overfiend* paved the way for the broad US video releases of masterpieces like *My Neighbor Totoro, Ninja Scroll* (1993), and others.

Sailor Moon (Japanese debut 1992, US 1995) made a splash stateside with young girls, and it still attracts a sizable following, as the recent direct-to-video release of *Sailor Moon: The Movie* proves. *Dragonball* (Japanese debut 1986, US 1995) and *Dragonball Z* and more hyper-energetic *anime* imports soon carved out turf once considered the exclusive domain of Warner Brothers, Nickelodeon, and Hanna-Barbera.

Even Disney studios have had to acknowledge the *anime* revolution. The Disney subsidiary Miramax recently secured the rights to release Hayao Miyazaki's entire body of work in the US, beginning with *Princess Mononoke* (1997). Despite a successful opening at the prestigious 1999 New York Film Festival, rave reviews, and placement on many critics' "Top Ten" lists, *Mononoke* has played only a select few urban theaters to date. Perhaps it's the PG-13 rating, prompted by the film's bursts of violence and its complex weave of ecological fantasy and adult moral sensibilities that has kept Miramax from opening the film wider. At the time of this writing, it appears Disney & Miramax have buried *Mononoke*'s chances for theatrical success, and Disney has released only one Miyazaki feature, *Kiki's Delivery Service*, to video. Hmmmmm.... could it be that they are afraid of usurping Disney's claim to the cartoon-feature kingdom?

Perhaps they should be afraid. Disney had better get on the boat, and soon. Warner Brothers isn't napping, having released the monster hit *Pokemon: The First Movie*; move over, Bugs Bunny. *Anime* is a profitable fixture in video stores while judiciously pruned (Japan has a far higher tolerance for violence in children's entertainment) juvenilia like *Dragonball*, *Sailor Moon*, *Digemon*, and *Pokemon* flourish on American airwaves. Only time will tell how long *Pokemon* will reign supreme, with there's no doubt that anime are here to stay. In the meantime, do you have a Charizard card you can spare?

March 2:

RANDOM HEARTS (1999) draws its sorrowful romance from the novel by Warren Adler. Washington D.C. internal affairs investigator Dutch (Harrison Ford) loves his wife (Susanna Thompson); Congress-person Kay Chandler (Kristin Scott Thomas) is comfy with the domestic bliss she enjoys with her hubby (Peter Coyote) and daughter Jessica (Kate Mara). Cruel fate upsets their respective applecarts when a fatal air disaster unveils a covert affair between Dutch's wife and Kay's husband. The subsequent entanglement of cop and congresswoman's emotional lives is the substance of this very odd coupling, which edges from a somber drama about infidelity into—well, I'm not sure what. Alfred Hitchcock carved *Vertigo* (1958) out of similarly disturbing emotional turf, and director Sydney Pollack (casting himself as Kay's campaign manager) has a credible track record punctuated with challenging fare like *They Shoot*

Horses, Don't They? (1969). Hitchcock, he's not: Pollack shies away from the genuinely ghoulish premise to craft a soulless, heartless romance. Steeped in David Grusin's wistful jazz score, the film is cool and austere when it should be hot and obsessive, lost in deeper denial than its characters. Ford is dour throughout, digging for the truth; Thomas (the European *femme fatale* of *The English Patient*) an ice princess, skirting the revelations for the sake of campaign, career, and her daughter. Not once do they express any believable grief, resentment, disgust, or madness, thought that's what drives them. When they suddenly, inexplicably leap into each other's arms, any remaining credibility flies out the window.

Like James Stewart, Ford trades on a solid screen persona he's created over 25 years. Working with directors like Alfred Hitchcock and Anthony Mann, James Stewart traded on his "nice guy" movie persona to create a fascinating gallery of compellingly flawed, psychologically-complex characters: the obsessed mavericks of the Mann westerns; the voyeur of *Rear Window*; the heartsick, borderline-necrophile of *Vertigo*. Harrison Ford denies himself such explorations, though offbeat gems like Peter Weir's *The Mosquito Coast* (1986) were promising. The package-deals and test-screening-driven 1990s Hollywood scene Ford plays in now yields only safe, sterile perversities like *Six Days, Seven Nights* (1998) and *Random Hearts*, which could have, should have provided an opportunity for something very different. *(Rated 'R' for nudity, language, adult and sexual situations, and one scene of gun violence.)*

A far, far better film and romantic meditation on the toll of infidelity is writer-director Malcolm D. Lee's **THE BEST MAN** (1999), co-produced by Spike Lee. Young Chicago author Harper Stewart (Taye Digs) shies from any commitment to his lovely girlfriend Robin (Sanaa Lathan), but his emotional aloofness is eventually shaken to the core by a weekend wedding reunion with his old NYC hood pals. There's football-star groom Lance (Morris Chestnut) and bride-to-be Mia (Monica Calhoun); social worker Merch (Harold Perrineau, giving a great, understated performance) living under the thumb of his manipulative, domineering girlfriend Shelby (Melissa DeSousa); and simmering provocateur Quentin (Terrence Howard, also in fine form), determined to hold a mirror up to everyone. They've been trading off an advanced copy of Harper's new novel, stressed by their interpretations of its autobiographical elements as they recognize themselves and their friends in its pages. They're also angling to get Harper together with his one-time maybe-sweetheart Jordan (Nia Long), whose own career ambitions have kept her clear of emotional partners.

The Best Man is an engaging, meaty weave of likable characters, and the climactic bachelor party and wedding day provide a truly satisfying conclusion to the mounting teasing and tensions. Recommended—and whatever you do, *do not* shut off the video when it's over: There's a pay-off moment before the final credits that you *do* want to see![28] *(Rated 'R' for language, nudity, adult and sexual situations, and one brief scene when male characters comes to blows.)*

STIGMATA (1999) is the top temptation on the new release wall. Perhaps as a result of the growing

---

[28] The *Video Views* reviews (or abridgements) of *The Best Man*, *The Highwayman*, *The Insider* and *Star Wars: The Phantom Menace* (see next volume) were also published in *VMag* #29, April 2000, pp. 42-43.

Christian market, Hollywood has edged many of its recent *The Exorcist* and *The Omen*-inspired religious horror films into more devotional territory (as in *The Seventh Sign*, 1988; Michael Tolkin's *The Rapture*, 1991; and others). Apocalyptic scenarios in these films evolve into parables about redemption rather than damnation, even as the narrative set-ups echo horror movie conventions. Patricia Arquette is the mortal vessel of *Stigmata*, possessed not by a demon, but by the spirit of a deceased priest whose outrage at the Vatican cannot be silenced by death. In a surprisingly anti-Roman Catholic narrative recalling the Los Angeles-based Jack T. Chick religious comic-book tracts, the film mounts a muddled but explicit attack on the Catholic Church's politics, vanity, and abusive concentration of power, embodied by the character of an evil cardinal (Jonathan Pryce) willing to go to any extreme to bury the truth.

The climactic exorcism sequence reverses *The Exorcist* dynamic: here, Jonathan Pryce's exorcist tries to cast out a *divine* spirit to further his own goals. Gabriel Byrne (who played Satan himself in *End of Days*, 1999) is the Church investigator who believes (and begins to fall for) Arquette. *The Exorcist* had torrents of spewed pea soup, but *Stigmata* is awash in water—drops, drips, founts, and vast *seas* of blood-tinged water. Director Rupert Wainwright tells the tale effectively to a point and conjures atmosphere galore, but I just couldn't suspend my disbelief with all that H2O everywhere. It's stylish overkill to an absurd degree: here's Arquette, living in an upper-floor Pittsburgh apartment, and the water just keeps on coming. She doesn't spread towels on the floor or get a mop; nobody downstairs bangs on their ceiling/her floor or complains to the landlord or calls the health department or fire department or shows up at her door with a sump pump. Early on in these grim proceedings, Arquette suffers a stigmata-seizure in her bathtub, spilling water everywhere and being rushed off to the hospital—but my concern for her was deep-sixed by the vain hope that, while she was away recuperating, somebody, *anybody* would turn off the water in her tub. But no. She's home later, all bandaged up with a friend over to take care of her, and Arquette stands looking at the tub overflowing on the floor, and her friend says "Come to bed"—that's *it*, "Come to bed," not, "Hey, what you doin' fool? *Turn off the water!*"—and the water keeps dripping and *dripping* and—*(Rated 'R' for language, blasphemy, partial nudity, sexual situations, gore, dubious interpretations of the Bible, and waaaaay too much water.)*

There's a bit more logic at work in Disney Studio's **THE EXTREMELY GOOFY MOVIE** (1999). Instead of excessive water spillage and evil Vatican plots, there's an excess of skateboarding and nasty frat boys scheming to trip up Goofy and his son Max, whose freshman year in college is being cramped by Dad. And when your Dad is Goofy, I mean, *really* Goofy—well, you get the idea. The skateboard and rollerblade antics might be more appropriate to junior high than college, and Goofy's anachronistic association with the 1970s may put off adults who link the character with the 1940s and '50s, but hey, relax and roll with it. Goofy's been a co-star fixture of the Disney cartoon empire for almost seventy years, and it's nice to see him back in his own vehicle. For that matter, it's nice to hear Pauly Shore (providing the voice for Max's buddy Bobby) again. The original *A Goofy Movie* (1994) was one of the most pleasant surprises to emerge from the Disney stable in recent years, a lively, genuinely funny animated feature that scored theatrical success despite the studio's lack of confidence. Apparently, they didn't learn their lesson: this sequel has gone direct-to-video, but it's a pretty entertaining outing, too, and would have been a hoot on the big screen. *(Rated 'G,' suitable for all ages.)*

For the record, here's my VMag *"Vid View" review (February, 2000, pg. 37) of* Stigmata*:*

STIGMATA (1999) is the latest ominous offshoot of *The Exorcist*, only instead of a pudgy nymphet providing upscale Georgetown housing for Pazuzu, we get wane & willowy Patricia Arquette manifesting the stigmata of Jesus Christ as she is possessed by the spirit of a devout priest. Before you can say "Holy hand-holes!," she's in the shit, or should I say, soup. *The Exorcist* had strategically-aimed pea-soup projectile vomit, but *Stigmata* is awash in drops, drips, founts, and vast seas of blood-tinged water (possession chowder, Manhattan style, if you know what I mean, and I think you do). Director Rupert Wainwright conjures atmosphere galore, and the lapsed Catholic in me is a sucker for these cinematic Jack T. Chick-tract narratives, but I just couldn't suspend my disbelief with all that damnable water everywhere. I mean, here's Arquette, living in an upper-floor city apartment, and the water just keeps on coming, and *nobody* downstairs bangs on the floor or bitches to the landlord or yells at the super, much less calls the health department or fire department or shows up at the door with a sump pump or a mop or sponge or tampon or *something*. Gabriel Byrne is all sullen in the Jason Miller role, pondering his lack of faith and the attendant agonies of it all, and the water just keeps on dripping into Arquette's apartment, sometimes in reverse motion, hinting that perhaps the neighbors aren't going ballistic due to some blessed recycling program unknown to secular science. Then there's Jonathan Pryce as the evil Vatican rep, sending my own disgust with organized religion into spin cycle while Arquette has a bleeding frenzy in her bathtub (no, it's really not her time of the month—see, these bloody holes keep appearing in her palms, and—oh, never mind). So now she's spilling water everywhere and being rushed off to the hospital. I lose track of my simmering loathing for the Pryce character and hope somebody, *anyfuckingbody* will turn off the water in the tub. But no, she's home later, all bandaged up with a friend over to take care of her, and she just stands there like a idjit, looking at the goddamned tub overflowing on the floor, and her friend says "Come on to bed"—*not "Hey! Turn off the fucking spigot!!"* And the water keeps dripping and dripping and *dripping and—(Rated 'R' for language, nudity, sexual situations, blasphemy, gore, dubious interpretations of the Bible, irreverent caricatures of the priesthood, and too much water.)*

March 9:

With the prominent exceptions of *Dr. Strangelove* and *A Clockwork Orange*, Stanley Kubrick's films always received cool (often hostile) critical and audience response upon their initial releases. His final film, **EYES WIDE SHUT** (1999), completed days before his death, earned the same. A friend of mine proclaimed the film "throbbingly banal," as succinct a description of the hermetically-sealed vacuum the film creates as any other I could offer. But banality has often been the core of Kubrick's best work—the calculated pacing of *2001: A Space Od-*

yssey, the leisure observations of *Barry Lyndon*'s moral decay—and I found *Eyes Wide Shut* as compelling, mesmerizing, and haunting as Kubrick's previous masterpieces. This, his final film, completed days before his death, will bear the test of time.

The story is absurdly simple: a young doctor (Cruise) is driven by his wife's (Kidman) bedroom confessions of desire for another man (though her only infidelity was desire and her fantasies) to court, for one long night, his own sexual curiosity. As the evening progresses, his sojourn edges closer to death, jeopardizing his cautious distance as an observer, a voyeur, a nonparticipant afraid to engage with his own fantasies. Overly hyped for its erotic content and the false promise of capturing the couplings of Tom Cruise and Nicole Kidman onscreen, *Eyes Wide Shut* is classical Kubrick: antiseptic, austere, hypnotic, and maddeningly introspective and restrained, despite its volatile emotional terrain and the voluptuous and venomous heat that drives its dreamlike narrative. That heat is smothered, not fanned; as ever, Kubrick's methodical dissection of the arcane alleys of human nature and emotion is driven by his "intellect, vast, cool, and unsympathetic" (to paraphrase H.G. Wells' description of the Martian intelligence in *The War of the Worlds*). His depiction of the New York City nightlife and streets (a British set, strangely barren and remote) are those of a dream, not reality. On its own terms, this meditation on the fragility of human sexual relations is a potent cinematic experience.

This is decidedly not everyone's cup of tea. Philip Saville's *Metroland* (1997) covers similar emotional and conceptual turf in a more comfortable, familiar manner, should Kubrick's exploration put you off. If it's traditional eroticism you seek, this is an exercise in futility (you might want to rent this week's *Emmanuel: First Contact* instead, or just visit the adult room). The infamous orgy sequence (a typically Kubrickian masque, calculatingly uninvolving despite all the flesh on display) wasn't cut per se for US release; Warner Bros. masked offending portions of the screen with digital images of clothed bodies to ensure an 'R' rating, reportedly with Kubrick's involvement and approval. Sadly, this US version is all we're allowed to see on video and DVD, as well. Warner claims this is contractual with the Kubrick estate, but don't forget that Warners also refused to release the uncut *Natural Born Killers* to the video market (Stone's contract allowed him to package the uncut version with another label), and is *still* refusing to release uncut prints of 1970s classics like *Performance* (1969) and *The Devils* (1971) domestically. The DVD extras include a surprisingly moving pair of interviews with Cruise and Kidman, demonstrating the depth of their personal bond with Kubrick. Recommended. *(Rated 'R' for nudity, adult and sexual situations, onscreen lovemaking, drug-abuse, and language.)*

The title of **BREAKFAST OF CHAMPIONS** (1999) refers to a martini, but this film is like one of those insane candied milkshakes. Kurt Vonnegut's idiosyncratic writing has defeated many filmmakers, yielding good films (*Slaughterhouse Five, Who Am I This Time?*, and *Mother Night*) and at least one disaster (*Slapstick of Another Kind*). Robert Altman acolyte Alan Rudolph (*Welcome to L.A., Choose Me, Mrs. Parker and the Vicious Circle*, etc.) is the latest director to court catastrophe and give one of Vonnegut's recent novels a go, and the results are decidedly mixed—like that milkshake I just mentioned.

Manic Bruce Willis (with bad hair) is kingpin Midland City car salesman Dwayne Hoover, suffering a midlife crisis as—in an apparently unrelated narrative thread—obscure sf author Kilgore Trout (Albert Finney in appropriately surly form) hitchhikes his away across country to be the guest of honor at the grand opening of the Midland City Arts Festival. Hoover's family are unhinged: his wife Celia (Barbara Hershey) is addicted to pharmaceuticals and television, and his son Bunny (Lucas Haas) lives in the family bomb shelter and performs ersatz muzak at a local club. Hoover's employees are off their rockers, too, prominent among them his succubus secretary (Glenne Headly) and Nick Nolte's vein-popping turn as Harry LeSabre (at one point Hoover proclaims, "I've never let the fact that you have the name of a Buick come between us"). There are interlopers, too, such as Wayne Hoobler (Omar Epps), who moves in and lives on Hoover's car lot solely because of the alliterative similarity of their names.

Initially, the in-your-face insanity of the film is oppressive and off-putting; the direction and performances seemed pitched at a constant level of hysteria. The critics roasted the film, and I have no doubt most of you will want to shut it off after the first half hour—but stick with it. There's a sublime central sequence between Dwayne, Celia, his gun, and her TV set that kicks the rest of the film into gear. In the end (as in many of Vonnegut's novels), the chaos coalesces into the satisfying and oddly moving fateful conjunction of Hoover's nervous breakdown and a passage from Kilgore Trout's novel *Now It Can Be Told*. Mark Isham's musical score liberally incorporates the 1950s lounge-lizard exoticism of Martin Denny, lending this eclectic spew what little cohesion it has. Vonnegut has a cameo as a TV commercial director,

Vonnegut's venerable character Elliott Rosewater (Ken Campbell) makes an appearance, and Rudolph isn't above sly self-references: Bunny's outrageous hairstyle echoes Keith Carradine's coiffure in Rudolph's stylishly controlled *Trouble in Mind* (1986), my personal favorite of his films. *Breakfast of Champions* is a mind-skewing mess, but it's well worth the ride, if you can stick with it—though only intrepid video viewers with a taste for the bizarre or rabid Vonnegut fans are likely to do so. *(Rated 'R' for language, nudity, drug and alcohol abuse, adult and sexual situations.)*

THE HIGHWAYMAN (1999) sells itself as another slice of contemporary film *noir*, like the recent (and highly recommended) *Best Laid Plans*. But this quirky Canadian road movie is an odd, unclassifiable original, and as such worth a look. Ziggy (Laura Harris of *Suicide Kings* and *The Faculty*) is an opportunistic teenage girl eager to shake her clinging boyfriend Walter (Gordon Michael Woolvett), break free of her dead-end job in a jewelry store and find her long-lost father. She gets her chance when she impulsively helps a jewel-heist at her job, hooking her caboose to the sociopathic thieves "Breakfast" (Jason Priestley of *Beverly Hills 90210* and the fine *Love and Death on Long Island*) and Panda (Bernie Coulson). Much to her frustration, Walter tags along for a cross-country crime spree that lands Ziggy at the door of the man she has tagged as "daddy," the unbelievably put-upon Frank Drake (Stephen McHattie). Frank needs relief from the shambles-of-a-life collapsing around him; Ziggy offers a purgatory of release and redemption. To say any more would give away the story, which twists and turns to an unexpectedly satisfying finale. The cast delivers in spades, with top-billed Priestley's unstable "Breakfast" taking a back seat to Harris' complex, compelling Ziggy throughout, as her insatiable hunger for the family she was denied merrily drives them all to hell in a handbasket. Kudos to Priestley for co-producing this lively dark comedy; *The Highwayman* is an engaging surprise; check it out. *(Rated 'R' for language, violence, and adult situations.)*

March 16:

DARING DEREN: Women's Film Festival Celebrates Maya Deren

"Cameras do not make films; film-makers make films. Improve your films not by adding more equipment and personnel but by using what you have to the fullest capacity. The most important part of your equipment is yourself; your mobile body, your imaginative mind, and your freedom to use both."

- Maya Deren,
"Amateur Versus Professional,"
Film Culture #39, Winter, 1965.

The very rare opportunity to see Maya Deren's marvelous body of work on the big screen this weekend (presented by the Women's Film Festival) allows us to discover or rediscover how Deren put herself, body and soul, into her films. She indeed placed herself at their center as performer, director, and creator. Her expressive face and body language, her eyes, and her adventurous exploration of cinema as an interpretive tool to share her personal dreams, nightmares, and visions with audiences still mesmerize and capture us. Though she left this mortal plane of existence in 1961, we still see her reflection; still hear her voice echo, though we may not know it is Maya we are seeing and hearing.

In *Meshes of the Afternoon* (1943, her first film), Deren was the troubled dreamer, haunted in and about her own home by a faceless cowled figure, a key, a knife, and her own doppelganger. Though inspired by the surrealist filmmakers before her, Deren's precisely calculated structure of the waking dream that plunges into nightmare was a revelation. In *At Land* (1944), she was an almost elemental being who emerged from the sea, crawling over surf, sand and a banquet table to flirt with a game of chess and then follow one of its spilled play pieces over the rocks, back into the sea. She was as powerful an elemental being in the medium of cinema, indelibly shaping its language and potential.

When Maya Deren committed her very personal visions to celluloid in the 1940s, the term "underground film" did not even exist (the moniker wasn't coined until 1959). Deren's works, like those of her immediate peers Kenneth Anger, Harry Smith, and Sidney Peterson, were referred to as "experimental films," a clumsy label implying amateurism, which at least signified such films' daring nature and distinction from mainstream Hollywood fare. The European term "avant garde film" was also adopted, but the works of Deren and her peers were distinctively American, bold, brazen, and crafted from the heart.

Once the term "underground film" was embraced, Deren was rightfully proclaimed the Mother of Underground Cinema. Deren's role was indeed matriarchal: she wholeheartedly devoted herself to cinema and the growing movement of independent young artists whose work freed the cinema from the confines of narrative theatrical conventions and the bondage of the Hollywood film industry, with its tightly-structured commercial studio and distribution systems. Deren nurtured the new generations of alternative filmmakers as a creator, a teacher, an advocate, and by lucidly committing the communal ideology to print in her monograph *An Anagram of Ideas on Art Form and Film* (1946). Unable to find a commercial distributor for her films, Deren mounted her own theatrical venues beginning in 1946; these proved so successful that she booked her own touring exhibition of her work, establishing the model for self-distribution which prompted others to open their own underground theaters (starting with Amos Vogel's Cinema 16, established at Deren's own debut showcase in Greenwich Village) and distribution networks. Working with Vogel, Deren co founded the first filmmakers' distribution and promotion cooperative, the Creative Film Foundation, which also rose sorely-needed funding for other directors. Her friendship with key underground filmmakers like Stan Brakhage had a deep and lasting impact on their own influential underground works. Her vision, her touch, is evident throughout the history of the movement and its most lasting works.

Ritual, magic, and mysticism played a fundamental role in Deren's remarkable body of work. Magic was, so to speak, in the air: fellow experimental film pioneer Kenneth Anger was an acolyte of notorious British occultist Aleister Crowley's "magick," and Anger's later works were indeed designed as "magickal" cinematic invocations. Deren's unique path prompted her to explore the voodoo religion, traveling to Haiti and filming authentic voodoo rituals from 1947-52. Deren eventually actively participated in the religion and rituals, an experience that profoundly affected her and yielded a remarkable book, *The Divine Horsemen* (1960). The extensive footage she shot was never edited or completed to Deren's satisfaction, though it was posthumously edited by Cherel Ito and released by Mystic Fire Video as *Divine Horsemen: The Living Gods of Haiti* (1985).

Prior to her Haitian experiences, Deren's film magic was profoundly personal and introspective. She was one of the pioneers of "trance cinema," creating celluloid experiences that embrace the alluring internal logic and rhythms of dreams and nightmares. *Meshes of the Afternoon* was a landmark "trance film," coaxing us into the shared experience of what is either a woman's transformative merger with dream reality, or her claustrophobic confinement, dread, and a devastating fulfillment of her self-destructive impulses. Not until Roman Polanski's *Repulsion* (1966) would the mainstream cinema explore similar emotional terrain with such unflinchingly confrontational, tactile clarity. Deren's poetic, personal fantasies charting internal emotional and psychological landscapes moved a generation of fellow West Coast underground filmmakers to embrace Deren's work as a point of departure: Kenneth Anger, Curtis Harrington, James Broughton, and Sidney Peterson crafted their own distinctively gothic strain of personal "trance film" psychodramas throughout the 1940s and '50s. Harrington ultimately chose to cross boundaries into Hollywood, extending this genre into theatrical features like *Night Tide* (1961), *Queen of Blood* (1965), and *What's the Matter With Helen?* (1971), edging Deren's influence further into the pop-cultural consciousness. Subsequently, directors like John Parker (*Dementia*, aka *Daughter of Horror*), Roman Polanski (*Repulsion, The Tenant*) and David Lynch (*Eraserhead, The Elephant Man, Blue Velvet, Twin Peaks*) have carried the syntax of Deren's "trance cinema" further into the mainstream.

Deren also founded "dance cinema." Though motion picture cameras had captured dances on film since the 1890s, they had done so to record theatrical experiences (passive observation and archival recorder) or as staged events within musical extravaganzas like Busky Berkeley's Depression-era "all-singing, all-dancing" epics (dance as an element of artifice and spectacle). Deren made dance and dance movement the absolute expressive focus of *A Study in Choreography for Camera* (1945), *Meditation on Violence* (1948), and her final film, *The Very Eye of Night* (1958), an exquisite piece designed to be shown in its negative form, establishing a fresh cinematic vocabulary for others to follow. Deren's profound influence can subsequently be seen through Shirley Clarke's *Dance in the Sun* (1953, in collaboration with dancer Daniel Nagrin[29]), *Bullfight* (1955), and *Moment in Love* (1957, both with dancer Anna Sokolow). The "dance film" became a genre in and of itself, further explored by underground filmmakers like Ed Emshwiller, Norman McClaren, Stan Vanderbeek, and Hilary Harris—all of whom cited Deren as a formative influence. Since the early 1980s, music videos have continued to build upon the foundation Deren created.

Maya Deren completed only six films in her lifetime, but the influence of her groundbreaking creations and efforts are still felt today. We are privileged to have the opportunity to see her work in a local venue. Deren's

---

[29] For the record, I once met dancer Daniel Nagrin when he came to Johnson State College in Johnson, VT during my technical theater student years (1974-76). When I asked him about Shirley Clarke, he confessed to recalling little.

films are occasionally shown in urban theater retrospectives in New York City and San Francisco, but the last Vermont theatrical showing of Deren's work I know of was in the early 1970s in Burlington, Vermont. I was lucky to see them then, and look forward to the chance to catch them again at the Hooker-Dunham Gallery Theater this week.

Go, with open eyes and heart, and see for yourself why Deren was indeed the Mother of the Underground Film.

March 16:

THE BONE COLLECTOR (1999) isn't for weak stomachs or weak-kneed viewers. Ever since the arrest of serial killer Henry Lee Lucas and the publication (and Academy Award-winning film version) of *Silence of the Lambs*, crime thrillers have edged into what was once the exclusive terrain of writers like Robert Bloch (author of the novel *Psycho*) and reviled exploitation and horror films. Novels like Caleb Carr's *The Alienist* (which *The Bone Collector* evokes in its title sequence and decisive clue), movies like *Se7en* and *Kiss the Girls*, and TV programs like *Millennium* have entrenched the genre's graphic extremes into distinctively mainstream entertainments. *The Bone Collector* is the latest entry in the nasty-serial-killer-police-procedural sweepstakes, starring a bed-ridden Denzel Washington as Lincoln Rhyme, one-time NYC detective extraordinaire paralyzed by an accident who has lost the will to live—but none of his investigative skills. Enter a serial-killer cabbie leaving inscrutable clues at the scenes of his surgically-precise sadistic murders, and young cop Amelia Donaghy (the extraordinary, pout-lipped Angelina Jolie of *Girl, Inter-*

rupted). The one-two punch of the killer's arcane murderous schemes and Amelia's latent forensic skills awakens Rhyme's own instincts and zest for detection, and thereby hangs the tale.

The twists and turns sometimes strain credibility, and Washington looks awful good given his situation, but if you can excuse such Hollywood "necessities" and the unsavory sadism of the murders themselves, this is an engaging (though unexceptional) potboiler. Washington and Jolie are engaging as always, Queen Latifah adds spice as Washington's nurse (named Thelma, a nod to Thelma Ritter's role in Hitchcock's *Rear Window*, which this film owes a clear debt to), and solid character actor Michael Rooker lends an anchor as the unlikable Captain Cheney. Rooker made his mark in the title role of *Henry: Portrait of a Serial Killer* (1989), a low-budget made-in-Chicago gut-wrencher that remains the most unflinching, non-exploitative serial killer movie ever made; if the makers of *The Bone Collector* were even aware of the association, they only milked it for its "red herring" value. They should have paid closer attention: the harrowing *Henry* will be remembered long, long after *Bone Collector*'s light-weight, one-night-stand entertainment has become a dim memory. Nevertheless, fans of the mystery-suspense genre, Denzel Washington, or Angelina Jolie may find enough meat on *The Bone Collector* to savor that single night. *(Rated 'R' for language, violence, gore, explicit forensic imagery, and the horrific nature of the crimes depicted.)*

Don't be fooled by the superficial video box-art similarities of this week's teen flicks **OUTSIDE PROVIDENCE** and **DRIVE ME CRAZY** (both 1999); they're nothing alike. *Drive Me Crazy* is a completely forgettable formulaic "by-the-numbers" teen romantic comedy, adapted from a juvenile novella, *How I Created My Perfect Prom Date* by Todd Strasser—and the book title really says it all. There's little to recommend in this shallow, superficial tale of estranged next-door neighbor teens Nicole (Melissa Joan Hart, TV's *Sabrina, The Teenage Witch*) and Chase (scruffy, likable Adrian Grenier) who scheme to make their ex-partners jealous by pretending to be "an item." They, of course, end up falling for each other as the prom night approaches. Hart sleepwalks through her role, but Grenier does all he can with the thankless part of the reckless rebel whose surprised to find camaraderie, succor, and love by embracing the jock lifestyle to further their ploy. Though the well-worn material offers him none of the opportunities the far superior coming-of-age tale *The Adventures of Sebastian Cole* (1999; coming soon to video [reviewed in *Blur, Vol. 2*]) offered, Grenier almost makes the usual "frog-to-prince" transformation believable. It's as harmless a diversion as the thin teen-love books it's derived from, and a safe bet for younger viewers seeking romance. *(Rated 'PG-13' for occasional suggestive language, teenage drinking and vomiting, one beating, and one non-explicit sexual situation safely averted.)*

Outside Providence is something else entirely, a semi-autobiographical coming-of-age tale with resonant heart and brains to spare. The double entendre title refers to both its physical and metaphoric geography: we meet teen slacker Timothy Dunphy (Shawn Hatosy) living in one of the blue-collar white communities on the outskirts of Providence, Rhode Island, adrift in an aimless environment and seemingly beyond the reach of any divine providence or intervention. Tim's aimlessness is echoed by his friends (including a party-demon aptly nicknamed "Drugs") and broken family (led by tough-talking widower father Alec Baldwin), until he stupidly rear-ends a police car. Dad deals with the situation with a haircut and dramatic change in lifestyle, dropping Tim into an upper-crust prep school, and thus the story begins.

The notorious Farrelly Brothers—Peter, Michael and Bobby—scripted *Outside Providence*. They were the creators of raunchy, raucous comedies like *Kingpin* and *There's Something About Mary*, here adapting brother Peter's novel (while fellow native Rhode Islander Michael Corrente directed, lending a strong sense of time, place, and character to the film). Since the makers of *American Pie* publicly acknowledged their debt to the ground-breaking gross-out comedy of the Farrelly's *There's Something About Mary*, you might expect *Outside Providence* to be another 1990s teen sex, beer, and hormone-soaked jokefest (though *American Pie* was much more than that, too). Instead, *Outside Providence* registers as a modest, honest snapshot of Tim's adult awakening and first tastes of self-respect. Completely out of his element and over his head, Tim adapts and asserts himself with quiet integrity and dignity, and therein lays this gem's greatest surprise. The incidental details touch on the usual antics—student rivalry with the nasty dorm supervisor; the dorm-room pranks; the habitual abuse of the put-upon scapegoat at the bottom of the pecking order; casual drinking, drug-use, and foul language; Tim's romance with a blonde (attractive Amy Smart from *Varsity Blues*) from the nearby female prep school. But the particulars of Tim's story, as he relies on his own self-assurance, sense of fair play, and inherent decency to make his way, elevates the film to a class of its own. Tim negotiates the obstacles in his path, unafraid to act on his innate empathy and respect for others, while anchored by the genuine gravity of Baldwin's "tough love," his own love for his younger brother, and fierce loyalty to his friends and peers.

Outside Providence is indeed funny and touching, a fine entertainment, and Shawn Hatosy's central performance is as engaging as Baldwin's sharp, offbeat turn. But there's more here than meets the eye, as the film reminds us why the coming-of-age comedy-drama cliches linger by reinvesting in the truths they embody. It reminds us how "pranks" are sometimes the only way for youngsters to address and correct authoritarian abuses of power; how our impoverished spiritual culture leaves teenagers to invent their own clumsy rites-of-passage, and how resourceful some young adults can be; how sudden loss can fuel profound change; how intoxicating "first love" can be, and its potential for initiating a deeper sense of self and shared responsibilities. And it reminds us how much of ourselves we sometimes find in such coming-of-age tales, however young or old we may be. Heartily recommended! *(Rated 'R' for strong language, casual alcohol and drug use and abuse, and adult situations—though the sexual situations are non-explicit and tastefully handled.)*

March 23:

The hottest new release this week is undoubtably **POKEMON: THE FIRST MOVIE** (1999), which is subtitled *MewTwo Strikes Back* and preceded by a short cartoon entitled *Pikachu's Vacation*. If you haven't heard of *Pokemon*, you either don't have kids or grandchildren, or live on another planet. Created by Satoshi Tajiri for Nintendo's Game Boy system, *Pokemon* (which literally means "Pocket Monster"—no, that's not a sexual innuendo) spawned a wildly-successful *anime*

(Japanese animated cartoon) series and branded the current generation of American youth as indelibly as Mickey Mouse, Davy Crockett, G.I. Joe, Barbie, and the Teenage Ninja Mutant Turtles marked prior generations. It should come as no surprise that *Pokemon: The First Movie* broke box office records when it opened theatrically late last year. Nor should it come as any surprise that you, hapless adult that you are, probably cannot make head or tail of the *Pokemon* phenomenon.

Well, it isn't *meant* for you or I, is it? You might want to leave this video to the kids, too, unless curiosity gets the better of you. Any adult stumbling unprepared into the opening cartoon short *Pikachu's Vacation* will quickly feel dazzled, dazed, punch-drunk, and perhaps (depending on what you were up to in your reckless youth) wondering if that acid-flashback they warned you about finally kicked in. You know: this is your brain, this is your brain on *Pokemon*. It's certainly not a "bad trip," but it is intoxicatingly giddy and giggly and gag-inducing, and unless you've a few kids with you willing to explain everything, you won't have a clue what's going on. Pokemon come in a procession of colorful and very noisy sizes, shapes, and species, they all incessantly repeat their names for easy identification, and every damned one of them seem to parade through this nonsensical slapstick "story" about cuddly Pikachu's "vacation" on Pokemon Island. (It's like a premonitional womb-dream of the Godzilla movies to come, if you could remember your womb-dreams, and they'd anticipated the Toho Monster Island mythos you would later grow up with, with all the Toho monsters there in fetal form, too. Oh, sorry—I'm sure I've lost you by now; OK, back to *Pikachu's Vacation*.) The antics of these weird, infantile, almost elemental beings make the

Teletubbies seem like the citizens of an Ayn Rand novel or a subversive David Lynch movie. Bizarre as the Pokemon designs and hyperactivity may be, its internal logic is too cause-and-effect-oriented to be considered truly surreal. But *Pikachu's Vacation* is close: Dada and Dali might have approved.

The feature, which is also directed by *Pokemon* maestro Kunihiko Yuyama, is far more coherent, but not nearly as hypnotically compelling. A long pre-title prologue establishes its juvenile science-fiction premise as a team of scientists plunder an ancient shrine to secure the fossil remains of Mew, "the most powerful Pokemon to have ever existed, now believed to be extinct." Silly scientists: as any five-year-old in the room can tell you, little Mew is spying on them as they poke around the ruins. Quicker than you can say "MewTwo," they've cloned a self-centered super-powered Mew clone named MewTwo (natch). MewTwo flexes his awesome telekinetic powers and shucks his captors. He later stages a faked Pokemon Master tournament to weed out the best of the breed and clone his own genetically-enhanced Super Pokemon army. Enter—finally!—the stars of the cartoon series, Pokemon trainers Ash, Brock, Misty, and their respective Pokemon pals, including the ever-adorable Pikachu, as they respond to the tournament invite and are caught in MewTwo's scheme to take over the world.

Pokemon isn't a particularly engaging *anime*: the animation itself is crude, the most inventive design elements are dedicated to the Pokemon creatures themselves, and the climax tumbles into tearful *My Little Pony* and *Care Bears* territory (which my own now-teenage daughter over-exposed me to when she was younger). But who cares what I think? I asked three local

Pokemon fans and card collectors what they thought of the movie when I interviewed them for the *Reformer* "*Anime* Alternative" article back in February. 7-year old Chris Johnson of Brattleboro and his cousin Gregory Johnson of Guilford really liked the movie and were particularly enthusiastic about the fight between Mew and MewTwo, but Chris thought it was hokey when MewTwo bragged about being the most powerful Pokemon. "He thought he was the best, that was dumb;" Chris didn't buy it. Comparative Pokemon veteran 11-year-old Kirby Veitch of Townshend thought "the Pokemon fight at the beginning of the movie was awesome," but he found "the end of the movie was very dumb and almost idiotic... that turned it into a Barbie-doll kind of movie... after the fight with MewTwo, it's Barbie-Doll." See, stupid me, I thought it was too much like the Care Bears. Man, I am getting old. Can I go back to that fetal womb-dream about Monster Island again? See, I know my way around Godzilla, Rodan, Mothra, Ghidrah, Baragon, Varan, and— *(Rated 'G,' suitable for all ages.)*

Thankfully, Steven Soderbergh's **THE LIMEY** (1999) is an adult entertainment—though it, too, reminded me I'm getting on in years, as a tight ensemble of 1960s counter-cultural icons casually act their age. Director Soderbergh (who quickly rose to prominence with his debut feature *Sex, Lies and Videotape* in 1989) made his mark in the crime genre with the subdued but effective *The Underneath* (1995) and his fine adaptation of Elmore Leonard's *Out of Sight* (1998). He breathes considerable life into Lem Dobbs' script about graying Cockney ex-con Wilson (Terence Stamp) who flies into Los Angeles seeking the truth about (and Shylock's proverbial "pound of flesh" for) the death of his estranged daughter Jennie. Working with local confidant Eddie (Vermont resident Luis Guzman of *Boogie Nights* and others, delivering another fine supporting performance), Wilson cuts a bloody swathe through L.A.'s underbelly and upper crust with brutal efficiency, following Jennie's former lover Terry Valentine (Peter Fonda) from his posh rock'n'roll promoter digs in Hollywood to their final confrontation on the grounds of Valentine's Big Sur hideaway.

I don't want to build false expectations. *The Limey* is a calculatedly low-key, minor, but effective character piece, but its awfully good on its own modest terms. The film becomes a meditation on the promise of a bygone era gone to seed by virtue of its cast of offbeat '60s and '70s movie icons (Stamp, Fonda, Leslie Ann Warren, Barry Newman of *Vanishing Point*, and Andy Warhol star Joe Dellassandro). Wilson's personal purge and quest for redemption is anchored with vivid flashbacks of a very young Terence Stamp (clipped from Ken Loach's *Poor Cow*, 1967), ingeniously lending weight and context to Wilson's vendetta; furthermore, *The Limey*'s narrative style knowingly evokes leaner, meaner '60s and '70s role models. The storyline, casual brutality, and deliberate pacing echoes the underrated Michael Caine vehicle *Get Carter* (1971), while Soderbergh's deliberately fragmented and layered visual and aural style recalls John Boorman's seminal *Point Blank* (1967). Thus, what could have been an ordinary crime potboiler becomes an evocative cinematic mosaic, a kinetic tapestry composed of piecemeal reveries and flash-forwards juxtaposed with fits of "here and now" immediacy when the action lurches forward.

Soderbergh and author Dobbs bristle at the mention of *Point Blank* in their engaging DVD commentary, citing the earlier influences of the 1960s European New Wave, but that's tough: Boorman made the leap first with *Point Blank*. Soderbergh and Dobbs also bristle at each other throughout their DVD commentary, making for lively listening. The other notable DVD extra (besides the usual trailer, separate music track, and crystal-clear visual and sound) is the "60s Docu-Commentary" track featuring Terence Stamp, Peter Fonda, Leslie Ann Warren, and Joe Dellassandro, which I found even more engaging. Recommended, particularly on DVD. *(Rated 'R' for language, violence, and casual brutality.)*

March 30:

Have you heard the buzz? Christian filmmakers finally shook up Hollywood with their latest opus, **THE OMEGA CODE** (1999), which snuck under the entertainment industry radar last fall to score in the October 1999 Top-Ten Boxoffice lists. More populist action-thriller than horror film, casual viewers might be forgiven for considering *The Omega Code* a condensation of *The Omen* sans the Grand Guignol mayhem. It is, indeed, a Millennium-age epic in which a savvy media "self-help" promoter (Casper Van Dien) finds himself swept into the court of a powerful political figure (Michael York) who just happens to be the Anti-Christ, busily orchestrating the Final Days prophetized in the Bible while desperately seeking the Final Code necessary to completing his bid for world domination.

The Omega Code hits video shops this week, opening up a whole new vista for devout filmmakers intent on carrying their message to wider audiences and beating Hollywood at their own game—by playing, for the time being, by Hollywood's rules. *The Omega Code* boasts acceptable star power (York, Van Dien, Michael Ironside), an international scope (filmed on location in Jerusalem, Rome, Vatican City, and Los Angeles), a modest multi-million-dollar budget (reportedly $7.2 million), and a briskly-paced thriller narrative that delivers more bang-for-the-buck than bloated secular extravaganzas like the similarly-themed *End of Days*.

Though *The Omega Code* delivers a compelling evening entertainment, it also scores on its own terms, establishing a beachhead for a new generation of filmmakers eager to engage with audiences beyond the reach of the churches and Christian bookstore markets. It's a whole new ballgame, as they say, and the angels just scored a home run.

The themes of *The Omega Code* are familiar enough, popularized in the 1970s by gory horror epics like *The Omen* series and its imitators, and bestsellers like Hal Lindsey's *The Late, Great Planet Earth* (in fact, Lindsey is credited as the "Biblical Prophecy Consultant" for *The Omega Code*). Ira Levin's novel *Rosemary's Baby* (1967) midwived the modern pop-cultural concept of the Anti-Christ, establishing "the Beast" as a pop-cultural bogeyman who addressed collective Millennial fears with increasing urgency.

But the Anti-Christ is a very real figure for devout Christians and fundamentalists. Belief in the Anti-Christ, the false Messiah, dates from a body of apocalyptic literature in Judaism that lies between the two Testaments of *The Bible*, written prior to the founding of the Christian Church. The concept of a final war between good and evil was evident in many religions (Persian, Babylonian, and Judaism) and myths (the Norse "Ragnarok") before Christian ideology embraced the theme. The term "Anti-Christ" appeared only in the First and Second

Epistles of John. However, The Book of Revelations and passages of The Book of Daniel remain the primary source for contemporary belief in the Anti-Christ (where he was referred to only as "the Beast," denoting an incarnation of Satan), the Mark of the Beast, the Second Coming and Battle of Armageddon and the Last Judgment.

The Christian belief in the Anti-Christ took a very specific form early in the Church's history. An influential sermon from about 360 A.D. ascribed to St. Ephrem described the anti-Christ as a charismatic being, who was not an incarnation of Satan but his organ. According to this sermon, this handsome being would fool all men with his kindness and righteousness, until securing power as a ruler and devastating the earth in the process of conquering his foes. This sermon informed William Bousset's *The Anti-Christ Legend* (1895), religious philosopher Vladimir Soloviev's *War, Progress, and the End of History* (1899) and almost every Christian apocalyptic interpretation, analysis, prophecy, or fantasy since—including *The Omega Code*. The film's villain played by Michael York, Stone Alexander, embodies St. Ephram's interpretation, purring persuasively and orchestrating escalating violence in the Middle East while pretending to mediate, currying favor among world leaders while scheming their demise.

The Omega Code's roots also lie in a fringe filmmaking community that has rarely scored any success outside of the Bible Belt. Independently financed, regionally-produced "roadshow" Biblical films established their own markets during the silent era, nurturing regional distribution venues that eventually yielded nationwide successes like *The Prince of Peace* (aka *The Lawton Story*, 1949). Only Johnny Cash's *The Gospel*

Road (1970), the Pat Boone vehicle *The Cross and the Switchblade* (1972), and *Jesus* (1979) penetrated mainstream theaters.

Alongside the Biblical recreations of the life of Christ and the Saints or contemporary morality plays like *The Restless Ones* (1965), Christian films often edged into horrific turf by bringing cautionary "hellfire and brimstone" imagery to the screen. Many religious independent filmmakers incorporated "hell" footage clipped from the various silent film versions of *Dante's Inferno* into their own shorts and features, offering glimpses of damnation awaiting sinners and wayward souls. Amid Hollywood's exploitation of the Anti-Christ theme in *Rosemary's Baby* (1968) and *The Omen* (1976), fundamentalist Christian filmmakers helmed their own cinematic dramatizations of the apocalyptic prophecies in Ron and June Ormond's *The Burning Hell* (1974) and *The Grim Reaper* (1976), Earl Owensby and C.D.H. Reynolds's *A Day of Judgment* (1980), and others. These were essentially Christian exploitation horror films, playing drive-ins, churches, revivals, and meeting houses in the South, the Midwest, and the Bible Belt.

Far more ambitious in their scope and fervor than any prior entries in this particular venue were the Mark IV Prophetic Films series, *A Thief in the Night* (1973), *A Distant Thunder* (1978), *Image of the Beast* (1980), and *The Prodigal Planet* (1983), the first Christian fundamentalist Anti-Christ epics. Filmed by producer/director Donald W. Thompson in and around Des Moines, Iowa, this ambitious, apocalyptic quartet interpreted the Book of Revelations as dystopian science-fiction, chronicling the events following the Rapture, the prophetized time when all devout souls would bodily enter heaven, leaving the rest of the population to fend for itself against the minions of the Anti-Christ. Thompson finally unveiled his ersatz Anti-Christ in *Image of the Beast*: a silver-haired gent seated upon a throne of silver-painted plywood boxes, wearing a calculator on a gold chain and a prominent tattoo (the Mark of the Beast) on his forehead, amid a set representing his Jerusalem temple adorned with tacky gold statuary. It was quite a letdown after over five hours of totalitarian violence, faceless soldiers, ominous helicopters, concentration camps, and endless preaching. Thompson's amateurish direction and impoverished productions short-changed his ambitions, rendering his vision of a cruel militaristic single-government police state tyrannically overseen by the Beast laughable to all but the faithful. Nonetheless, the Christian road-show circuit kept the series playing for almost two decades, claiming many converts and eventually establishing itself as a popular video sell-through series in Christian bookstores and via mail-order.

Despite their paucity of means, these films and a growing number of evangelical-horror bestsellers specifically written and published for the growing Christian bookstore market (including Frank E. Peretti's *This Present Darkness*, 1987, and *Piercing the Darkness*, 1989; Dave Hunt's *The Archon Conspiracy*, 1989; etc.) paved the way for far more polished works. By the close of the 1980s, video had prompted the collapse of the Christian rental film libraries. Ironically, the ever-popular horror, science-fiction, and action genres would finally provide more commercially-viable vehicles for Christian filmmakers; it should come as no surprise that the *Star Wars* series and Steven Spielberg's *Raiders of the Lost Ark* (1981, featuring the Biblical Ark of the Covenant) inspired young Christian authors and filmmakers. Tim LaHaye and Jerry B. Jenkins' post-Rapture science-fiction novel *Left Behind* ushered in the 1990s as the first Christian literature to register on mainstream book industry best-seller lists, spawning sequels and a popular juvenile series, *Left Behind: The Kids*. The breakthrough video release of Peter and Paul Lalonde's *Apocalypse* (1996) launched their trilogy of Biblical "End of Days" sf thrillers, *Revelation* (1998, starring Jeff Fahey) and *Tribulation* (2000, starring Gary Busey), and paved the way for *The Omega Code*.

These films were Christian in content without being overtly evangelistic, and *The Omega Code* follows suit. It's clear that script writers Stephan Blinn and Hollis Barton consider Dr. Gillen Lane's (Casper Van Dien) sins those of hubris, cynicism, a lack of faith, and the constant placing of his career before his marriage and family, but there's no preaching about it. Lane suffers until his eventual awakening prompts divine intervention, but the incompetence of the minions of "the Beast" is a constant ally. The villains' dialogue is also suggestively spiced with barbed references to "human evolution," echoing fundamentalist derision for Darwinian theory, but you have to be paying close attention to catch such threads (the truly devout are already attuned). From its opening sequence, *The Omega Code* embraces the syntax of the Hollywood thrillers it emulates, complete with conspiracy plots, mercenary assassins, and its *Omen*-like score (by Harry Manfredini, who scored the notorious *Friday the 13th* films) and imagery (ominous crows, cowled figures, a cabal of Biblical scholars and prophets dedicated to usurping "the Beast"). But the violence is understated and essentially bloodless, and the climactic special effects showcase dedicated to the divine rather than the demonic.

With its Hollywood cast and budget far beyond the means of its roadshow predecessors, *The Omega Code* earned rousing boxoffice success (claiming the Number 10 spot in October 1999 weekend theatrical earnings) and attention from the mainstream press. Produced by Matthew Crouch under the umbrella of his father Paul Crouch's Trinity Broadcasting Network, the film was marketed to Christian audiences via TBN previews and promotion and church-related advertising and exhibitions. It's the first production of its kind to be aggressively promoted in the mainstream video market. The ongoing success of *The Omega Code* promises future Christian productions will reap more mainstream distribution distribution and venues. *Left Behind: The Movie* is currently in production with a budget of almost $18 million in place, and rumors of Hollywood distribution interests.[30] Apocalyptic Christian video action games have begun to carve out a niche for themselves, too. Valusoft's *The War in Heaven* (1999) is among the first, allowing the player to engage with the game as either a divine or fallen angel.

Perhaps as a result of this growing Christian market, Hollywood edged many later *Omen*-inspired religious horror films into more devotional territory with W.W. Wicket and Carl Schultz's *The Seventh Sign* (1988), Michael Tolkin's *The Rapture* (1991), Gregory

---

[30] *Left Behind: The Movie* enjoyed wider theatrical distribution than *The Omega Code* – I saw it at a local cinema in Greenfield, MA – *after* its video release, *sans* a major studio distributor. Mel Gibson's self-financed *The Passion of the Christ* (2004) proved to be *the* breakthrough Christian film, smashing boxoffice records while fulfilling the potential *The Omega Code*'s comparatively modest success initiated.

Widen's *The Prophecy* (1995), the recent *Stigmata* (1999), and others. Apocalyptic scenarios in these films evolved into parables about redemption rather than damnation, even as the narrative set-ups echoed horror-movie conventions. But *The Omega Code* demonstrates that the Christian community is no longer content to let Hollywood continue plundering their ideology. Their best and brightest filmmakers have taken the reins, heralding a new generation of Christian cinema that will reach more viewers and command far more attention than their precursors ever mustered. They're going mainstream, and heaven is the limit.

Keep your eyes and hearts—and wallets—open.

March 30:

THE SIXTH SENSE (1999) was slighted by the Academy Awards, but don't let that keep you from one of last year's best movies. Like *The Blair Witch Project*, *The Sixth Sense* proved to a boxoffice juggernaut and a return to the evocatively suggestive horror film aesthetic established by producer Val Lewton in the 1940s (*The Cat People, I Walked With a Zombie*, etc.). In fact, *The Sixth Sense* is closest in tone and spirit to Lewton's unusual *The Curse of the Cat People* (1944), a touching B-movie that transcended its lurid title to sensitively portray the imaginative fantasy life of a troubled little girl who also had visions and spoke to ghosts.

The Sixth Sense is a horror movie—more specifically, a ghost story—but it plucks your nerves en route to the heart, arriving at a lovingly orchestrated final act that is as profoundly moving as it is terrifying. After a frightening confrontation with an adult former-patient (Donny Wahlberg) accusing the doctor of failing him, child psychologist Dr. Malcolm Crowe (Bruce Willis, delivering his finest performance since Terry Gilliam's 1995 sf opus *12 Monkeys*) seeks atonement and redemption by attending to a similarly-troubled young boy, Cole Sear (played by the extraordinary Haley Joel Osment). Cole sees "dead people" everywhere, day and night, a psychic ability he keeps from his mother (Toni Collette) while struggling to maintain his own tentative balance. Crowe's attempts to help Cole deal with such literally-chilling encounters (the temperature drops during the spectral visitations) culminates in a number of surprises which are best left for you to discover (please, don't spoil it for your friends and family!).

There was precious little in writer/director M. Night Shyamalan's first two features, *Praying with Anger* (1993; not yet on video) and *Wide Awake* (1997), to suggest he was capable of mounting such a masterpiece. Shyamalan's tale is blessed with ideal casting, particularly that of eleven-year old Osment, who registered years ago as Forrest Jr. in *Forrest Gump* (1994) and in movies like *Bogus* (1996, playing an orphan who interacts with an "imaginary friend"). Osment refined his considerable skills on TV programs like *Murphy Brown, The Jeff Foxworth Show*, and *Ally McBeal* (as a terminally-ill boy who wants to sue God), but he conjures real screen magic here. The ingenious tale, performances and every aspect of the production rewards repeat viewings. *The Sixth Sense* is "rental-priced" (the video costs over $100 retail; as usual, the DVD is affordably priced for sell-thru), so don't be surprised to find yourself haunting your local independent video shop for a return visit. The DVD sports engaging extras (but no commentary track) about the making of the film, it's carefully planted clues and strict "rules," and an amusing surprise (be sure to click on the graphic of the wrapped box on the second page of the "Bonus Materials" menu for a glimpse of Shyamalan's earliest film efforts). Highly recommended! *(Rated 'PG-13' for mild language, brief glimpses of the aftermath of violence during the spectral visits, and some genuine scares.)*

Another excellent young performer graces and elevates **CRAZY IN ALABAMA** (1999), actor Antonio Banderas' directorial debut which adventurously (but unsuccessfully) interweaves two tentatively-related narratives set in the early 1960s. Vet actress (and Banderas' wife) Melanie Griffith is at the center of the more whimsical of the two story threads as Lucille Benson, who kills and beheads her brutal husband (all offscreen) and hits the high road for Hollywood to fulfill her dreams, toting her hubby's head in a Tupperware container—but only after confiding in her teenage nephew Peejoe (Lucas Black). The nasty local sheriff (Meatloaf Aday) targets Peejoe, whose determination to stand up to the corrupt official only increases after he alone witnesses the sheriff's casual murder of a young black civil-rights activist. Either story would have made an engaging film, but the mix of the two doesn't really come off.

The rough equation of the era's oppression of women with the racial prejudices that fueled the volatile Civil Rights movement is made explicit in the courtroom finale (presided over by judge Rod Steiger, delivering another eccentric autumnal performance); perhaps if we had witnessed Lucille's dire situation rather than simply being told about it, the film might have fulfilled its high aspirations. Nevertheless, it's Peejoe's plight that holds our attention, and Lucas Black more than holds his own against Meatloaf's menace and character actor David Morse's dignified turn as Lucille's brother (and Peejoe's

Uncle). Black's lanky screen presence and Alabama drawl anchored the TV series *American Gothic* (1995-96) and, most memorably, Billy Bob Thornton's *Sling Blade* (1996). It's a real pleasure to see Lucas again, and he carries the film admirably. *(Rated 'PG-13' for mild language, adult themes and situations, and civil-rights riot violence.)*

There's a procession of young actors and actresses baring all in **BODY SHOTS** (1999), seeking sexual oblivion awash in alcohol while finding precious little to cling to. This dispassionate, sometimes cruel dissection of the 1990s hedonistic club scene isn't for the timid or prudish—nor is it really for those seeking titillation. It's an ugly, opportunistic ride with upscale young urban professionals consumed by their cravings for carnality without consequence, the rush for sexual intimacy without emotional foundation or heart. In short, we're in Bret Easton Ellis territory, in the cinematic realm of *Less Than Zero* (1987, from the Ellis novel), *Bright Lights, Big City* (1988), *The Accused* (1988), and the scathing *Your Friends & Neighbors* (1998). Granted, the promise of seeing your favorite up-and-coming stars indulging in unrated sexual activity may be a draw, but be warned that the film doesn't let you enjoy the charms of this cosmetically-attractive crew. Their collective revel in seductive swagger, swinish excess, self-debasement, and self-destructive gropings clearly isn't meant to be "fun viewing," though fun is all they're after.

The unpleasant tenor of the film is immediately established with glimpses of "The Aftermath" (the film marks its chapters), as hung-over attorney Rick (Sean Patrick Flanery) crawls out of bed with lawyer Jane (Amanda Peet) to urinate on the closed toilet lid in her bathroom; he barely attempts a clean-up. Meanwhile, traumatized and bloodied Sara (Tara Reid) is at the wheel, risking collision and pulling over her car just long enough to "heave-ho" before she finally stumbles into Jane's apartment, saying she was raped. It's all downhill from there, as the film rewinds to "Foreplay," chronicling the scores, misses, hazards, ravages, and loneliness of anonymous one-night stands. Only Trent (affable Ron Livingston of *Swingers* and *Office Space*) emerges relatively unscathed and somehow likable, enjoying the only playful consensual sexual encounter of the film (a sadomasochistic fling with "cat woman" Emily Procter) as his try-anything emotional callousness and low expectations are rewarded. The rest of the cast—Sybil Temchen's shallow party girl, Jerry O'Connell's loutish football star, Brad Rowe's adrift "nice guy"—are left to wallow in their own brine. Your move, but this one's for mature viewers only, available in both 'R'-rated and an "Unrated Director's Cut" *(for explicit language, alcohol abuse, vivid sexual situations and encounters, nudity, rape, and one ugly man-to-man beating)*.

About the Author

Stephen R. Bissette is world renowned for his 30+ years of work in comics (*Saga of the Swamp Thing, Taboo, 1963, Tyrant*, etc.) and now savors life as an artist, writer, lecturer and instructor. He presently teaches at the Center for Cartoon Studies in White River Jct., VT, and lives in Windsor, VT with his wife Marjory.

Visit his website at www.srbissette.com

S.R. Bissette's Blur, Volume 2 is also available from Black Coat Press.